D0274554

How to Iron a Shirt

500 household tips and tricks I wish my mother had told me

This edition published 2013 for Index Books Ltd

Parragon
Chartist House
15–17 Trim Street
Bath, BA1 1HA, UK

www.parragon.com

ISBN: 978-1-4723-3430-5

Printed in China

Author: Manidipa Mandal
Editor: Fiona Biggs
Illustrators: Kunal Kundu, Suresh Kumar, Rajita Kashyap, Nitin Chawla
Layout: Eleven Arts
Cover design: Tracy Killick

Picture acknowledgements
The publishers would like to thank the Advertising Archives for the use of the lady with a hoover image on the front and back cover and Mary Evans Picture Library/Classic Stock/H. Armstrong Roberts for the use of the lady with shirts image on the front cover and spine.

Contents

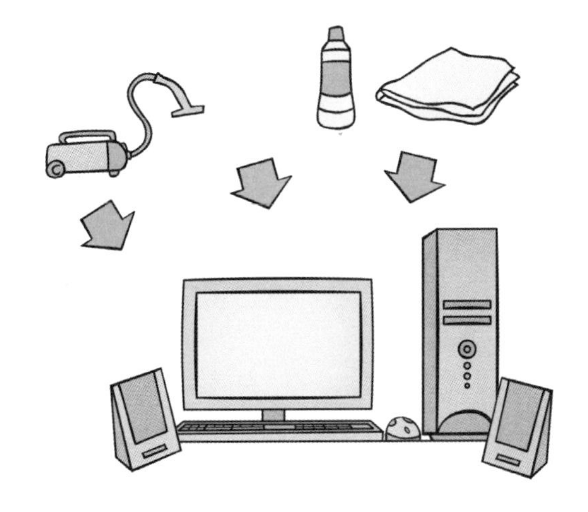

The Organized Home: Scheduling and systems 4

The Organized Home: Storage 19

The Organized Home: Safety, first aid and home remedies 37

The Organized Home: Greener living – recycle, reuse, renew, ration 56

Home Care: The big clean-up 80

Stains 98

Garments and Accessories 108

Furniture and Furnishings 130

Do It Yourself 145

Pest Control 155

Pet Care 167

Bringing Up Baby 194

Home Aesthetics 222

Welcome to Our Home 232

It's a Wrap 241

Index 256

The Organized Home

Scheduling and systems

Time management is key to running an organized household – having your own systems and drills in place minimizes scheduling conflicts (and family rows!)

Keeping time

1. Chalk it up at breakfast

Notice-board notwithstanding, the family keep missing messages!

- Buy dark stoneware mugs and tumblers with a matte surface. Chalk urgent reminders on their first cuppa!
- Include good wishes, loving notes and compliments in your morning scrawls too!

2. Water retention

Water-retaining granules don't just save you time and effort, they mean you can go away for the weekend without organizing a house-sitter.

- Mix some into your garden compost and potting compost so that your plants will hold more moisture for longer.

3. Make that call!

You may be tempted to shoot off an email asking for immediate action. However:

- The best way to get something done is to make a call.
- For what can wait, an email forestalls telephone tag games!

4. Picture plan

Ask your child to paint seven themed pictures (or make collages) to hang in the hall, one for each day.

- Use these to remind the family that Wednesdays are football nights, Fridays mean food shopping trips, etc.

Children will take pride in their art while strangers won't be privy to your weekly plans! The children will remember their chores better too, having lavished care on them!

Handy helpmates

5. End the pen hunt

Hunting through your deep bag for your pen is frustrating. To keep it close to your notebook:

- Choose a diary with its own bookmark, or use sturdy fabric glue to attach a ribbon or braid to a plain one – put it in the middle of the book so putting the pen in won't strain the spine.
- Tie or sew a lightweight plastic pen to the end of the braid, and then clip it to the diary – on the outside cover or in the middle.
- A soft-covered notebook allows flex; in an organizer with a roomy binder cover, tie the ribbon to a binder ring.

6. Shop by the centimetre

No point buying pull-out baskets deeper than your shelves!

- Always carry a carpenter's, or tailor's, tape measure with you.
- Devote a page in your organizer to the measurements of all your rooms, the depth of all your fitted storage.
- Jot down the measurements of all holding spaces like alcoves and room above shelves.
- Carry the shoe sizes and measurements of all your family – saves waiting in dressing room queues or dragging unwilling kids along.

7. Mix and match bedlinen

Never run out of clean sheets or matching pillowcases. Buy multiples in *coordinating* colours and patterns.

- Except for whites – it's best to buy three identical sets of those.
- Don't match the colour and pattern of pillowcases and sheets exactly.
- Pick coordinating patterns and colours. For pale blue striped sheets, choose pillowcases in toning blues, solid or a different stripe; or choose a darker solid colour (say, plum) that will go with blue stripes, pink ginghams and cream damasks; or get different patterns in the same colours!

What's best about mix-and-match is zero boredom!

8. Writing on the wall

Many families use notes to schedule and coordinate activities, or maintain a diary of birthdays and anniversaries on a notice-board (whiteboard, blackboard or cork).

Make your board work harder:

- If you use pens, attach different coloured ones to easily locate where each person might be on, say, Friday night.
- Errands for each person could also be left in 'his' or 'her' colour.
- Attach a cord to the cap of each pen and pin it to the board – it won't get misplaced or carried away. Do a quick check before shopping for any refills needed.
- If you use chalk, keep a box of each colour on a narrow shelf just below the blackboard.
- Add an extra colour for all-family events.
- Also handy: a separate colour for must-remember occasions and doctor's appointments.

In and out of the closet

9. The everything box

No, you don't have time to sort the laundry *and* the post *and* lunchboxes each night. Even if you did, there's still more! Get an 'everything box' for each room:

- It should be large, yet compact enough to keep coins and keys safe. It should be low enough to hide under the bed and small enough to carry around.
- Put all clutter in it each day – get everyone to collect their own belongings.
- Set a sorting time each weekend – 20 minutes should do.
- Get everyone together for quicker resolution of what belongs to whom or goes where.
- Anything you can't decide on stays in the box. But if no one claims (or uses) it in a month, give it away or discard it.

10. Before the big shop...

A change of seasons, a landmark birthday, a new school year – anything can trigger a buying spree.

Tidy the cupboards before you shop:

- Don't just aim to 'declutter' – tell yourself (and the children) that you need space for new buys.
- However, don't actually assign cubbyholes for additions – that will be an irresistible pressure to buy.
- Take everything out and put it back neatly – chances are your cupboards need a tidy.
- When you see what you have, you'll realize what you need.
- If you find an item you're sick of, that's dated or tired, or a never-worn, perhaps you know someone who will love it.
- Now you can go shopping with better perspective – and a list!

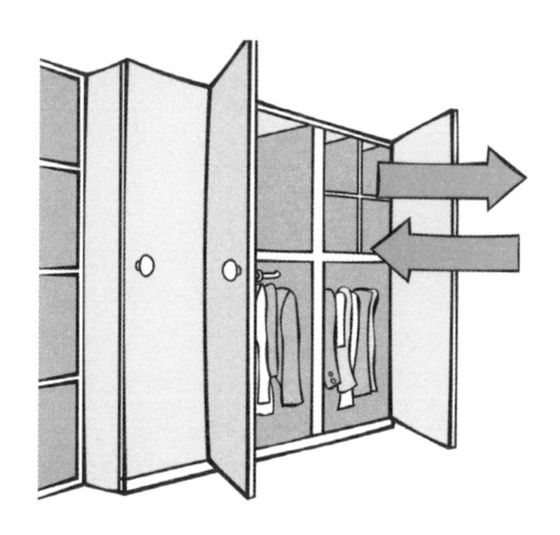

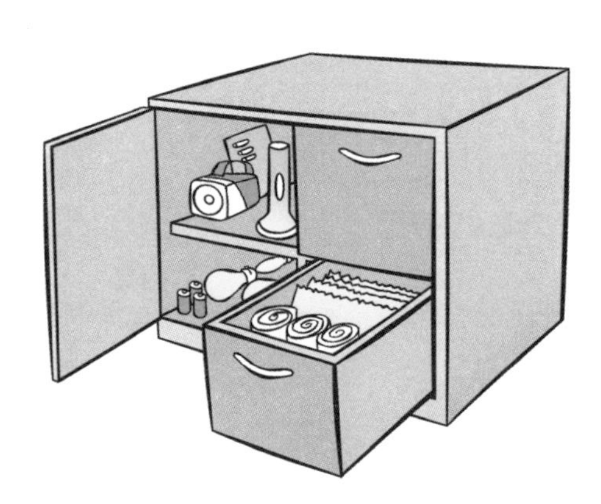

11. Utility cupboard must-haves

These are the fix-its you need:

- Light bulbs, an assortment.
- Fuses, various.
- Batteries, half a dozen in all the usual sizes.
- A couple of torches.
- A good supply of bin liners.
- Extra bags for the vacuum cleaner.

■ Primping planner

12. Handy hand cream

When is the best time to use hand cream? Just after your hands have been in sudsy water.

- Keep a heavy-duty hand cream near all soap-and-water areas – kitchen sink, bathroom basin, potting shed and laundry room.
- For longer-lasting benefits choose a brand that resists a couple of washes.
- Buy cream in pump dispensers or decant cream into pumps – they're easier to use with damp hands (which is better for your skin).

Rank and file at the desk

14. Old ball and chain

Tethered to the desk with no prospect of getting active outdoors?

- Swap your chair for a Swiss ball. Choose between sitting upright or rolling off!
- With even the tiniest movement, your abdominal core muscles will need to flex to maintain your balance. A working workout!

13. Order of dress

When getting dressed, follow this sequence to minimize stains, discoloration and damage to clothes and accessories:

- Perfume and make-up first – that includes hair products!
- Give it time. Some cosmetics can smudge onto clothes; alcohol (in perfumes, hairspray, deodorants) can affect fabric dyes, especially on silk, which doesn't take dye in too deeply anyway.
- When sure you won't 'wipe off', get dressed.
- Put jewellery on last for maximum protection. Pearls are particularly vulnerable to damage from the alcohol in perfume.

15. Home work for more playtime

Working from home can mean more 'play'!

- Multitask and refresh yourself by alternating household duties with bread-earning!
- Take a 10-minute break every hour – you need to move around for your health's sake. Stretch, run up and down the stairs, do ab crunches or curl weights.
- Set a kitchen timer to prompt you to rest your eyes every 15 minutes – look away from the screen, into the distance. Roll your eyes up at the ceiling, down at the floor, from side to side. Now turn your head to do it again!
- On breaks soon after breakfast or lunch, substitute a quick errand for exercise – put the washing on, feed the cat.
- Advertise your work hours far and wide – because you're working from home doesn't mean you're 'at-home' to work all the time.

16. Slow down the information highway

Instant information and continuous connectivity can put you under pressure to be a super-speed superhero! But you don't have to respond to technology 'instantly'.

- Answer emails immediately only if it's an emergency; otherwise don't reply until it's 'mail hour'.
- Better still, turn off the alert and check no more than twice or three times a day.
- If it's urgent, an intelligent colleague will say so in the subject line. Use your discretion regarding the 'high priority' button!
- If it's an emergency, people will call if you don't respond to emails.
- Avoid non-urgent calls in the middle of a deadline crunch. Put the answering machine on and ignore chat requests till you have the time.
- Keep your mobile phone on a silent or discreet setting – check who's calling and decide whether they can wait.

17. Pocket those papers

Household papers need filing. Then again, it's laborious sorting mail into 'mortgage', 'school', 'household', etc. daily.

Have a single-file system for daily mail – it'll be less intimidating and faster and it's efficient enough:

- Get an accordion file with 12 pockets and label them for each month.
- Get 48 clear-plastic envelopes – 12 each in four colours — to fit the pockets. Use an indelible marker to label these 'Week 1', 'Week 2', etc.; colour-code simultaneously.
- Put one 4-week set of envelopes in each filing pocket.
- When a bill, notice or letter arrives, aim to deal with it early and file accordingly. If a payment's due on the 15th, aim to pay by the end of week 1 – and place in the correct envelope.
- At the beginning of each week, fish out the relevant envelope and deal with everything in one go. Set aside time for this every weekend.

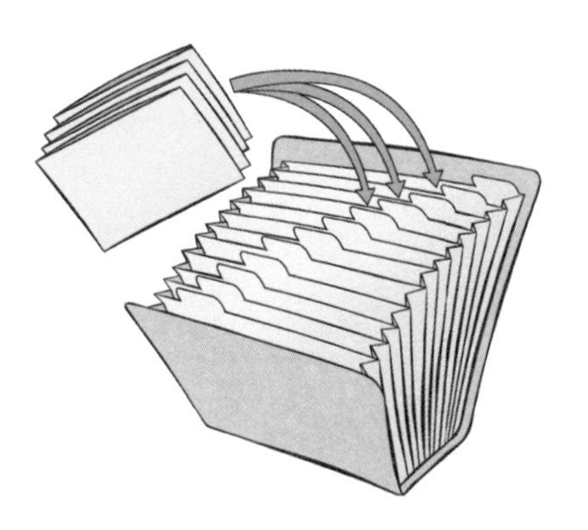

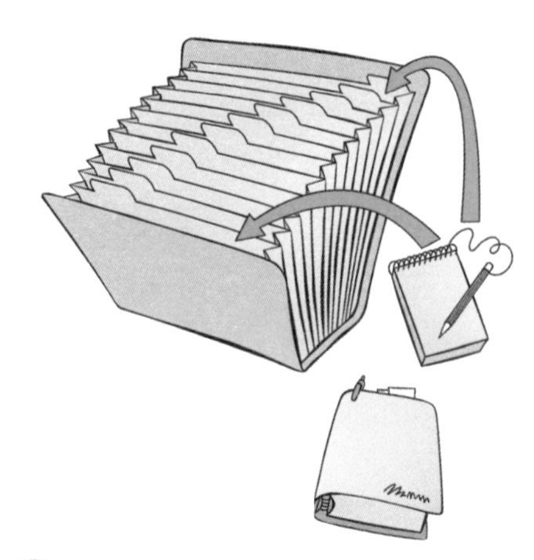

18. Piggyback those pockets!

Now make the single-file system (*see Tip 17*) more efficient!

- Treat your file as an extension of your organizer. When sorting mail, get your organizer too.
- Keep a little notepad and pencil in the file – the first or last section is easiest to find.
- Transfer all appointments to individual slips of paper and put them in the relevant envelope.
- When you settle the bills, bring out the family calendar and transfer your schedule to it!

Best bit? It recycles every year!

19. Stamped!

You've pocketed the lot (*see Tip 17*) but are still unsure whether the chore was completed.

- Get a rolling 'professional' rubber stamp made stating 'Paid!', 'Returned!', 'Replied!', 'Wishes Sent!', 'Gift bought:______', 'Checked' and 'Done!'.
- Buy an inkpad and refill. Store both in a box beside the file. Add a stapler, some stamps, a nice notepad and a box of pins.
- As you finish tasks, stamp them out!
- For gifts, pen the details.
- Answer the mail.

You're finished!

20. File away!

Make a date – yourself, coffee and those pesky ring binders!

- Schedule filing for every second Saturday, say, or quarterly. If there's not much paperwork, you could get away with yearly (a month ahead of filing your tax return!).
- If your file bulges, you need to clear it out more often. To a dozen (one for every month) identical ring binders, add labels 'Electricity', 'Mortgage', 'School', 'Receipts', etc. Or choose a really deep, sturdy one with divider cards.
- Get another tabbed pocket file for 'annuals' and long-term records. Label tabs 'Medical', 'Bank', 'Insurance', 'Car', 'House', 'ID', etc. Add loose pockets as needed.
- A third bunch – manuals, instruction booklets, guarantee cards – goes in an expanding accordion or big box file plus plastic envelopes. Once in five years, armed with a glass of good wine, weed out dated documents.

21. Coupon bank

Keep cutting out those money-off coupons and then forgetting to use them?

- Get a large version of a money bank with a transparent window for the coupons you cut out.
- When you've finished the weekly payments (*see Tip 17*), put the coupons you've to use up soon in your wallet. Discard any you're unsure about.

No bulging wallet and you get time to think about the 'Buy 1, Get 1 Free' vouchers.

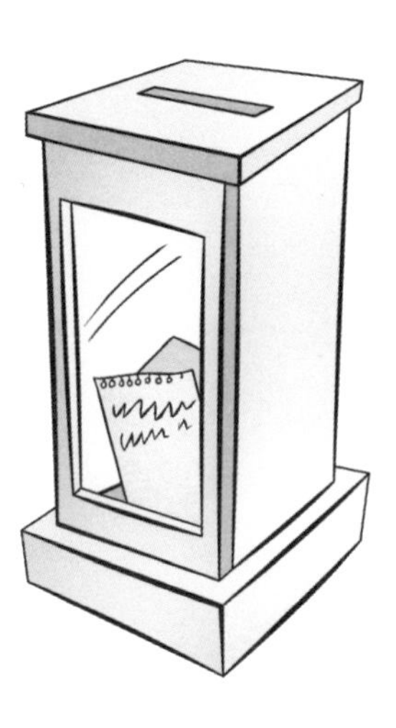

22. Net pay!

Set up direct debits for all monthly bills:

- Utilities such as water and gas
- Mortgage and insurance
- Recurring deposits
- School fees
- Loan instalments

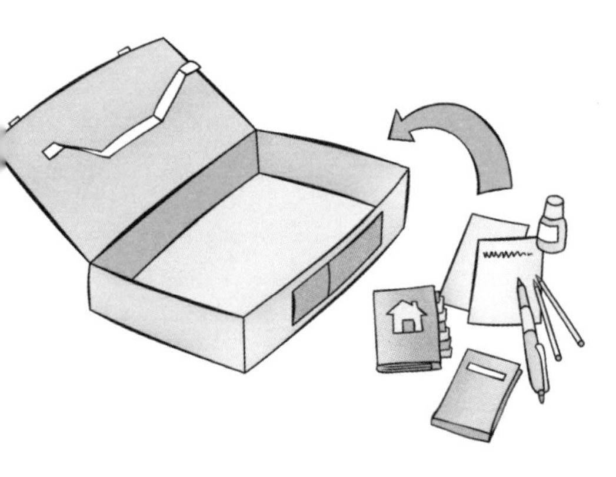

23. Don't juggle, multiply

Do you know your daughter's best friend's number? Does she know your best friend's, for emergencies?

- Put them all together in a box file with a pen, refills and correcting fluid.
- Get several address books, with space for anniversaries, birthdays and email addresses.
- Label 'Family & Friends', 'Children' (or one per child), 'Work', 'Services & Supplies'.
- Update the children's diaries every major school holiday, or even monthly if you can.

24. Emergency rescue!

Make your address box (*see Tip 23*) your emergency rescue service:

- List emergency numbers at the front or back of each – most address books offer 'Notes' pages.
- Add a trusted family member's number – with their consent.
- For the 'Work' diary, add the numbers of your most reliable colleagues and contacts. Duplicate those alphabetically too.
- In the 'Service Directory', add your favourite takeaways, the plumber and electrician, and the closest pharmacy.
- Have the best babysitter options and best friend's mother's number in the front of the children's diaries.
- Carry a copy of all frequently called and emergency numbers in your wallet.
- Add photocopies of the list to your partner's and children's wallets.
- Give a copy of that same list to your 'emergency family member'.

Penny pinchers

25. Switch for savings!

With service providers, play kangaroo – if they aren't offering the best rates, hop to another.

- Shop around before a new financial year begins; agents hoping to improve their bottom line may offer bargains.

Check service providers for:

- Telephones
- Cable TV
- Internet connection
- Electricity and gas

Check financial outgoings and income for:

- Bank savings accounts, fixed deposits and mutual funds
- Credit, debit and ATM cards – note reward points and interest charged
- Loan and mortgage payment rates – check for pre-payment penalties, rollover policies and flexibility

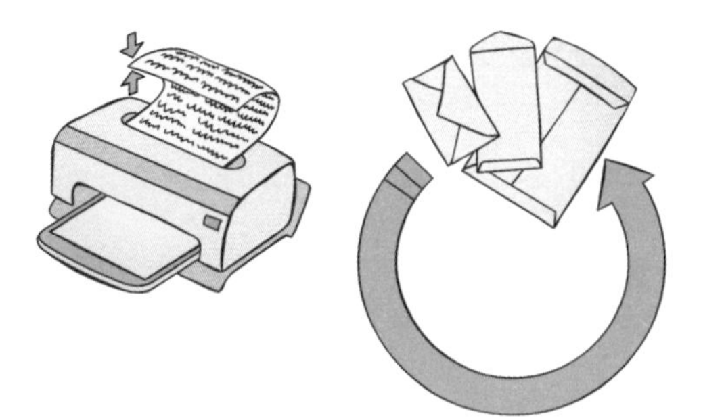

26. Saved from work

If you're working from home, cutting a few corners where it doesn't hurt will help pinch those hard-earned pennies.

- Print documents for reference (rather than for sending out to someone) on both sides of the paper.
- Print on the draft quality setting of your printer rather than letter quality.
- Save the coloured ink for when you really need it; print regular documents in black.
- Avoid printing white space (waste of paper) and elaborate visuals, especially large photos (waste of ink). Most websites offer information in a text-only or printer-friendly format. (Hint: try the site map or choose the HTML version of a website.)
- Recycle envelopes – they can be handy 'folders' for short projects of 'work in progress'.
- Use energy-saving practices (*see Tip 144*).

27. Tiny tasks

If you have growing children, review the roster of chores frequently and delegate more. Here are some jobs even toddlers can help with:

- Putting rubbish into the wastepaper basket.
- Emptying all the wastepaper baskets into the main bin once a week.
- Keeping the family pet's water bowl filled (a squirt bottle is least messy for a child still acquiring motor coordination skills).
- Feeding smaller mammals, birds and fish – just keep an eye on how they are doing. It's wonderful training for the responsibilities of a more demanding pet like a dog.
- Watch and advise; communicate your standards; offer praise for a job done well – but never 'do it better' or redo what has been done.

28. Lock up when leaving

Moving house?

- Prime furniture for transport by locking all drawers and doors to prevent accidental opening (and consequent splintering/shattering).
- If you can't lock a movable portion, see if you can remove it; pack separately.
- Pad all corners; protect jutting parts (knobs and hooks) with bubble wrap.

29. While you were out

Going on holiday? Make some arrangements to ease your homecoming.

- Stop post delivery up to a day after your return date (ask the post office to hold it for you).
- Stop the newspaper. If you are a direct subscriber, try to arrange for a friend to pick it up. It won't pile up announcing that no one's home!
- Stop regular deliveries. Shop for cartons of UHT milk to keep in the larder till you return (check expiry dates so it's good to use even beyond then).
- In summer, pay someone to mow your lawn. In winter, hire someone to shovel any snow off your driveway. The house won't look 'abandoned'.
- Installing timers? Make sure there are separate switches for each room set to different hours. The shifting on-and-off cycle appears more natural.
- Don't forget the sprinkler timers. Ask a friend to take an occasional walk around your garden if you'll be gone for more than a fortnight – for maintenance and the appearance of occupation.

The Organized Home

Storage

Innovative and dedicated storage solutions are possible for every room: from your wardrobe to your workstation, from utility rooms to nurseries, from larder to family living zones.

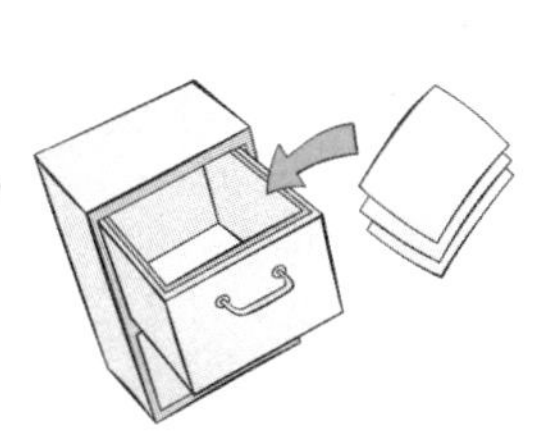

■ Hard(er)-working hideaways

30. Drawers versus shelves

Fed up with stacks of stuff toppling when you need to pull out that large pot from the bottom of the pile? Drawers can be more practical than shelves, but unless you're planning your home storage from scratch, you may end up with not enough drawers.

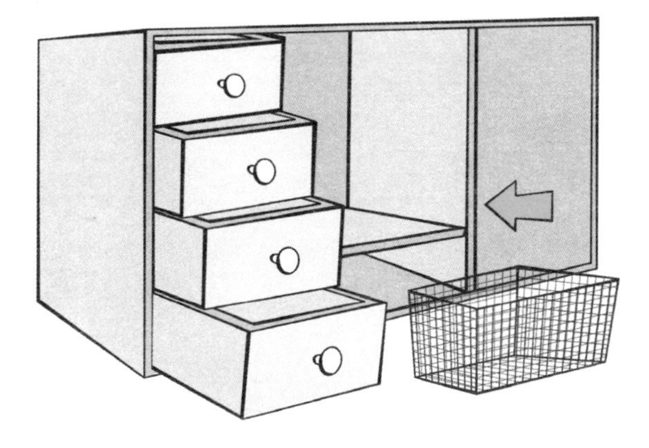

- If you have cupboards rather than drawers, fit some sliding wire baskets under the shelves – you'll be able to see what's in them at a glance.
- If you have enough drawers and are still short of storage, add trays and inserts to maximize the use of horizontal space.

31. Enlarge your cupboard capacity

For the same reason that a drawer can hold more stuff, certain additions to your storage can help you stock more without stacking:

- Tiered racks that divide shelves into horizontal layers
- Tiered carousels
- Ultra-slim shelves in the door
- Hanging rods and hooks on the backs of doors

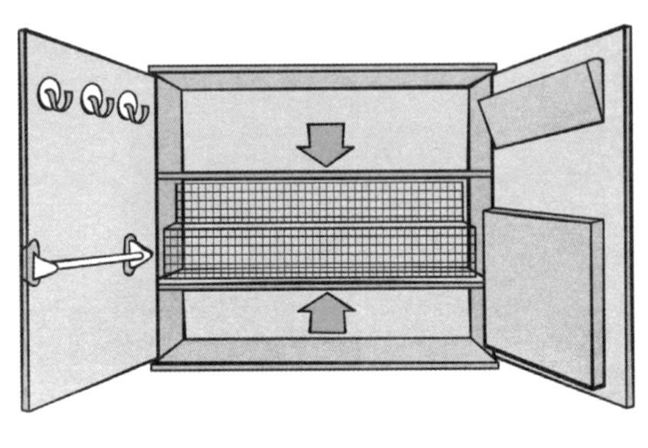

32. Storage with a view

Window seats make a great dual-purpose addition to any room with recessed windows.

- A lift-up seat hides seasonal or occasional items; place cushions on top.
- For readier access, fit lightweight baskets or drawers to hold paperback books, extra cushions and pillows, toys, cleaning equipment or surplus bathroom supplies.
- Open shelving's good for larger or frequently used items: towels in the bathroom; childhood toys in a young adult's room; large ceramic bowls or copper utensils in the kitchen; heavy stone sculptures; or a basket of candles or seashells.

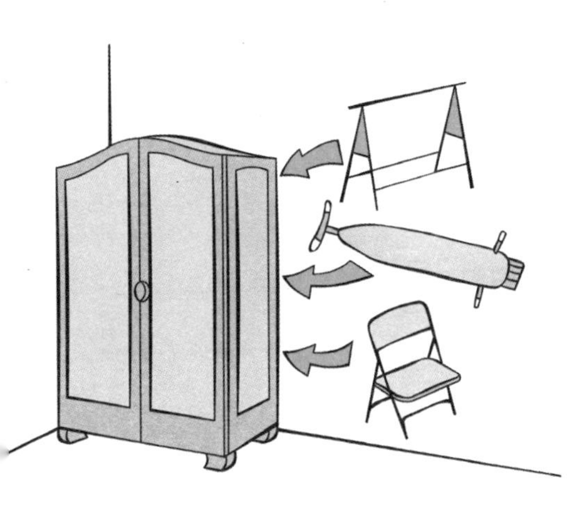

33. Standalone stowaways

Use space behind standalone furniture as 'slim storage space':

- Stand cupboards, dressers and chests of drawers a couple of inches away from the wall; you might not miss that extra space – especially as standalone furniture on legs frees up floor space visually.
- Slide in an extra folding table, a couple of trestles, folding chairs or the ironing board.
- Make sure you can reach it easily when you want it – the stowaway item shouldn't be pushed too far back, with other objects preventing you sliding it out easily.

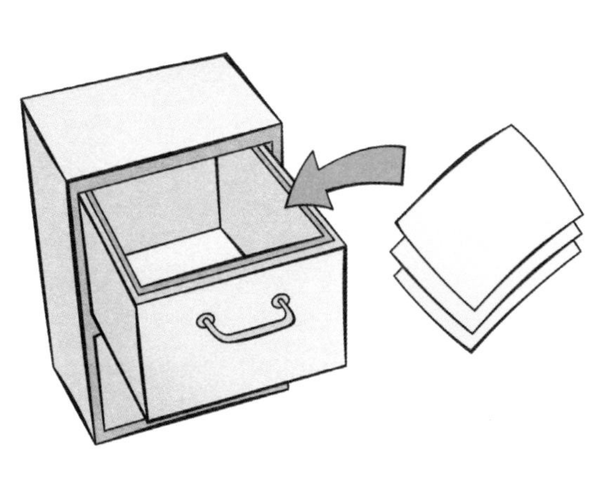

34. Paper liners

Paper liners are great for protecting drawers and shelves, as well as their contents.

- If you've got breakables sliding around and knocking into each other, however, switch to felt sheets – it should minimize shifting and prevent those chips.
- If you have a problem with moths, look out for lining paper that's been impregnated with lavender or cedar essence.

■ Kitchen (and larder) buddies

35. Top up your shelves

Deep shelves or uneven stacks of dishes on smaller shelves waste vertical space. Stacking high makes removal difficult. Some solutions:

- Screw or superglue the lids of lightweight spice jars to the underside of a slim shelf – screw the jar in. Simply unscrew to use.
- On sturdy eye-level shelves, screw some cup hooks into the cabinet 'ceiling' or under the shelf.
- Add a slim wire drawer or a woven basket on rails under the shelf – for lids, baking paper, baking sheets and occasional cutlery.

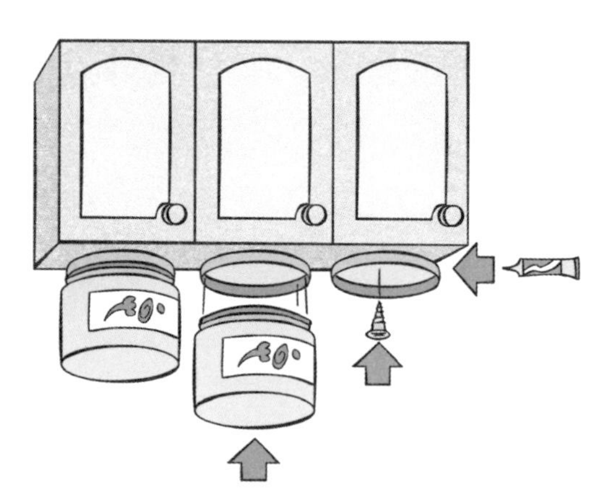

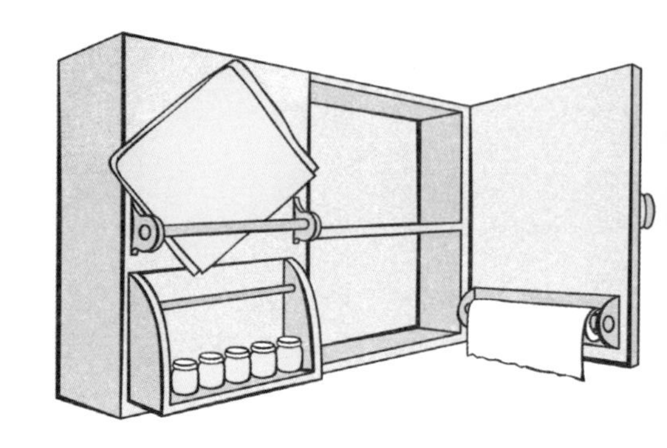

36. Stack in the door

The insides of kitchen-cabinet doors are perfect for slimline storage, and almost every shelf has a few empty inches in front where you can slide something in.

- Slim wire racks or short towel bars can hold pot lids and lightweight chopping boards.
- Slim shelves house spices neatly and allow an at-a-glance view.
- Hanging rails can hold flat utensils and extra tea towels.
- Attach foil and paper dispensers to the insides of doors – neater than having the caddy in the open where fumes and pests get all over them.

37. Cubbyholes for cutlery

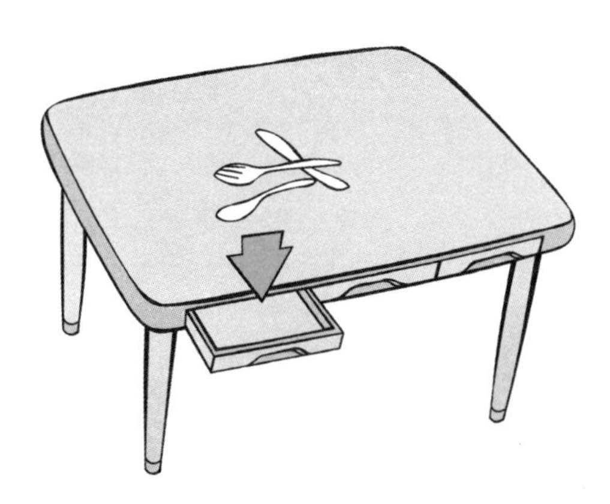

There's no need for cutlery to take up an entire kitchen drawer.

- All but the tiniest table should have room underneath to have a couple of inches of drawer space added flush beneath the surface. That's enough to store your everyday cutlery.
- It's also a handy place for napkins and table mats – just where you need them.

38. Guard your goblets

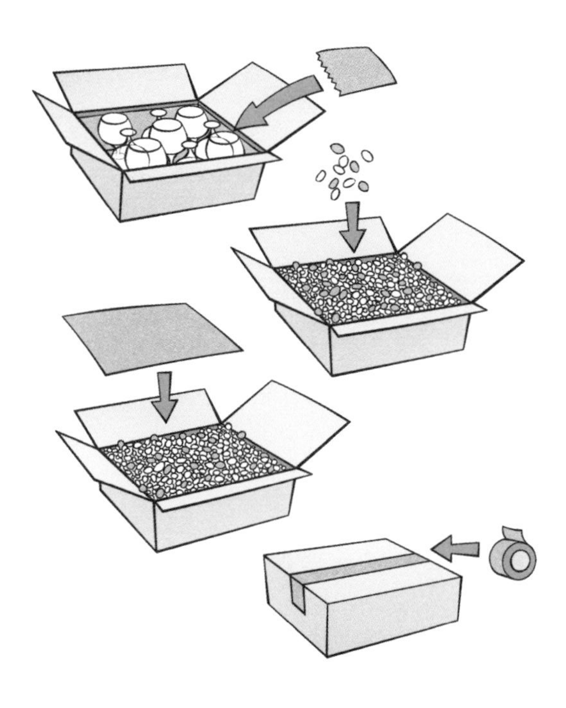

A good way to keep your special crystal safe from chips and cracks.

- Line a sturdy cardboard box with a layer of felt. Place your glasses so they don't touch – leave an inch between – with every alternate goblet placed upside down.
- Shake packing pellets (styrofoam beads available at stationery and DIY shops) over the lot to fill the gaps and the empty cups.
- Add a layer of felt and a sheet of corrugated cardboard on top; fill with packing pellets to the top and seal with masking or parcel tape.

39. Frills and filters

Ever wonder what to do with that pack of paper doilies at the back of the cupboard?

- Those frilly doilies may no longer be in fashion, but they're great for interweaving with your fine china to prevent scratches.
- For smaller saucers and for cups, try using coffee filters.

■ Clutter-free clothes storage

40. One season at a time

Store only this season's stuff in your wardrobe.

- Decide how many seasons (not retail, climatic!) you really have where you live.
- Put this season's things into the wardrobe.
- Break up all-season garments (T-shirts, shirts, blouses) into seasonal collections by colour, pattern or material.
- Store the rest by season.
- Use vacuum storage bags; or plain large zipped or re-sealable bags (get the extra air out using a vacuum cleaner, unzipping just enough to fit the nozzle).

This will be better for your clothes – they won't get squashed in the wardrobe.

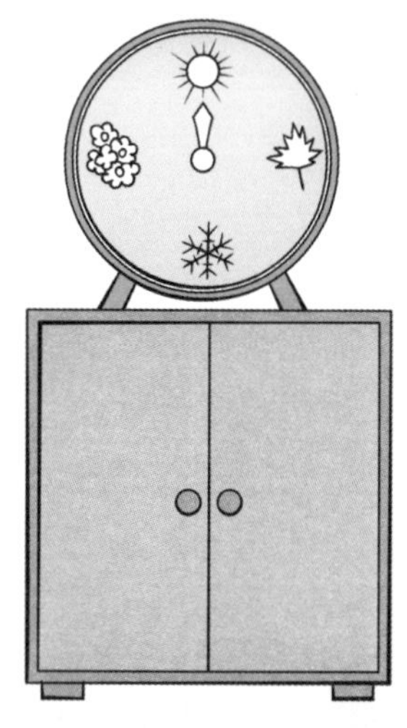

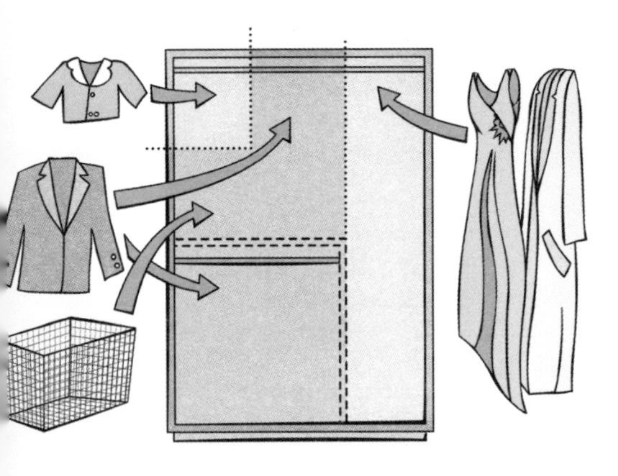

41. Halve your hanging space...

...to store twice the number of garments!

- Divide full-length hanging areas into a two-tier one.
- Leave just enough full-depth hanging space to fit in about half a dozen more long garments than you have – about 2 inches for long dresses, 3 for coats is plenty.
- Organize clothes by length. Use the space under mid-length dresses by adding storage boxes, baskets or removable shelves. That's a handy nook for handbags and shoes too.

42. A few of my foldable things

Not all garments *need* to be on a hanger.

- It's better spacewise to fold or roll up garments that hold their shape without hanging (knitwear, T-shirts, etc).
- Fold and stack stretch fabrics only if you have shallow drawers and shelves.
- Jeans and casual trousers can be folded too, as can dresses and long skirts in stretch fabrics.
- Fold socks in half and interleave to keep the pair together.
- Knickers can be rolled up; but bras need to lie flat.

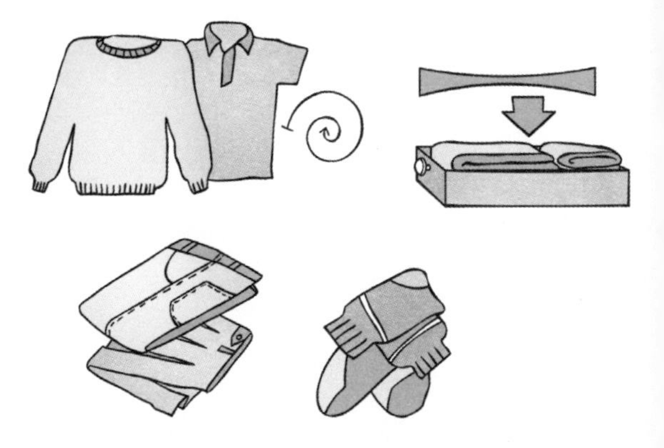

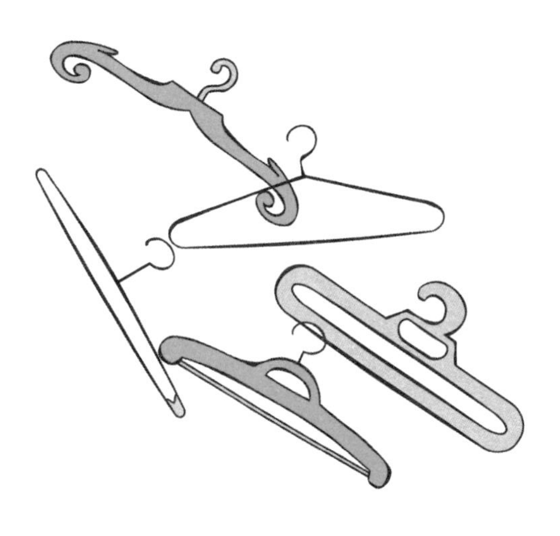

43. Hang-ups

Some garments *do* need hanging.

- For skirts, use hangers with rubberized clips, or hang by the loops on the waistband or side seams.
- For formal trousers, use dedicated trouser hangers or smooth wooden hangers (snags and splinters will damage the fabric). When folding, align the inseams.
- Use curved, sturdy coat hangers for outerwear and suit jackets.
- For tops and dresses in delicate, textured or slippery fabrics, use padded hangers.
- Choose straight-shouldered hangers for strappy garments, or pass a ribbon through the straps and tie loosely to hold them together.

44. Shoe-in space

Dusty shoe boxes and odd shoes squashed at the bottom of the wardrobe?

- Store your shoes in clear plastic drawers or hanging pockets. Not only can you see what you have at a glance, your shoes will be better protected from dust, humidity, mildew and pets than they would be in the original cardboard box.

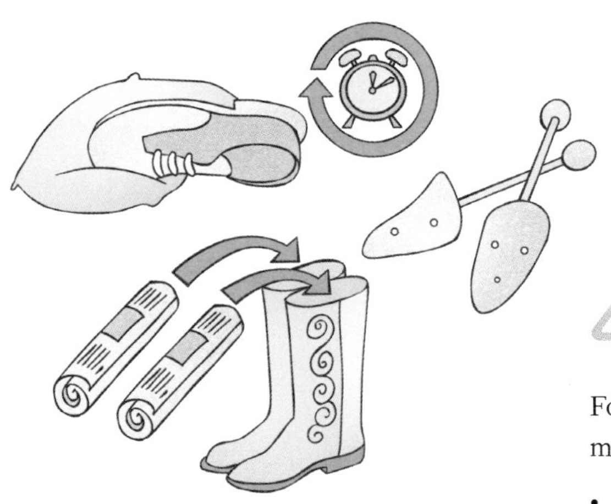

46. Tubed tops?

For delicate and decorated garments, minimize friction with tubing!

- Clear plastic tubes (such as those tennis balls come in) are perfect for protecting delicates.
- Tumblers can also be used for garments and accessories that scrunch up small.
- Try to stick to the same type of tube.

Note: This method will not prevent crushing. It is best for knits and garments that can be ironed, or that won't show creases (e.g. a fully beaded scarf).

45. Leather on wood, silk in paper

To keep your best pair of shoes in good shape, a little post-wear consideration is needed.

- Avoid wearing the same pair on two consecutive days. Give shoes, leather especially, at least 24 hours to dry out and return to their original shape.
- Use wooden shoe trees to help leather shoes keep their contour.
- If you don't have boot stretchers, roll up two magazines and pop one down each leg.
- Wrap strappy evening sandals and satin slippers individually in acid-free tissue paper and place each pair inside a sturdy box.

47. Set and match

Perfectly matched sets of bedlinen are not very versatile in terms of changing your decor. In addition, losing, staining or tearing any one item means a full-set replacement – not very budget-friendly. Go with co-ordinates instead *(see Tip 7)*.

- If you *must* match, store sheets and second pillowcases (folded) inside one pillowcase to hold the set together. Easy to find, easier to carry.
- Use all white – even if your linen isn't all from the same set, nobody will notice.

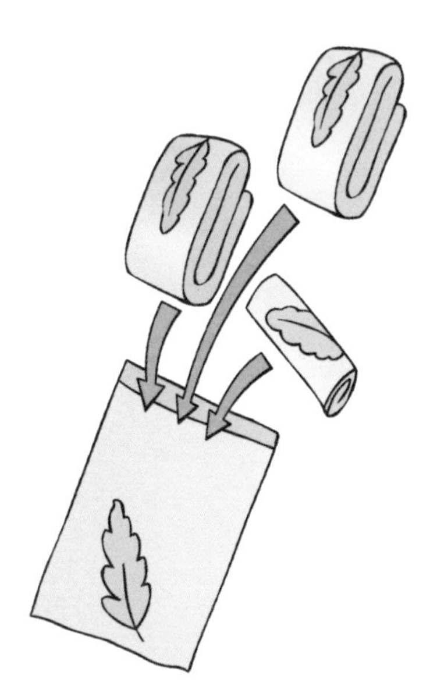

48. Umbrella stand

These seem to have fallen out of fashion, although it hasn't stopped raining! An old metal pot caddy makes the ideal umbrella tidy.

- Drips won't pool inside your container.
- If you live in a seriously wet climate or have carpeting or wooden flooring in the hall, you could put a large plant saucer under the caddy.
- The pot-holder is probably moisture-resistant – after all, it was designed to withstand watering – so a mildew-treatment is all you need to render it brolly-proof.

■ Better bathrooms

49. Remote hook-up

Sick of hunting for the remotes? You have two choices:

- Have a dedicated remote-control box in each room.
- Alternatively, glue a bit of Velcro to each remote and attach its counterpart either to the side of the TV or to the shelf or wall behind. Let them stick together now!

The real key to success, though, is remembering to put the remotes back after every use.

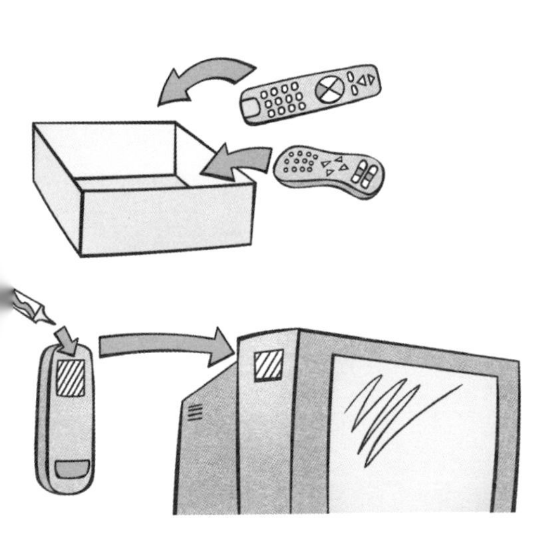

50. Rail against the door

For large families, the average length of towel rail can be a tight fit on busy mornings.

- Consider a ladder-style radiator rail instead.
- Choose a pedestal basin with a built-in rail under the rim.
- Add a rail at waist height behind the door.

Child-sized clutter busters

51. Children's hideaway in plain sight

Choose at least one large and stylish piece of storage furniture for the living room.

- A storage cube that doubles as an ottoman
- A rattan chest
- A closed picnic basket
- An old-fashioned trunk

Keep it empty for emergency storage of household clutter and children's things that you need to clear away in a hurry when you have company at short notice. It's especially useful if you work from home and clients might drop in to your 'office'.

52. Child-high shelving

High shelves keep things out of the reach of little fingers. But shelves in the children's room should be low enough for them to access safely.

Run a narrow line of shelving around the room at picture-rail height with a row of pegs beneath, wherever larger furniture doesn't interrupt them. They can use the space for favourite toys and books, even a small radio or CD player, as well as for hanging bags, jackets, scarves, etc.

When they're older, that space can house their model aeroplanes, CDs, jars of seashells or beads…

53. Sticky blackboard buddies

For the children's room, it's worth investing in magnetic blackboard paint. It's handy for them and saves space too.

- Paint the cupboard doors or half a wall (behind the desk, perhaps) with it.
- Drawings, timetables, photographs, pin-ups and other keepsakes can go on the same surface they scribble on.
- It's versatile enough to stay useful for toddlers to teens.
- If you're worried that all the dark matte paint will darken the room, paint the *inside* of the cupboard doors instead! Visual clutter vanishes too!

54. Dish up the paperwork

You don't need expensive filing systems for household paperwork.

- Sort papers into folders and expanding/accordion files that are colour-coded by subject – household bills, children's school papers, identification documents, etc.
- Reclaim an old wall-mounted dish rack with a lick of paint. The slots for the plates are perfect for sorting your files!
- Shelves are an added bonus – perfect for a box of stamps, a set of envelopes and notecards.
- Hooks for hanging cups can be used to dangle some cleaned-up paint cans for pens and pencils!

Oddments and ornaments

55. Stuck sharp

A magnetic board mounted on the inside of a cupboard door will safely store an assortment of small, sharp metal objects.

- In your sewing and craft cupboard you can use it for hanging small, lightweight scissors, stray pieces of hardware, knitting needles, even coils of wire.
- For the DIY cupboard, you can line up all your tap washers, different gauges of fuse wire and other electrical wiring.
- In your bathroom cabinet, it can hold tweezers and hair grips.
- In your laundry cupboard, it's ideal for safety pins.

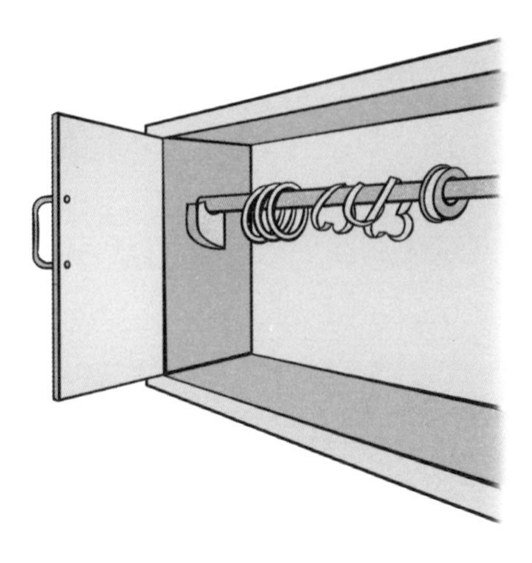

56. Don't spare the rod

Biscuit cutters, napkin rings, bangles, scrunchies, rolls of ribbon and spools of thread – more than a dozen of these become a pain to store.

- Fit some wooden dowels or curtain rods inside your closet. Instead of screwing the ends into the walls, rest them in cupped brackets to lift out easily.
- Run the objects along the dowels, by type.

This way you can see everything at a glance – and find what you want without rifling through the lot.

57. Tangle-free trinkets

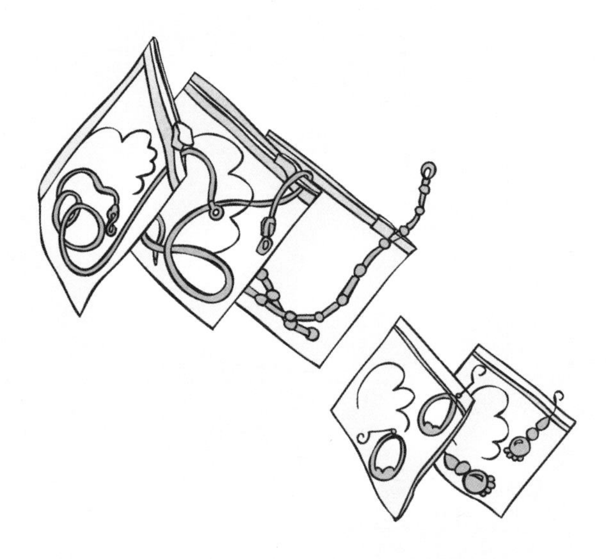

Necklaces forever in a tangle?

- Place them in individual zipped or re-sealable bags – allow the clasp to protrude beyond the slider track when you seal! Easy to find.
- Store earrings with hooks the same way, with the ends of the hooks protruding outside the bag. Makes it easier to open the bag without tugging!

58. Mesh your accessories

Costume jewellery spilling out of the jumble basket?

- Frame a rectangle of fine wire mesh or window-screen netting.
- Mount it on the inside of your wardrobe door with hinges along one side so you can open it out like a book.
- Thread earrings and brooch pins through the mesh.
- Add small S-hooks, and your necklaces and belts (hang them by the buckle) can join them.

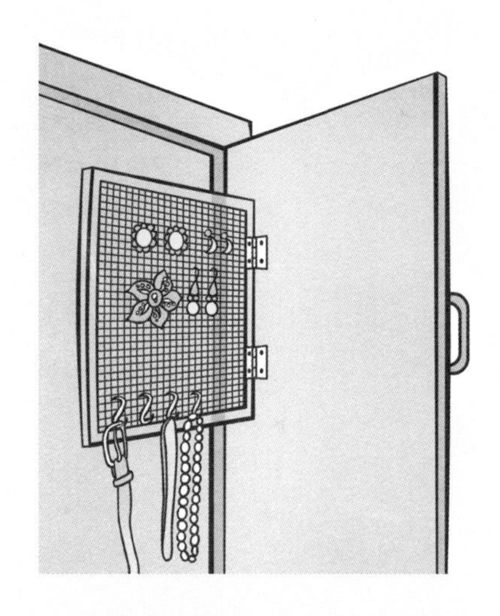

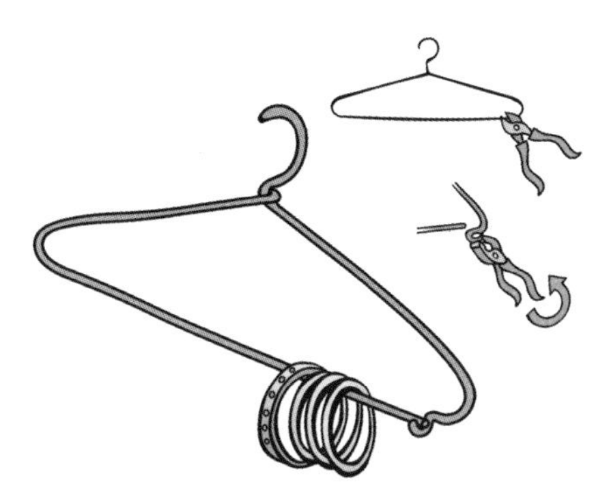

59. Hanging bangles

Bangles spilling out of a drawer? Hang them.

- Put on your work gloves and, with a wire cutter, snip through a wire hanger just where the horizontal turns up towards the hook on top.
- Using pliers, bend the curling corner into an open loop (U-shaped).
- File the free edges of wire smooth.
- Press the sides downwards a little, and the horizontal should sit neatly in the loop – the hanger is now rather like a giant safety-pin.
- Thread your bangles through – watch the weight or the wire will bend and bow!

■ Maintain your memories

60. Keeping keepsakes

Precious stuff clutters our cupboards and shelves, reducing immediate-access storage space.

- Special mementoes deserve their own treasure box.
- Choose a pretty, sturdy trunk for the collection.
- Get smaller cardboard and metal boxes that fit easily into it to house the little things.
- Get tiny decorated keepsake boxes for individual precious bits.
- Pack delicate items in acid-free paper.
- Use special fabric sleeves, envelopes or drawstring bags for expensive and vintage fabric or leather items.
- Replicate for each family member.

Unpack and enjoy those memories from time to time.

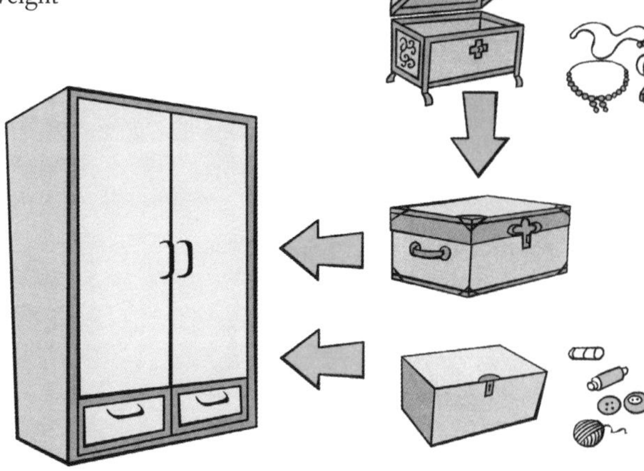

61. Once in a lifetime

For all those life-defining documents, you need to get a fire-resistant and water-resistant box. This is what you grab in an emergency evacuation, so keep it within easy reach (but in a safe place).

A heavy-gauge metal box or sturdy wooden box treated with fire-retardant material on the outside and lined with metal sheeting inside is best. Put in:

- Birth certificates
- School and college certificates/diplomas
- Passport and other state-recognized IDs
- Duplicate of driver's licence
- House deeds
- Marriage certificate
- Copy of your will/living will

62. Memory keeper

You can choose a very few defining memories from your memory box (*see Tip 60*) to put in your evacuation kit (*see Tip 61)*:

- Your wedding ring – if not on your finger
- The heirloom pendant (though it should really be in a safe deposit)
- Your baby's first photo
- Your parents' wedding photo

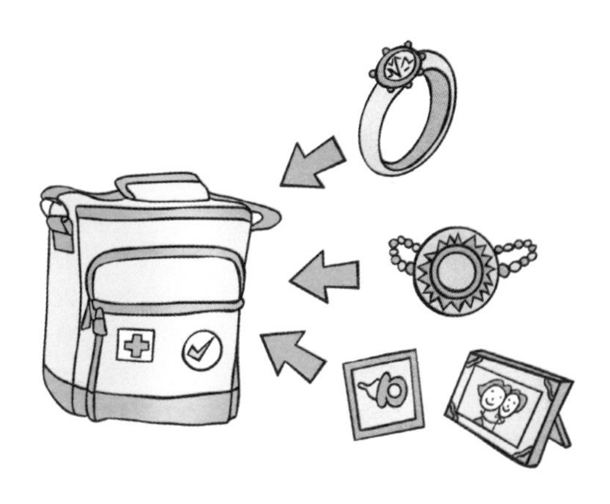

■ Keep it manageable

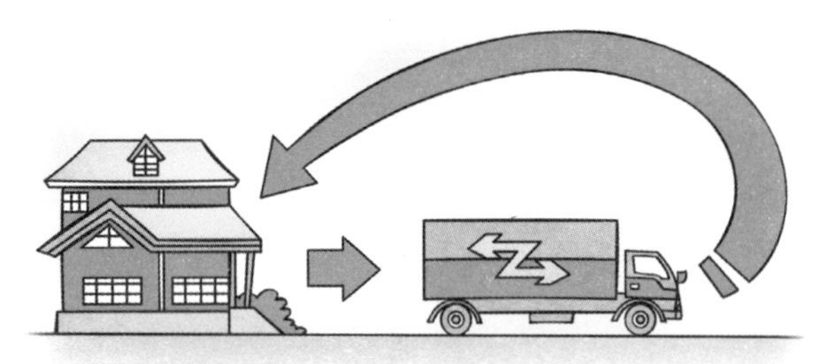

63. Practice moves

If your household seems clutter-prone, have a make-believe moving session every year. There's probably a lot you wouldn't bother to bring if you moved.

- Try scheduling the make-believe around New Year – call it 'moving into a new year' and children will readily make a tradition of the game.
- Get young children to draw their ideal room every year and make changes to their existing room accordingly.

64. Chalk it up

In humid climates, moisture can be difficult to keep at bay.

- Add bundles of blackboard chalk to drawers and shelves!
- Use them in the kitchen, bathroom, utility room and drawing room, as well as your wardrobe.

65. Keep things dry with gel

Problems with mould and damp when storing those precious items?

- For expensive equipment and accessories – camera lenses, fine leather bags – silica gel is the dehumidifier of choice.

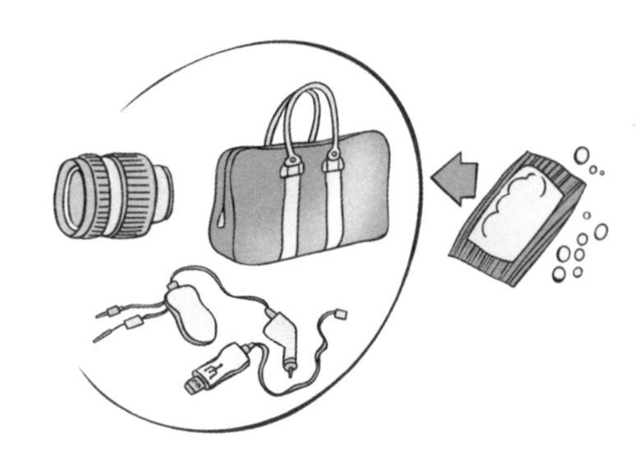

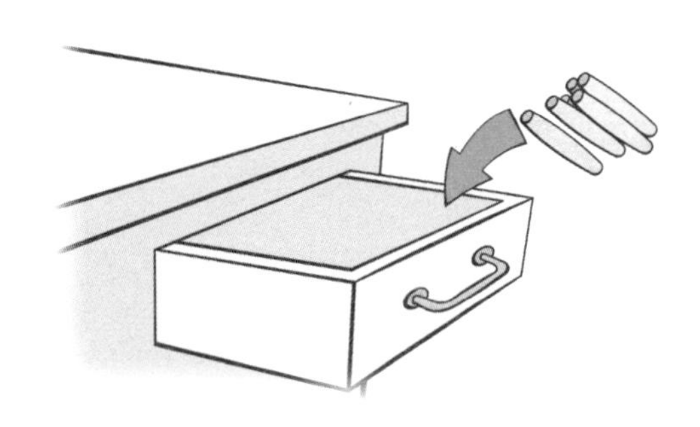

The Organized Home

Safety, first aid and home remedies*

Here's what you should keep to hand for safety and security at home; what precautions to take; and what to do when accidents do happen.

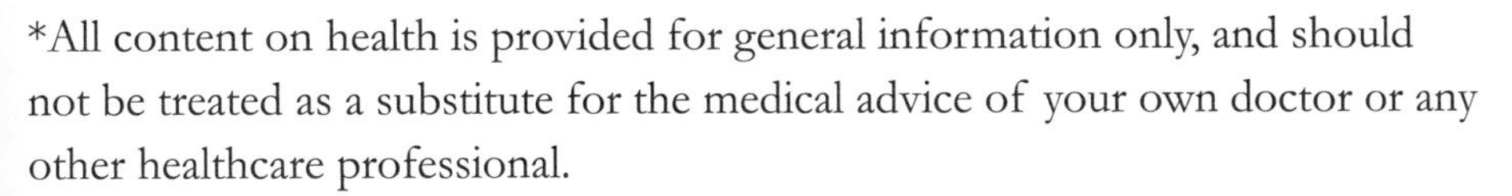

*All content on health is provided for general information only, and should not be treated as a substitute for the medical advice of your own doctor or any other healthcare professional.

■ Store up safety

66. The Essential Medicine Cabinet

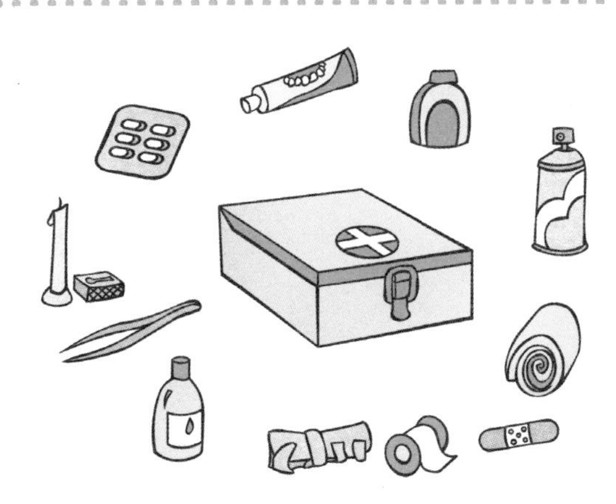

Collect the listed items in a sturdy metal box. Top up monthly.

- Toothpaste (basic white) – relieves the itch of minor insect bites.
- Borax – mix a mild solution in warm water for cleaning out minor injuries, sores and boils.
- Anaesthetic sports spray – for painful rashes and stings.
- Sterile gauze, a roll of sterilized cotton and cotton pads for bandages.
- An assortment of medicated adhesive bandages; sticking plasters.
- Splints.
- Antiseptic liquid.
- Pointed tweezers, a candle and a matchbox.
- Antipyretics, painkillers – clearly labelled with dosage and date.
- Emergency numbers (*see Tip 23*).

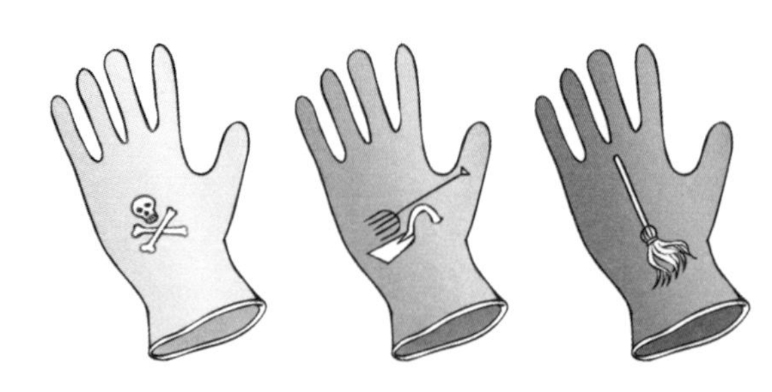

67. Peas for the pain?

A packet of frozen peas makes a versatile ice pack – the peas roll around like pellets, nicely shaping the bag around awkward spots like knees and elbows. What's more, it's a great freezer standby, so you don't need a separate space for your supply!

- Remember to put a thick folded towel against your skin before applying an ice pack to protect your skin from serious freezer burn! (Do the same for a hot pack.)

68. Pull on your gloves

Keep colour-coded sets of rubber gloves. They'll protect your hands from cuts and burns (chemical and electrical), and may even save your life.

- The yellow ones are for working with toxics.
- Keep thick and sturdy blue or green ones for DIY and gardening.
- Pink gloves are for general clean-ups.

■ Skin-deep – trouble on the surface

69. Sunburn!

It's not just unsightly or painful, it can even call for medical intervention.

- Cover the area at once with a clean cloth or towel, until you can get some cold water to sponge the area as well as to sip and rehydrate yourself.
- A light application of calamine lotion is soothing and helps healing.
- However, if that doesn't soothe the discomfort, you should see a doctor.
- Do not break any blisters that form!

70. Stung by a plant!

Summer brings with it a few plant pitfalls . . .

- Should you fall foul of poison ivy or nettles, a cool layer of calamine lotion should help.
- If it doesn't subside, you should see a doctor.

71. Itching insects!

If you're bitten by an insect that's left your skin stinging or itching:

- Check that the area is clean.
- If there's no debris, a paste of equal parts vinegar and baking soda should disinfect the wound and neutralize any mild venom.

In the flesh – broken skin

72. Know your enemy

If you can tell a doctor what bit you, you may not need to go to casualty.

- If it's a spider (if there are poisonous varieties in the vicinity), get to the doctor *at once*.
- For mammalian or non-poisonous reptile bites, wash with soap and water, apply a clean dressing, then call your doctor.
- For a severe bite with profuse bleeding or an unidentified insect bite, get yourself to the hospital fast!
- You may need a tetanus shot within 24 hours – your doctor will advise.

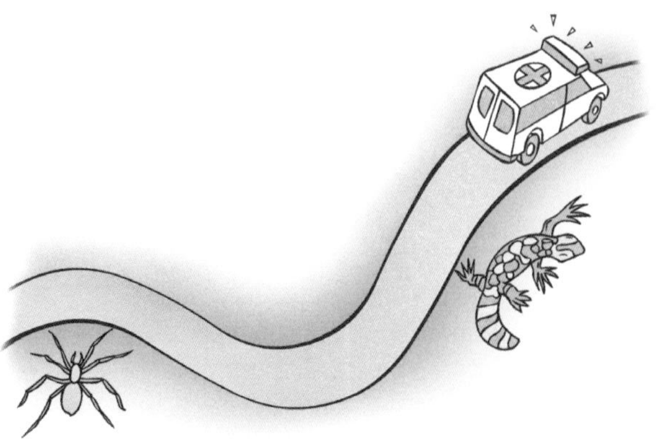

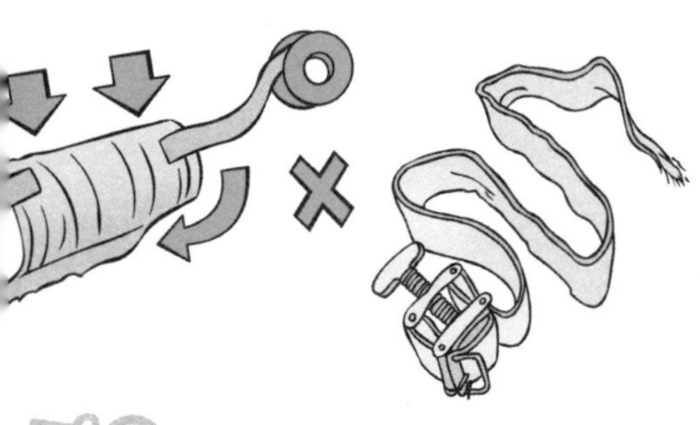

73. I got cut!

If it's deep enough to bleed profusely:

- Press a clean cloth or dressing pad against the wound to stem the flow.
- Elevate the cut area above the level of your heart, if possible.
- Holding the cloth pad firmly in place, bandage the wound.
- Do not lower the cut area until bleeding subsides.
- If the bandage gets soaked, quickly remove it and dress afresh, still applying firm pressure. Then seek medical attention.
- Do NOT use a tourniquet. Cutting off circulation is likely to do more harm than good.

74. Splinter in my thumb

Don't tug it out!

- Clean with soapy water.
- Disinfect tweezers in a candle flame for several seconds.
- Wait until cool – do not touch or wipe! (Ignore soot deposits.)
- Try to avoid touching the skin – grasp the splinter close to its base and pull out.
- Lightly press the sides of the wound – an absence of blood might indicate that a bit of the splinter is still in. On the other hand, any small fibres left should be dislodged as the wound bleeds.
- Clean the wound again and dress.
- Check it with your doctor.

■ Down in the mouth – and throat

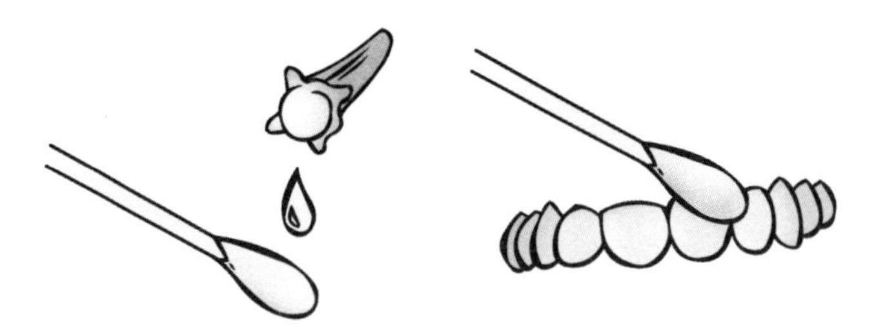

75. My tooth hurts!

One of the worst non life-threatening pains, toothache!

- Soak a small piece of cotton wool or the head of a cotton bud in clove oil; dab on the painful area.
- If it doesn't subside at once, leave in place for 2–3 minutes.
- However, don't lodge the cotton wool in your cheek and forget about it – clove oil can irritate the delicate membranes in your mouth and cause sores!
- See your dentist as soon as possible.

76. My throat is sore

This is an old-fashioned remedy but makes an effective palliative for the sore throat.

- Mix a little warm honey with lemon juice.
- Add a few drops of fresh ginger juice and some crushed basil leaves, if you have any handy.
- Take a spoonful every 20 minutes to 1 hour.

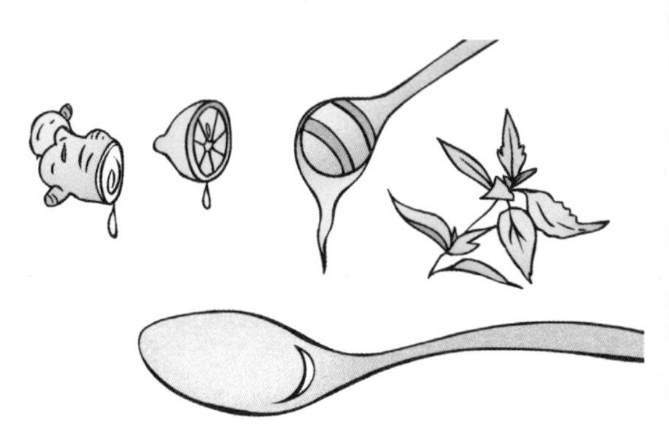

78. Lavender and vitamin E for burn scars

Skin often stretches drum-taut, when even a minor burn heals up.

- Lavender oil has long been a traditional remedy against the inevitable scars.
- A little Vitamin E oil will ease the tightness, enabling skin to stretch back to normal.
- To get both benefits in one, dilute the lavender oil with the oil from a Vitamin E capsule. Both are available from herbalists and natural pharmacists.

77. I got burnt!

It can be difficult to tell how bad a burn is at once, so you need to act immediately to minimize damage.

- Plunge the affected area into cold water for at least 10 minutes. A running tap, filled bowl or even bottled water will do.
- When the pain subsides a little, apply a sterile gauze pad and bandage.
- Do NOT use cotton wool or other lint-shedding material, or any ointment.
- Secure the bandage with a knot; do NOT use tape or sticking plaster.
- Get to a doctor.
- Do not puncture any blisters that form.

79. Wash the ashtrays

Ashtrays can be easily overlooked sources of fires.

- Always add a little water or sand to them to help extinguish butts.
- Never empty an ashtray into a full wastepaper basket.
- Sprinkle water into the ashtray before emptying or wash it out in running water.

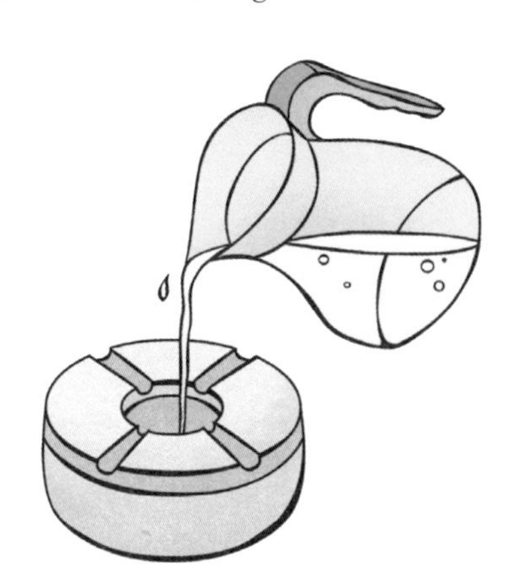

80. Contain the flame

Yes, our ancestors did it all the time; but we have safer means.

- Avoid moving oil lamps, stoves or candles while lit.
- Use battery-powered torches for emergency lighting, rather than a candle.
- Keep a couple of torches in each room where you can reach for them in the dark.
- Don't carry a lit taper to the fireplace, bonfire or candle – light it where it is going to be used.
- Be careful carrying a cake with lit candles or a Christmas pudding flambé.
- If possible, flambé using a flambé ladle, not on the stove.

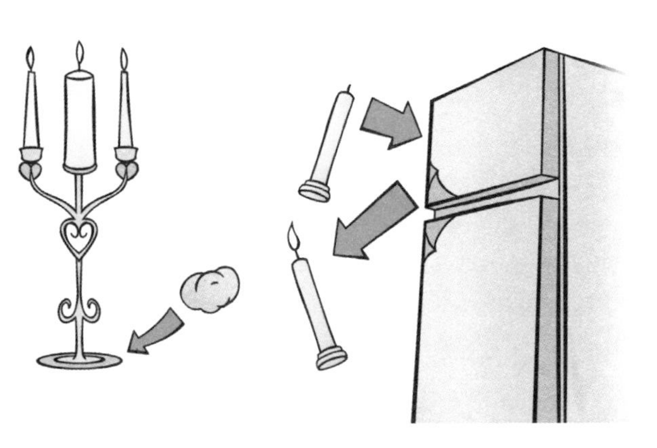

81. Candles standing against the wind

Tall candles in silver sticks or a mass of church candles bunched together on a platter – such an elegant, warm look for your table. But what if you topple one? Accidents happen.

- To minimize the chances of a hot wax disaster, add a spot of non-permanent adhesive at the base to hold them firm.
- Before lighting candles, place them in the freezer for 10 minutes. This will reduce dripping, helping them to stay in shape – and burn – longer.

82. Tumbling hot

Never ever switch off your tumble dryer or unload it before the entire cycle – including the cool-down phase – is complete!

- Unless it's helped to cool down, your piping hot laundry will be difficult to handle.

83. Not so hot!

Electric blankets can be brilliant – or, improperly used, a catastrophe.

- Never fold or tuck in an electric blanket.
- Unless it's specifically designed for use as an underblanket, never allow anything else to rest on it – a person, a pet, the jacket you just shrugged off or even a light coverlet or throw.
- Electric blankets are not safe for children or pets!

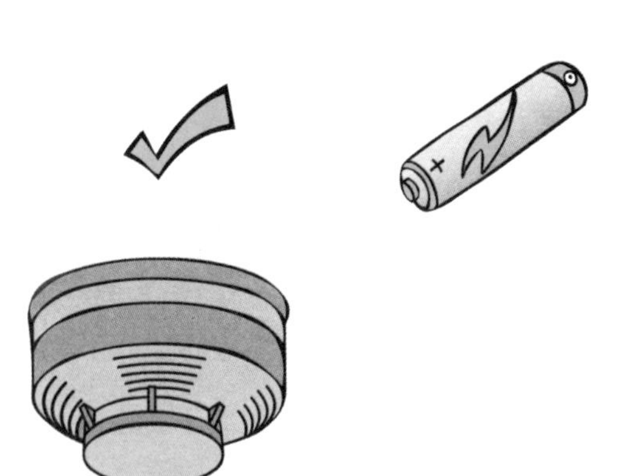

84. Fire alarm

Make sure your fire alarm is ready to alert you!

- Check smoke detectors during your weekly cleaning of each room and space.
- If your detector isn't wired to the mains electricity, replace the batteries regularly; set a reminder on your phone or an alert on your computer.
- Check fire extinguishers every year – New Year's Day is a good choice.
- Make sure there's a fire extinguisher in easy reach of hotspots: stove, oven, microwave, fireplaces, and outdoors if you have bonfires or barbecues in the garden.

85. Smother that fire!

It's a great idea to keep a few fire blankets in the house.

- If you can't buy any, get some large, thick canvas sheets with a tight weave and good drape.
- Keep one near the kitchen, one by the fire extinguisher for the back yard, one just outside the children's room (but out of a very young child's reach because it can smother), one in the hall downstairs and one upstairs (preferably near the stairs).

86. Sand blanket

Rather than relying on buckets of water or snow as fire safety back-ups, have some buckets of sand to hand.

- Water (liquid or frozen) can increase the danger of an electrical fire and is likely to make a fat-fed flame (such as cooking oil) worse. The blanketing action of sand is more likely to work in either case.
- Sand is also good for putting out fireworks. Have some to hand before you light up the sky.

■ Safety in motion

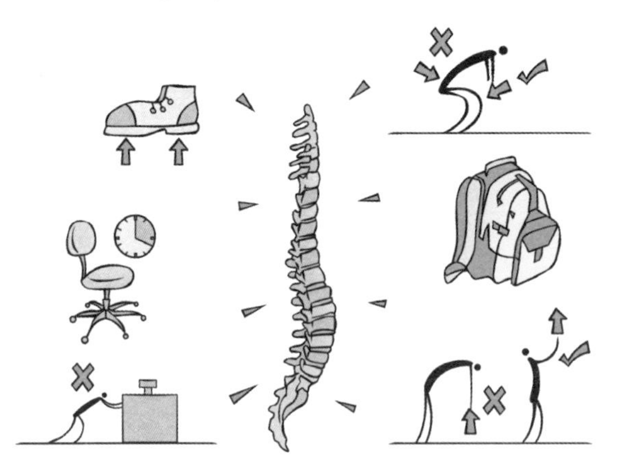

87. Ergonomics for safety

You don't realize how important your back is until you put it out. Put the mechanics of motion to work:

- Bend at the knees when lifting. Don't hinge from the waist.
- A shoulder bag is better than a handbag; a rucksack is safer than both.
- Divide loads evenly into two, one per hand.
- Don't 'pull up'; 'push up' instead – cradle heavy objects close to your body, arms underneath; don't let them drag your arms downwards.
- Wear well-cushioned shoes – even for household chores.
- Don't sit still too long. Pace or stretch every 20 minutes.
- Don't drag or shove heavy furniture; get help to lift and shift.

■ Unsafes away!

88. Hunt down the hardware

Stray screws, washers, sprockets, staples – sharp, small, rusty metal can kill! Do a daily sweep – you can use them again!

- Put a large magnet in a discarded shower cap or small polythene bag.
- Slip the open end over the vacuum nozzle.
- Hold in place with a rubber band, scrunchie or torn stocking.
- Pass over all hidden corners and under furniture. There's no need to plug in the vacuum – all iron will jump to it! Afterwards, remove the tie, invert the cap or bag and safely stow away your hardware (*see Tip 113*).

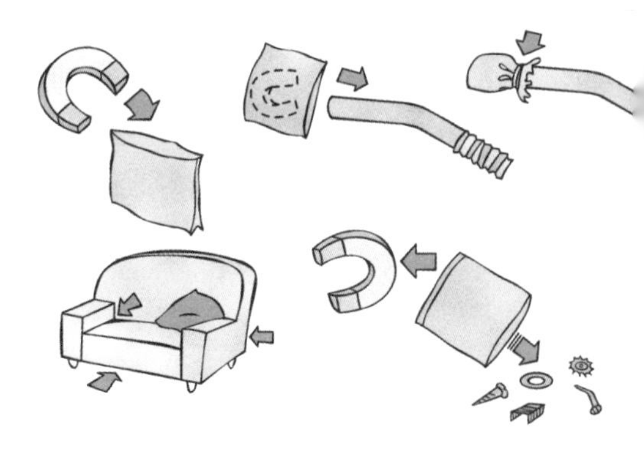

89. Safe storage

Many daily essentials are hazardous substances. Safety lies in careful storage.

- Keep corrosives away from metal.
- Volatile substances need a cool, ventilated home.
- Store flammables away from sparks.
- Keep hazardous substances away from children and pets.
- Place a copy of emergency numbers (*see Tip 23*) near such substances.
- Dry rags used with flammables (paints or solvents) outdoors – away from smokers! Store in tightly sealed metal containers.
- Protect hazardous substances against moisture – it corrodes containers.
- Never keep flammables and corrosives in breakable containers.

90. I smell gas...

At the very first whiff:

- Open all the windows.
- If it's a strong smell, evacuate the family and pets to the garden.
- Do not switch anything on or off – don't even try to turn off the mains. The smallest spark could set off an inferno!
- Do not use the phone – once you get outside, call your supplier from a mobile phone or neighbour's phone.

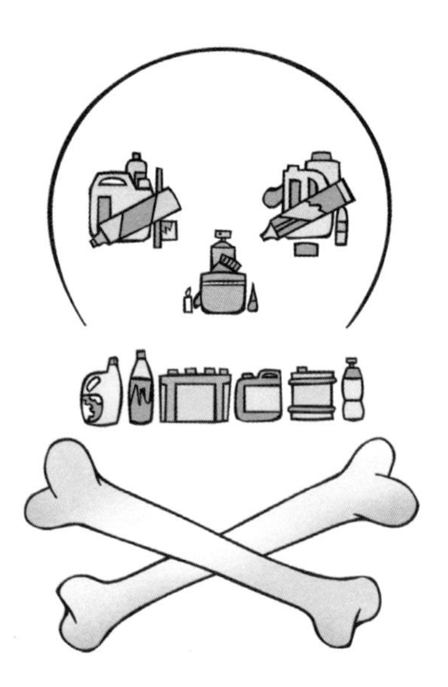

91. Household hazards

Treat these as hazardous and store accordingly (*see Tip 92*).

- Garage – motor oil, anti-freeze, batteries, brake and transmission fluids, fuel, kerosene, car wax.
- Workshop – paint, primer, varnish, stains, thinner, stripper, adhesives, mineral spirits, tar, anti-rust solutions, fixatives, solvents.
- Utility room – toilet cleaners, tile cleaners, drain unblockers, oven cleaners, stain removers, furniture polish, window spray, bleach, dyes.
- Garden and pets – pesticides, insect repellents, weed killer, pet products, pool cleaners, sealants.
- Indoors – mothballs, batteries, fluorescent bulbs, electronics, aerosols, smoke detectors, lighter fluid, shoe polish, hobby equipment, cosmetics, mercury thermometers, medications.

92. Danger – Plaster ahead!

If you have a young child it's a good idea to flag up the danger points:

- Consider pasting stickers with a child-friendly figure with a bandage on potentially dangerous objects. (Establish early on with the child that this is a 'BIG OUCH' sign!)

93. Lock up the keys

If you leave your keys near the door, they could easily be hooked out.

- Make sure keys can't be reached even with a long-handled tool. If you must have them near the door, hang them inside a key cabinet with a stiff bolt.
- Don't keep your keys in the same place as your money – a pickpocket going for one could get lucky with the other.
- Lock up all ladders and tools, especially if you keep them in outdoor locations such as the garden shed or garage.

94. Vault-worthy valuables

Expensive goodies belong in the bank's safe deposit box. If you must keep them in the house, at least make sure they can't be seen through windows.

- A cupboard that's right opposite or next to a window, let alone a door, is a poor place for valuables.
- Carry your jewels in your handbag and put them on at the party venue (and vice versa on the way back).
- Or at least wrap up so your bling is hidden by your collar or shawl.

95. Post-free zone

Don't let the post pile up while you go on holiday – it's an open invitation to burglars.

- If possible, get the post office to hold or redirect your mail.
- Otherwise, ask a friend or neighbour to look in daily and collect.

96. Personal is private

You may be just an internet search away; but the whole world needn't know your personal details.

- Shred documents that display personal data; dispose in batches over two to three days (to prevent reconstruction).
- Put surnames only on nameplates and ID tags – not full names.
- Don't state your name on the message on your answering machine. Never record your child's voice.
- Live alone? Get a friend to record your answering machine message; change monthly.
- Talking to a handyman or telecaller? Use the royal plural: '*We* would like…'
- NEVER carry passwords in your wallet!

97. Stay hooked up

- You should switch to cordless phones when you have a baby. However, don't pull the plug on the old handset yet. Should the electricity fail, most cordless phones won't work as the base unit requires power.
- Keep one handset for emergencies.

Secure your outdoors

98. Get a grip on the garden

Tidiness in the garden means safety.

- Always carry tools in a trug or gardener's caddy. Put it back as soon as you've finished using it.
- Have individual compartments for all tools, so you know at once if something's missing.
- Check and clean tools before storing.
- Put away pesticides and fertilizers immediately after use.
- Take them out one at a time if you're working with large containers.
- Promptly fill holes and ruts to prevent stumbles.
- Fix loose paving or damaged decking at once.

99. Lawn perils

When working on the lawn, watch out for these common pitfalls.

- If you use a powered mower, make sure you rake away any rocks or gravel – the mower could fling them out and injure someone.
- Don't leave the mower out of sight while you take a break.
- If you stop to go inside for a drink, make sure you can keep an eye on the equipment from the kitchen.

100. Good fences

Those are the ones that keep trouble out and contain the residents safely.

- Check fencing, posts and stakes regularly for splinters, breaks and protruding nails.
- Also look out for peeling paint, which can lead to rot and rust setting in.
- Make sure there isn't a gap under the fence that an animal could slip through – such as your pup burrowing out to explore.
- A gate that swings to and clicks shut on its own is always preferable.

101. Shout for safety

Teach the whole family your emergency drill – and practise it weekly (monthly should do with over-12s). Use a codeword signal as well as an alarm.

- Choose your codeword with care. Try 'Scramble!' or 'Scram!' or 'Scoot!'; not 'Emergency!'.
- Tell children they can use the emergency word to warn you if they feel threatened in public.
- Teach your dog to take his place in the drill.
- Make sure your codeword is short enough to use as a signal to your pet!

102. What's the drill?

Improvise based on your children's age and where you live.

- If there are neighbours within hailing distance, include a warning shout.
- 'Help!' should be among your infant's first words. However, guard against a 'cry wolf' tendency!
- Practise using a multiplicity of exits.
- Keep all emergency exits clear.
- Not all safety equipment is safe for children to handle; have a list of what is accessible to them, and teach them how to survive without the rest.
- Teach children that loud sounds, flashing lights and bright colours attract attention.

The Organized Home

Greener living – recycle, reuse, renew, ration

Do your bit to restore your old stuff to new glory, rather than cart it to the rubbish tip; make your garden greener, and your shopping list too; add some small steps to save.

■ Ecological rescue

103. Polo-necked warmers

The poloneck pullovers your child outgrows can easily be transformed into covers for hot water bottles.

- Simply detach the sleeves at the seams and sew up the sides.
- Raglan sleeves are particularly good as you don't need to take in the side seam – just closing up the armhole gives a nice shoulder to fit the bottle.
- Pop the bottle in and sew up at the base.

Some lovely warm memories to snuggle up to!

105. Intoxicating candlelight

Short stubby candle ends don't do much for your silver candelabra. However:

- They're the perfect height for sticking in the top of old wine bottles for a romantic café ambience – and you won't mind the drips messing up the holder so much, either.
- Place the bottle in an old ramekin to catch the drips before they reach the tablecloth, though.

104. Framed out of the box

Filling up the wall with framed prints is a bit passé. Put those old jam jars to use instead.

- Carefully roll up each of your holiday photos and pop into a jar.
- Add a little pillow of silica gel to each.
- Screw them shut and line them all up on a shelf at eye level.

These *will* get the conversation rolling.

107. Splash of cool

Does your old but serviceable umbrella turn your day greyer than the cloudy skies? Rescue it with a game of paintball.

- Pop the old umbrella in a large cardboard box and turn on its side.
- Cover up everything in the vicinity!
- Now shoot a smack of vivid colour or two with a paint gun. Fluorescent and glow-in-the-dark fabric paints are an especially bright touch.
- Leave it to dry. (If you don't have a paint gun, see if your child will sacrifice an old water pistol.)

106. Bar art

Got more olive oil, wine and vodka bottles than you know what to do with? Fill them up and colour your home bar crazy.

- Pour in some thick plastic emulsion paint into each bottle, swirl around and tip out the excess.
- Leave to dry completely.
- Wipe any dribbles and smudges on the outside with a rag dipped in thinner.
- Display on the shelf.

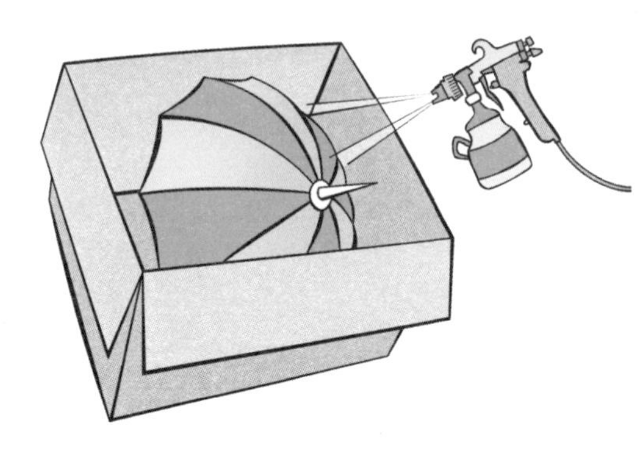

108. Shoe in the door

One half of your favourite pair of shoes is beyond repair, but it breaks your heart to show your old pals the door.

- Disinfect the mangled shoe and offer it to a dog kennel for a chew toy.
- Use the still stylish stiletto as a wedge to stop the door slamming!

109. Ice tub

That old inflatable paddling pool could be just the thing for grown-ups to drink from!

- You can fill it with ice to chill the beer bottles in for a big bash.

Handier than an ice chest, cheaper and not as space-hungry.

110. Gifting jars

Be a domestic goddess and give home-made treats as gifts.

- Save all jars and bottles, steaming off the labels; any leftover glue usually yields to make-up cleanser followed by alcohol-based toner.
- If the lid has a brand name on it, cut out fabric circles a bit larger than the lid and paste down with non-toxic glue.
- Stick on some ribbon or braid to hide the raw edges!
- After filling the jar, place a square of gingham, linen or muslin over the lid, secure with a rubber band and tie a bow around it.

111. Flowerpot caps!

It's difficult to keep small potted plants, especially kitchen herbs, adequately watered.

- Use old shower caps to keep the air humid and counter evaporation, and at the same time protect them from pollution and pet 'accidents' – you don't want a dog to spray your salad, do you?
- Of course, the plants do need to breathe too, so remove the caps every couple of days, or pull them on only when you're away on holiday and can't water or keep constant vigil.

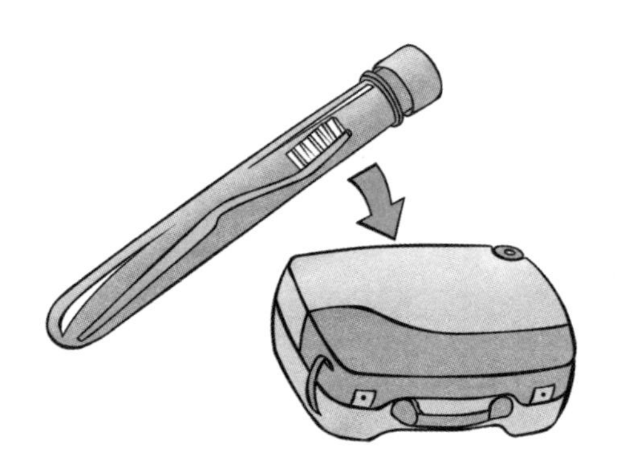

112. Toothbrush tube

Those old plastic test-tubes that herbs, spices and bath salts come in are good friends to travellers (never use glass tubes for this).

- No more waiting for the toothbrush to dry – and then forgetting to pack it. Pop it into a test tube and pack at once.
- Do replace any natural cork stoppers with rubber or plastic ones – the real thing will crumble.

113. Haute hardware

When you find stray metal bits and bobs lying around the house (*see Tip 88*):

- Put the odd shapes and sizes and those you recognize into your tool kit until you identify where they came from.
- For the more generic stuff – standard sizes of screws and sprockets– use your child's bead basket (over-tens only, please!) or your own workbasket.
- You can string them together as bracelets and pendants on a rubber or leather thong.
- For ponytail rings and elastic or leather wristbands or belts, sew or glue them on (use non-toxic fabric glue).

114. Loofah for the lot!

Buy these natural scrubbing aids by the dozen – the plainest you can find (no handles or fancy shapes to boost the price).

- Use them as an alternative to plastic scrubs in your eco-friendly kitchen. They're good for pots and worktops alike.
- Bring them back to the bathroom to scrub the basin and bath, and to clean gardening equipment.

Completely biodegradable, they – literally – don't cost the earth!

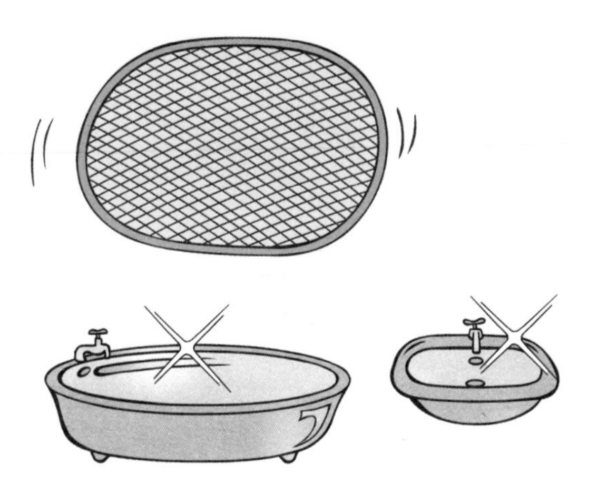

115. Packing peanuts for pots

Adding broken crocks and gravel chips in the bottom of pots keeps the roots of plants well-drained, but the extra weight makes the planters a pain to shift.

- Try re-using the polysterene beads used to cushion goods during transportation. They're lightweight, and it's a good use for a non-biodegradable material that's difficult to recycle.

116. Super sections

Hold on to those old egg trays and use them to store:

- Delicate Christmas baubles
- Spare light bulbs
- Freshly sprouted seedlings waiting for the pot

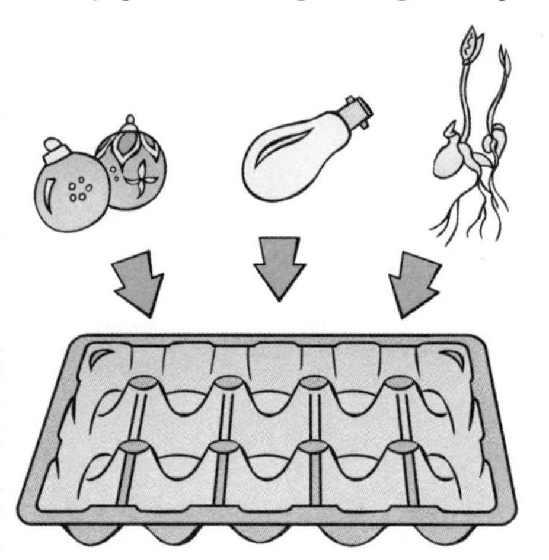

117. Soft stuffing

Stuffing handbags with tissue to help keep their shape is all very well, but the acid used to bleach the paper can damage the leather! And it's another unnecessary use of paper.

- Roll up old T-shirts or tights to pad bags instead.

You can also use the same technique for coat sleeves.

118. Short, stout, spouted – and string-y!

Got an old cracked teapot or kettle that you haven't the heart to throw away? As long as the spout is in place, you can keep your balls of twine in it!

- Pop the ball of string in and thread the free end through the spout.
- Repeat with as many spools as will fit in comfortably with a little room to roll around in. Shut the lid on them.
- When you want some string, just tug it out of the spout.

You can keep ribbon for gift-wrapping this way too.

119. Ramekin lights

Transform old ramekins into stylish LED candle holders.

- Spray-paint if chipped.
- Take a length of non-stick baking paper about 2½ times the circumference of the ramekin and about 5 cm/2 inches wide.
- Using superglue, fix the strip at a slight diagonal under the rim.
- Continue to overlap the parchment strip so it swirls to a second level.
- Glue fire-retardent tinsel round the rim.
- Tie on some cloves to exude a mild aroma.
- Add your LED candle.

Never leave unattended while lit!

120. Plastic mesh scrubbies – for free!

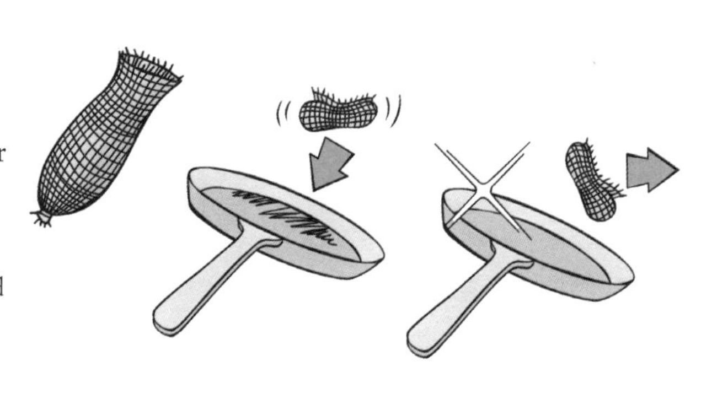

Save those little mesh bags the oranges or potatoes arrived in.

- Next time you have a greasy pan to clean, don't waste your usual scrubber on it (if used on a really gloopy mess, it will probably be beyond rescue or reuse). Use the clumped up mesh instead!

Now you can throw it away with a clearer conscience...

121. Scissors soapbox

Keep things separate in your dressing-table drawer:

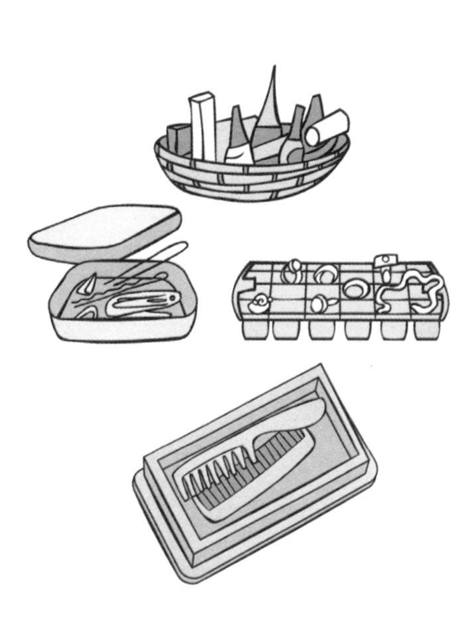

- Recycle biscuit tins, small baskets or a cutlery tray for lip colour and nail varnish.
- Mint or pastille tins could house hairpins and small clips.
- Ice trays can hold rings, brooches, cuff links and flexible bracelets or necklaces.
- Keep your watch in its box.
- Get a covered box for hair accessories.
- An old cigar box is ideal for combs and brushes.
- Cardboard soap boxes are perfect for tweezers, manicure staples, and scissors.
- A biscuit tube is perfect for cottonwool pads.

122. Filter again, and again

Paper coffee filters, like any other paper product, require trees to be cut down to make them.

- Switch to the reusable mesh type.
- The golden colour means you can wash them one last time and use them in craft projects like tinsel once they're really done for.

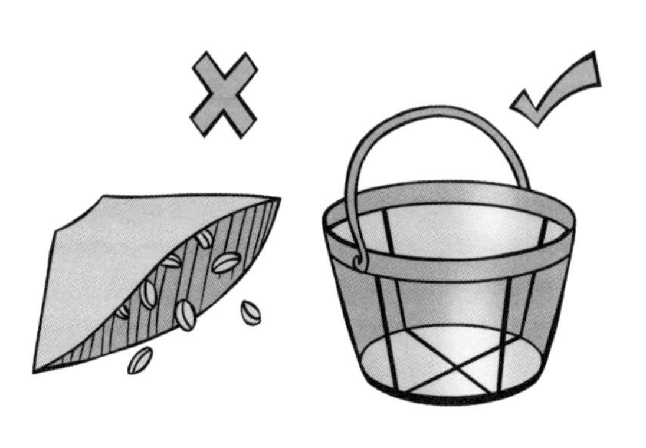

123. Spice rolls

If you have any old film plastic canisters from the days before digital cameras, you can use these plastic containers as spice jars.

- They are the perfect size and shape for small quantities of herbs and spices.
- The opaque material guards against deterioration caused by light.
- They are easy to get hold of for replacements.
- They are easy to label, on the lid or the side.
- They are lightweight and unbreakable.
- If you like, you can even use a drill bit to perforate the lids and make shakers.

125. Don't bin the books!

Many councils offer recycling services for books, or at least paper. But why spend energy pulping them when they can be re-read?

- Giving to a charity is the easiest option.
- Go to the nearest children's hospital or care home, with every paperback, magazine and boardbook you've finished reading.
- If possible, check with your council where the 'recycled' books go. If they are reselling, that's fine too!
- Or, pinch a few pennies: sell them to a second-hand store and treat yourself to a new book with the money!

124. Bin bounty

Decluttering shouldn't just be annual.

- Have standing bins for things to: give to charity; 're-gift'; and take to the collection centre.
- Line each bin with a drawstring sack so it's easy to gather up and take away later.
- Make your own sacks by doubling up and sewing the sides of old sheets or curtains. For the drawstring, either feed in cord through the hem fold (stitches picked out at sides) or simply tie the mouth shut.

■ Green house!

126. Refresh your recycle bin

Got your own compost heap? Good for you!

- However, if you don't tip out the compost bin at least daily, try popping in a charcoal briquet in the bottom to combat festering odours.
- Every month or so, scrub the charcoal out well (use a stiff toothbrush) in hot water to which bleach has been added and dry in the oven or on the barbecue grill to 'recharge' for action.

127. Greener greenery

Plants cancel your home's carbon footprint and reduce energy usage.

- Deciduous trees are better close to your home than evergreens. The leaves will shade you in summer, but after they fall in winter, your home will receive sunlight!
- If you need extra shade in summer, a creeper or vine across the western or southern walls is a good bet. Allow them to trail and shade windows where possible.
- If cold winter winds are more of a bother, plant evergreens as a windbreak to the north and west.

128. Limit the effects of sun

Strong summer sunlight will damage your furniture and carpets.

- Consider putting reflective film or other sun-control treatments on south-facing windows, especially if you have large expanses of glass.
- Double glazing also helps.
- Install awnings on the south and west.
- Keep curtains drawn during the day, especially to the south and west.
- Choose fabrics in paler colours and tighter weaves that are more light-reflective.

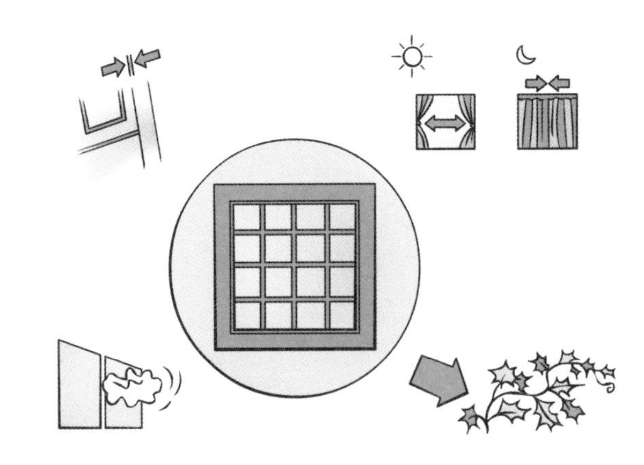

129. Keep the heat in

In colder weather, your windows can help reduce your heating bill.

- Make sure all gaps are well sealed. Weatherproof your windows.
- If they still feel draughty, consider putting a tight, insulating blind across them.
- Keep curtains drawn at night to minimize heat loss; open in the daytime to maximize solar gain.
- Make sure southern windows in particular are kept clean to let the most sun in.
- Don't allow plants to obstruct the sun coming in through the window or falling on and warming a wall.

130. A nice cuppa in the garden?

Many plants love an occasional feed of used tea leaves (or leftover cold tea), and several don't mind a shot of spent coffee grounds either!

- Not only are both great fertilizers, they also act as mulch if lightly spread over the soil, holding in moisture.
- As with any concentrated plant food, don't put too much too close to the root. Make it an occasional treat as an excess will kill the plant.
- Follow with a drink of water to dilute the nutrients and help them sink deep.

131. Peat-free peat!

Yes, peat is good for your garden. However, mining it isn't so great for the ecology.

- Switch to peat-free composts instead – a fabulous choice is 'coco-peat', made from coconut coir, which is a by-product of harvesting coconuts. Also, it is much quicker and easier to replenish than peat (which took millennia to develop).

132. Pave the path only

Why spread stone and brick around when there's precious water waiting to soak into the earth?

- Green cover holds on to soil and moisture – paving lets good rainwater run off into the gutter while exposed barren earth runs right away with the water.
- Have just a single driveway or path up to your front door. You don't need a maze of paved strips for the average-sized town property.
- To water, pull on your wellies and go wade in the grass! Or install timed sprinklers, adjustable for the season.

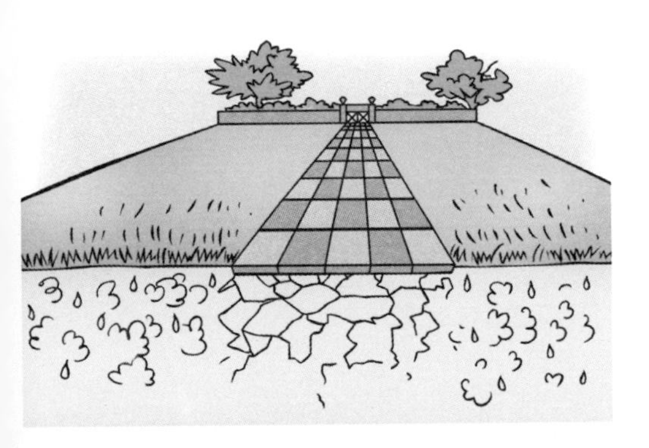

133. Butt before gutter

Don't lose water to the storm drains!

- Cut pipes to about 1 metre/3 feet above ground level.
- Add a water butt under each with a hole in the cover to accommodate the pipe.
- Make sure you can swivel the lid on the pipe!
- A charcoal brick in each butt will keep the water fresh for a week.
- If you have rain spouts, put a flexible garden hose down the mouth of each spout to catch the water without leaving an uncovered barrel beneath (this is dangerous as it can drown pets or small children).

134. Green fingers not required

You don't really need gardening skills to grow the hardy English ivy, golden pothos or peace lilies, yet all three are spectacularly good at filtering out household air pollution from common volatiles such as benzene and formaldehyde (they're everywhere – in your furniture, home-office equipment, filing cabinet, even kitchen and cleaning cabinets, not to mention your dressing table).

- All three have eye-catching sculptural shapes that give your décor an energizing 'lift'.
- Feng shui practitioners consider peace lilies good for absorbing the negative energies from electrical equipment. Put a pot next to the PC!

135. Water-based is best

Those harmful volatile toxins (VOCs, or volatile organic compounds) are most perceptible when you're in the middle of a paint job.

- Try to use water-based latex paints rather than oil-based paints for zero or low volatiles. It's the eco-safe thing to do.

136. Put a lid on fumes

Household volatiles are hazardous to air quality (*see Tip 135*).

- Buy water-based (such as zero-VOC paints) rather than solvent-based products.
- Paint with a brush rather than a spray gun.
- Switch to a propane or liquid gas barbecue rather than one burning solid fuel.
- Upgrade your fireplace too.
- Revert to a push lawnmower. If it has to be powered, electrical is better than petrol-driven.
- Avoid using leaf blowers. A rake will take only a little more time and effort.
- Get natural sprays rather than aerosol.
- Ban smoking indoors.

137. Faster wood

Avoid buying hardwood cooking utensils.

- Grasses grow faster than trees and bamboo is one fast-growing grass that yields wood quite similar to a tree's!
- Choose bamboo for utensils in the kitchen, especially those that see heavy use and a relatively short useful life – chopping boards and spoons.
- You can consider coconut wood for cooking utensils, especially the shell – coconut wood is moisture-proof.
- Keep the precious tree timber for furniture that you hope to pass down instead – it's that rare.

138. Look—free water!

Why buy mineral water when every tap in the house yields potable water?

- Tot up your monthly food bills. Check how much you spent on water.

Buy watertight metal flasks that you can sterilize. Fill up from the taps!

139. Glass that's greener from the other side

If you're shopping around for new glassware, consider recycled glass.

- Recycled glass products are now widely available (even in supermarkets!) in beautiful designs with a high-quality finish. And the cool green hue gives them a covetable vintage look.

■ Green your gadgets

140. Don't fan too freely!

Ventilator and extractor fans in kitchens, bathrooms and other work areas certainly are indispensable; but they do have their energy implications.

- Heated or cooled air is pulled out very quickly by these fans, resulting in higher energy bills.
- Switch them on for the minimum necessary time and switch off as soon as possible during extremes of weather – whenever you are using an air conditioner or heater that is!

141. In hot water

Avoid heating water unnecessarily. Turn on the boiler just before you need hot water and let it run for no more than 15 minutes.

- For just a little water, don't turn on the hot tap. This heats more water than you will use! Put the kettle on or heat a cup of water in the microwave.
- Insulate the hot water tank to minimize loss and wastage.
- Don't use hot water when cold will do.
- When cooking, use the smallest vessel and cover when bringing liquids to a boil.
- Adjust the dishwasher thermostat to a lower temperature.
- Set your washing machine to a cycle with a lower temperature.

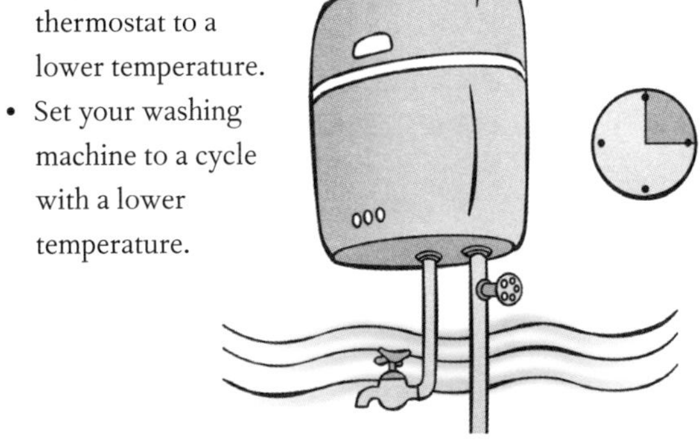

142. Cool it

Excessive cooling also wastes energy.

- Don't turn your fridge thermostat too low. The freezer should be at about -15°C/5°F and the main compartment 2.8–4.4°C/37–40°F.
- For long-term storage, invest in a separate freezer chest and keep it at -18°C/0°F.
- Defrost regularly. Never let frost build up to a depth of more than 5 mm/¼ inch.
- Cover liquids and wrap moist solids in the fridge. Evaporation from foods puts greater pressure on the compressor.
- Vacuum the coils regularly to help the fridge run for shorter periods at a time.

143. Laptop beats desktop

Portability isn't the only reason laptops are preferable to desktop PCs.

- They guzzle less energy.
- Plus, with having to plug it in and work around the wires every time you move – not to mention needing the socket for something else – you're unlikely to leave it on standby for as long!

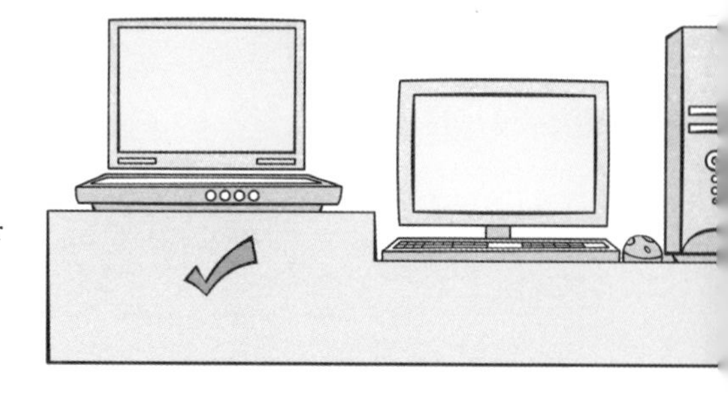

144. Conserve to save

Saving electricity not only helps the environment, it cuts your bills.

- Don't leave the modem connected or the computer on when not needed.
- Use the energy-saving settings of your monitor – let the screen go blank after 5 minutes of inactivity.
- Keep the brightness setting low and the contrast high – it's better for your eyes too.
- Use a dark background whenever you can – on the desktop, in your word-processing window, even on your web search.
- Turn off the screensaver.

■ Green light to power!

145. Light right

Get the lighting right and save on energy.

- Lights fitted with sensor switches, timers and dimmers save energy.
- Concentrate light where you need it. Use good task lighting – under-cabinet lighting for kitchen counters and a bright directional lamp on your desk; leave ambient lighting dim.
- To maximize the light you get from each bulb, use dedicated CFL fluorescent fixtures rather than fitting them inside existing shades.
- For spot lighting, use CFLs backed by reflectors. Good for the garage, workshop, laundry/utility area, basement or attic and task lighting.
- Send CFLs to your local recycling centre (they contain mercury).

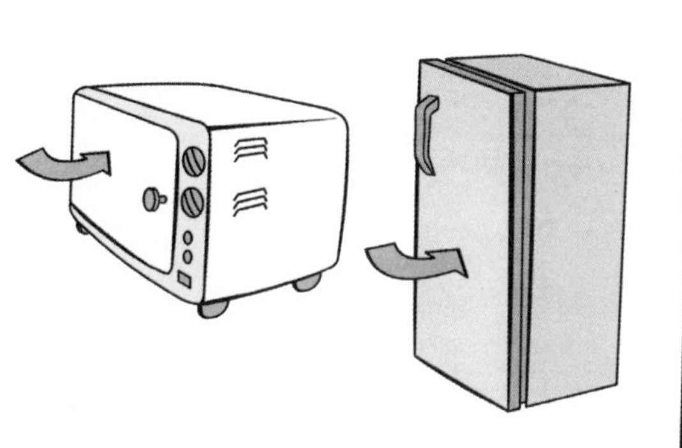

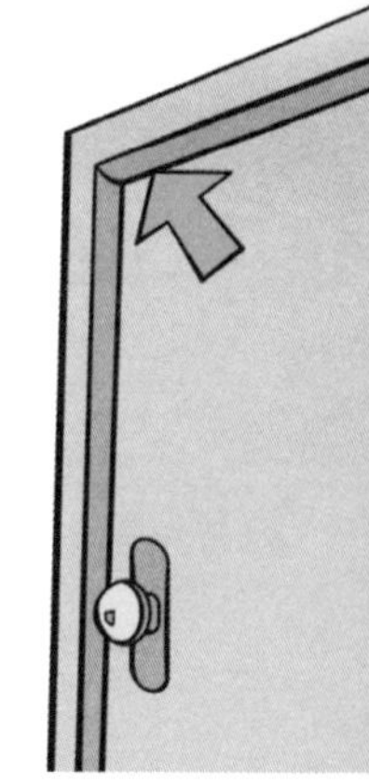

146. Bright LED

For decorative lights, CFLs may not be an option. However, there is a better choice than the traditional incandescent bulbs.

- Switch to LED – they use 80 per cent less energy and are even more environment-friendly than CFL. However, they cost quite a bit more, so you have to factor that in if you are thinking of all your traditional lighting requirements.
- For special occasions, however, the one-time cost of decorative LED is possibly one most families can happily absorb.

147. Keep the door shut

It saves untold kilowatts of energy and prevents pollution.

- Don't open oven doors too often, especially in winter, when cold draughts will make the temperature drop sharply.
- Don't keep refrigerator doors open too long either – for the reverse reason.
- Shut and insulate any gaps in doors between rooms with different sources of heating or cooling.

148. Plastic problems

Yes, do reuse those plastic milk and juice bottles – but not for more than two years, and try not to buy plastic in the first place.

- Once bacteria from saliva or sweat (on your hands as you unscrew the top), or even from the air, is introduced, there's no way to sanitize them completely.
- Plastic begins to decompose after a while. That's where the expiry date on packaged water comes from – water can't deteriorate, but its packaging can.

149. Let the car idle

Drive less, drive smarter.

- Shopping via phone or internet saves time, energy and fuel.
- Accelerate gradually rather than revving up.
- Replace your air filters and get the car tuned regularly to minimize emissions.
- Keep tyres well inflated.
- Drive more slowly on unpaved roads to avoid raising dust.
- Use the air conditioner only on the motorway; in slower city traffic, turn it off and roll down the windows.
- Remove the luggage rack when it's not required. It reduces fuel efficiency by adding weight.

Home Care

The big clean-up

Roll up your sleeves and muck right in for a sparkling clean home! We've got the equipment (and we're stocking some strange but super stuff under the sink); the short-cuts and time savers; the grime busters; and even help for some odd nooks and crannies that you (and time) forgot! Psst – for help with the laundry, look to the next couple of chapters!

The supply cabinet(s)

150. Complete clean-up caddy

Multitasking and mild is best for cleanliness. The 15 must-have implements are:

- Feather duster, with static-generating bristles
- Colour-coded lint-free dust cloths
- Mop for wet cleaning
- A dry mop
- Half a dozen pairs of white cotton gloves
- Multi-surface spray
- Anti-mildew tile/grout cleaner
- White vinegar
- Borax
- Pure household soap
- Wax polish
- A sack of plastic bags or bin liners for rubbish
- Mini-vacuum cleaner
- 2 pairs of thick rubber gloves
- Goggles
- Knee pads

152. Bleached clean!

Chlorine bleach is a stain remover and disinfectant.

- A weak solution is great for washing surfaces in the kitchen and bathroom.
- It's the safest bet for almost any surface in the nursery.
- A more concentrated solution (or the neat liquid) tackles most stains.
- It's even handy for plugholes, sinks and loos, as well as for disinfecting wipe-down appliances.

Keep the neat stuff away from plastics, acrylic, wood and marble.

Never use in conjunction with soap (or any detergent containing soap) as this will produce a poisonous green gas!

151. Where it's at

Sometimes, the difference between completing a job and not is whether you'll have to go up and down the stairs again for supplies. Keep specialized or frequently-used supplies in small baskets with carry handles, dotted around your home.

- A toilet brush and disinfectant in every loo.
- The full array of stain busters in the laundry room.
- Shoe polish and leather cream in the utility room.

The only multitasker to spread around is chlorine bleach. Keep small bottles in the kitchen, utility room and bathroom. Store away from soap *(see Tip 152)*.

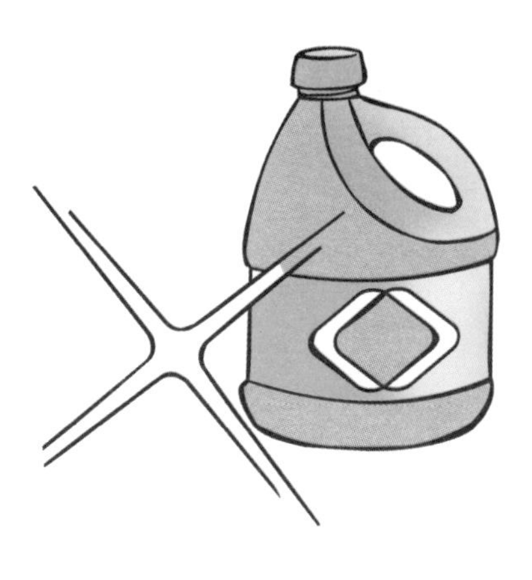

153. Better be big on borax

Besides acting as disinfectant (*see Tip 66*), borax is also a fantastic general-purpose cleaner – many 'natural' household products list 'borax' among the active ingredients.

A solution of borax is not as corrosive as the same strength of vinegar or lemon juice.

- Use a solution for almost all surfaces for regular everyday clean-up.
- Keep the tougher stuff for stains and deep dirt-shifting operations on a weekly basis (*see tips 155 to 157; but note 156*).

154. Strange stuff under the kitchen sink!

These unexpected additions to the cupboard under the sink should jazz up your cleaning routine:

- White toothpaste (basic) cleans most porous substances gently (stone and china) and shines metal fixtures.
- Mouthwash – quickly and easily removes garlicky and fishy odours; even curry seems to yield!
- Used lemon wedges and salt – together or with a dab of that toothpaste (for really stubborn stains), these shine up taps and metal sink bowls.
- Baking soda – good for dealing with milder food odours; fantastic for the stainless steel sink when made into a paste with vinegar.

155. Be good to wood

A monthly once-over polish is enough for most furniture and floors. A quick dusting every other day – even weekly – will suffice.

- Wipe down a well-waxed, laminated or varnished surface with a damp duster.
- A damp wipe-down in the kitchen at the end of the day with a very well-squeezed cloth and a solution of either mild detergent or bleach (to disinfect) is in order.
- Once every week or two, rub all wooden furniture with some vegetable oil into which a few drops of lemon oil or juice have been shaken.

156. Citrus is sweet – and strong

Besides leaving your home smelling of sunny Majorca, lemon juice shines all sorts of surfaces – laminates, ceramic tiles, stainless steel. It's great against grease and is a natural disinfectant and deodorizer.

- Reach for those used lemon quarters for stubborn splatters.
- Squeeze a few drops of juice onto a moistened sponge for a daily swipe.

Warning: Keep lemon away from stone worktops or quarry tiles; all stone will be burned through and stained by the acid and the stains are impossible to remove.

157. Vinegar for vim and vigour

Plain white vinegar will save you lots of elbow grease – and a pretty penny too.

It's invaluable for:

- Cleaning mirrors and windows.
- Removing limescale from vases and tumblers.
- Removing soap scum from tiles and shower panels, baths and basins.
- Removing the odours left by pet accidents, as long as the material can withstand bleaching – avoid using on coloured fabrics or untreated wood for this reason.

158. Don't mix cleaning agents

In general, mixing cleaning agents is almost always a bad idea. At best, an acidic and an alkaline cleaner will neutralize each other; at worst, the fumes can be lethal.

- Don't ever mix bleach with acid or ammonia. Both combinations generate toxic fumes.
- Always try to use one cleaning product, rinse well and wait to air out the space before trying a different one if the problem persists.

159. Happy hands

Dusting and dipping into hot water can really mess up your hands. Yet not every job can be tackled with rubber gloves.

- Smear a little petroleum jelly around your fingertips, working it well under your nails, before you tackle household chores.
- Slip on cotton gloves, pulling on rubber gloves over them when needed.
- Afterwards, just wash clean – no grime under your fingernails, either.

Bonus: You might find your cuticles nicely conditioned too, especially if you've had your hands in warm water!

160. Don't leave... yet!

After every shower – and this goes for every family member – do a quick tidy and wipe.

- Wipe down bath/shower, basin and surfaces with the appropriate implements – squeegee, sponge, tissue/paper towels.
- Dry that misted mirror.
- Bin all refuse – including hair clogging up the drainage.
- Put towels on rails or hooks, or in the laundry basket.
- Close the lid on the loo and flush.
- Make a habit of wiping the basin dry every time you wash your hands.

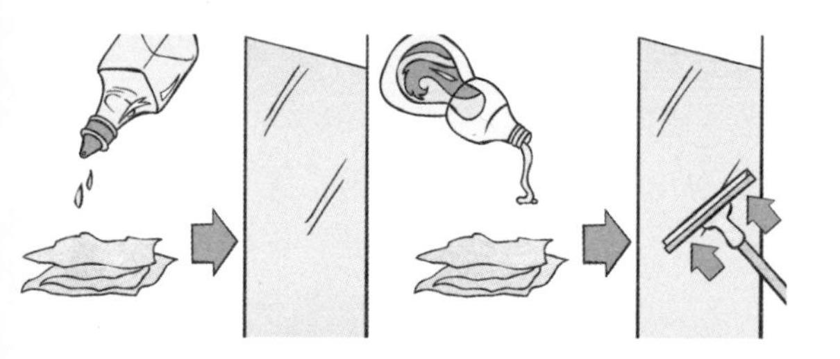

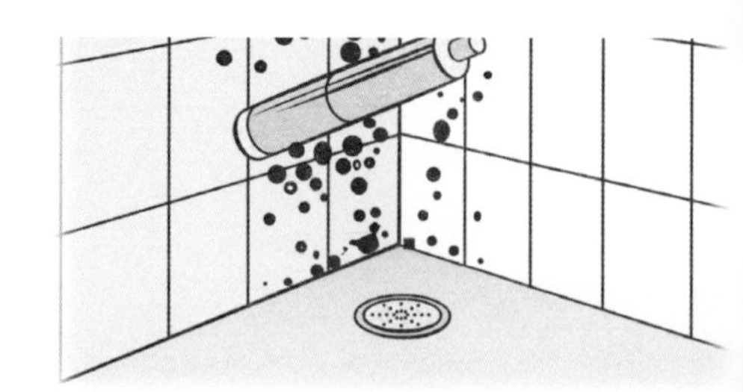

161. Scummy shower doors?

Hard water and soap suds can turn transparent glass into an ugly mess.

- Dip a cloth or plastic scrubber in white vinegar and wipe – this should shift the surface film.
- For a deeper scale, lather on some economy-brand shampoo and leave for a few minutes.
- Use a rubber-bladed squeegee to scrape it away.
- Spray on some vinegar for a squeaky-clean shine.

162. Mildew tactics

Regular wipe-downs after every shower and bath get tedious, even though they're effective for keeping stains at bay.

- Avoid using bleach, baking soda, borax, toothpaste and vinegar to shift scum, as they can compromise the sealant, which means the mildew problem usually keeps recurring.
- Reach for the anti-mildew cleaner at the first whiff of damp or dark smudge in the grouting! This is one specialist product that's worth its price.

163. Mist-free mirrors

It can be such a pain wiping the mirror clean after every hot bath or shower before you can see your face!

- Rub the surface lightly with a dry cake of soap or some neat shampoo each time you clean to keep the surface condensation at bay.

164. Spray the cloth, not the glass

Never spray glass cleaner directly on to glass – you risk damaging the window frame or mirror backing.

- Use the spray to moisten your cleaning cloth and wipe.
- Use a soft dry cloth to shine the glass and remove any excess fluid.

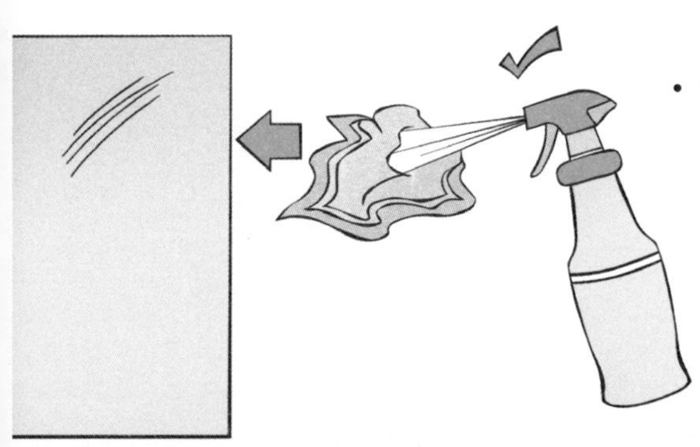

165. Worktops tough granite

Granite worktops are better at taking punishment than wood or marble, and won't show scratches in quite the unforgiving way that brushed stainless steel does.

However:

- Avoid all-purpose cleaners – the harsher ingredients in these cleaners will dull the stone over time.
- Clean with mild dishwashing liquid instead – it's gentler.

166. Sink freshness

Sometimes nasty niffs rise up from the kitchen drain.

- A sprinkle of baking soda down the drain should do the trick.
- Follow with some cider vinegar and cover with an upturned saucer.
- Finally, flush with boiling hot water.

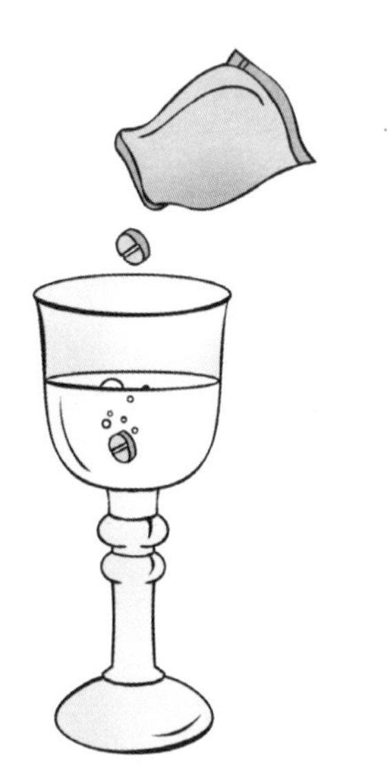

167. Crystal clear

Hard tap water is tough on fine crystal.

- To get your vases sparkling clean in a jiffy, fill them with some vinegar solution and leave overnight, then rinse out in the morning.
- If you're in a hurry, drop a couple of fizzing denture tablets into them and fill with warm water. Sit for a couple of hours, then rinse.

168. Wax off!

Clean wax from a metal candlestick:

- Wrap in a freezer-proof polythene bag and freeze for half an hour until the wax has become brittle.
- Rub briskly (through the bag) to remove the biggest drips.
- Tap lightly with a blunt knife to loosen.
- Those last smears? Lay down some newspaper, wrap the candlestick tightly in brown paper, scrunching it into crevices, and blast with your hairdryer.

Warning: Don't try this if the candlestick is made of glass, crystal or a mixture of two different metals.

169. Wax on glass

So you can freeze a brass candlestick to get the drips off. But glass or pottery?

- When cool, tap the wax gently to crack it.
- Ease and scrape off.
- Now get some kitchen paper, some scrunched up foil and the hairdryer. Direct the hairdryer on to the wax – don't let the glass get too hot! – and keep scrubbing away with foil.
- When a thin layer is left, wrap the glass in the kitchen paper and give it a final blast of hot air.

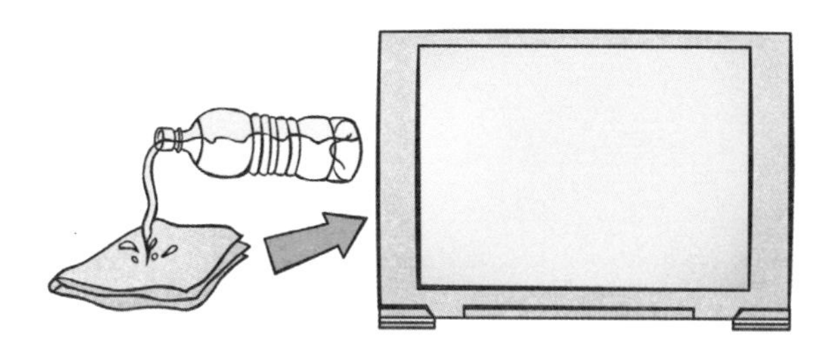

170. Only water for the TV

Never use those spray cleaners and glass-cleaning aerosols on the TV screen (or a computer monitor). The film left behind makes the dirt attracted by static stick to the screen!

- Remember to switch off and unplug from the power socket before cleaning.
- Use a soft lint-free cloth moistened with water.

171. Hand-in-glove cleaning

For smooth but fiddly surfaces such as slatted blinds, a dusting cloth or feather duster are not very effective.

- Pull on your white cotton cleaning gloves.
- Spray all-purpose cleaner directly on to the fingertips and swipe.
- To clean and wipe at once, spray cleaner on the right-hand glove and mist the left with water, then swipe with alternate hands.

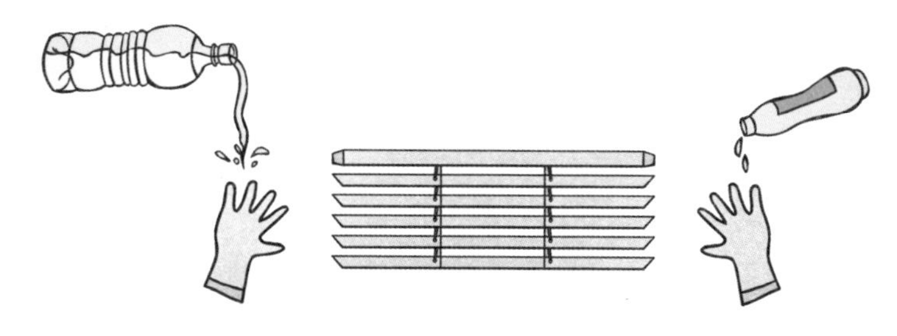

172. Cleaning nooks and crannies

All those intricately carved wooden frames, pleated lampshades, grooved panels and window sliders collect dust that's tough to shift. Although a thorough weekly vacuum will keep them in acceptable order, you'll need to get out your 'specialist' tools once in a while.

- For metal and stone crevices, an old baby toothbrush works best.
- For wood, glazing or ceramics, try a cottonwool bud.
- Fabrics can be brushed clean with either a toothbrush (sturdier fabrics) or a small fluffy paintbrush (delicates and intricate textures, such as devoré).

173. Pristine PC

This is especially important if you have a home office.

- Switch off and unplug from the power socket before cleaning.
- Turn over the keyboard, shake out any crumbs and dust, then vacuum with an air spray attachment.
- Clean the tops of the keys and side surfaces with methylated spirits or even a spritz of aftershave!
- Open up and clean the mouse.
- Damp dust the display, CPU and printer.
- Vacuum all vents gently.
- Wipe clean CD drawers.

Cleaning up the odds and ends

174. Wipe the washing line!

Putting out the washing?

- Wipe dust off the washing line or drying rack first, otherwise you'll end up with ugly streaks on freshly laundered clothes!
- Wash the line or rack once in a while too.

175. Bins for cleaning?

When your kitchen bin is ready for a scrub, make it multitask first.

- Empty the bin.
- Now use the bin as your mopping bucket – fill with whatever disinfectant solution you use to clean the floor, and get to work!
- By the time you're ready to pour the water away, the bin should be quite free of debris and germs! Now all you need to do is rinse and dry.

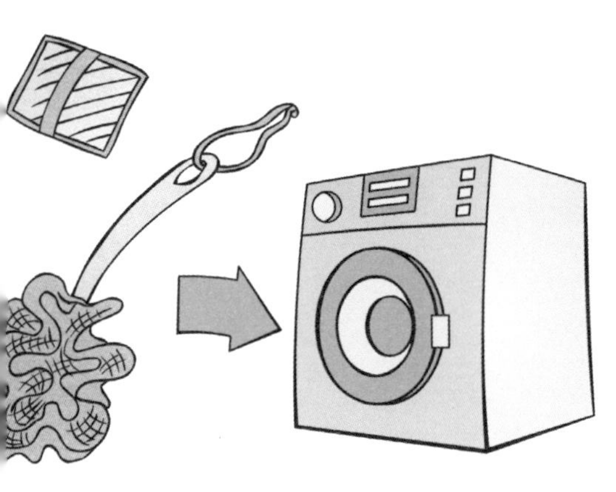

176. Rinse and machine

You probably rinse your sponges and bath mitts after a shower, and hang them up to dry. However, warm and moist fabric is a favourite breeding ground.

- Pop them in the washing machine with the towels once a week.
- Don't do that to a natural sponge, though, or it'll come apart mid-cycle! Swill in a basin of soapy water, rinse, squeeze and leave on a sunny window-sill to dry.

Porch and hallway help

177. Mud-busters

If you live in a muddy area you'll know just how much of the stuff can get tracked into the house.

- Place thick coir doormats inside and a bootscraper outside your front and back doors.
- Get a rectangle of beautiful window/railing fretwork for outside the door. You can spray-paint it every other season for upkeep and rust prevention.
- Or just use a length of sturdy fencing mesh laid into a thick, solid frame. It's cheap and easy to replace when worn.
- Every week, let it dry and clean it outside with a coir-bristled brush to dislodge the mud.

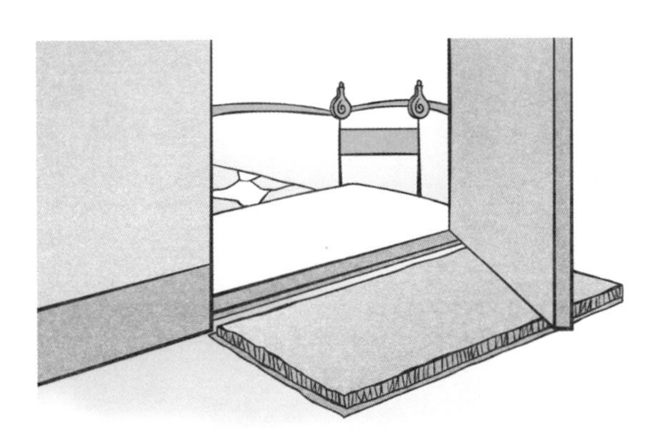

178. Banish grimy banisters

Can't get the grime out of those mouldings and crevices with the vacuum nozzle?

- Tie an old towel, lightly moistened, over a soft bristle broom or dry mop.
- Brush the banisters from top to bottom.
- Switch the towel inside out when dusty.
- Spritz the railings with water and go over them again, this time with a dry towel. (Spray lightly though, or you'll have to clean dirty drips off the wall below!)

179. On the way up or on the way down?

Should you clean the staircase on your way up or on the way down?

- Work from top to bottom if you're mopping or sweeping debris down a hard surface.
- If you have a runner or carpeting on the stairs, it's better to get the vacuum cleaner and start on the bottom step. You won't damage the pile by literally scouring it away with dirt and grit!

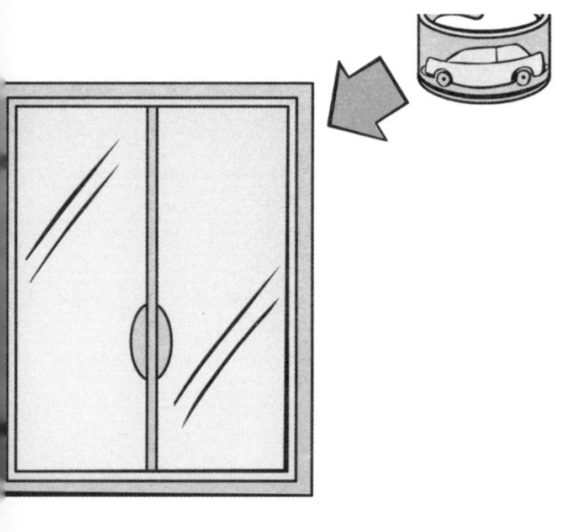

181. Side-to-side, top-to-bottom

Fed up with streaky, smeared windows?

- When washing windows, use side-to-side motions with your cloth on the inside. But on the outside, go up and down.
- That way, should you spot a stray streak, its direction will tell you whether it's on the outside or inside of the pane.

180. Good for cars, great for windows

f you have the modern aluminium-framed vindows, the best protection for this soft netal may be in your garage!

A couple of times a year, wash down the frames with warm soapy water.
Open the windows wide and let the sun dry them out.
Now give them a coat of car wax, and they'll be easy to look after all the rest of the year!

■ Clean-up by the clock

183. Emergency tidy!

Unannounced visitors at the gate! For a jiffy shine-up:

- Don those cotton gloves and dampen one hand with the multi-surface spray.
- Do a quick swipe of dusty and grimy spots, using the appropriate glove for each surface.
- Give metal fixtures a quick once-over too.
- Chuck the soiled gloves in the washing machine and answer that doorbell.

182. Super-fast spruce up

Guests at short notice? Pay attention to places they'll see.

- Close doors to bedrooms, playroom, home office, utility room and garage.
- Give the TV screen a wipe.
- Straighten rugs, plump up cushions.
- Open-plan kitchen? Put clutter in or under the sink.
- Wipe down the work surface and hob.
- Put cleaner in the downstairs loo.
- Get all unnecessary items off the surfaces and wipe down.
- Put out a nice soap and add fresh towels.

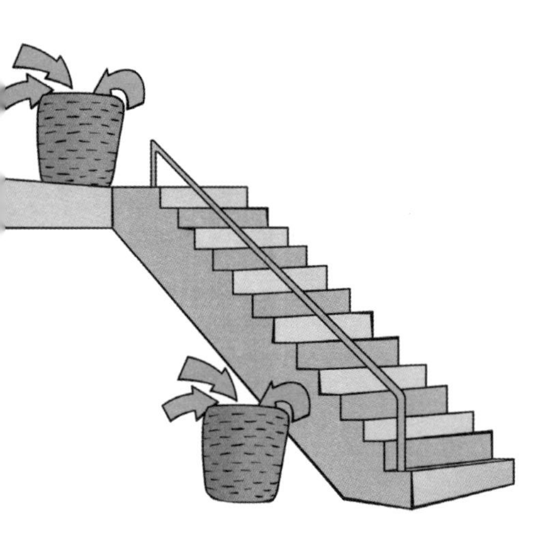

184. In the basket

If you live in an untidy household a stair basket is a fabulous idea.

- Place a wicker basket or small plastic crate at the bottom of the stairs, and another one at the top. Stuff that must go upstairs can be plonked in the downstairs basket throughout the day, and vice versa.
- It's the owners' responsibility to retrieve their possessions, upstairs and downstairs, before the basket fills or is emptied at the end of the week. Anything left is dumped in a (clean!) bin in the garage, loft or basement.

185. Living room straightener

Do a 5-minute straighten-up and collection before bedtime.

- Put away whatever you can.
- Plump up cushions.
- Remove things that don't belong (take stray coffee mugs and bowls to the kitchen, your handbag to the bedroom).
- Other people's clutter goes into the stair basket or collection box (*see Tip 184*).

Stains

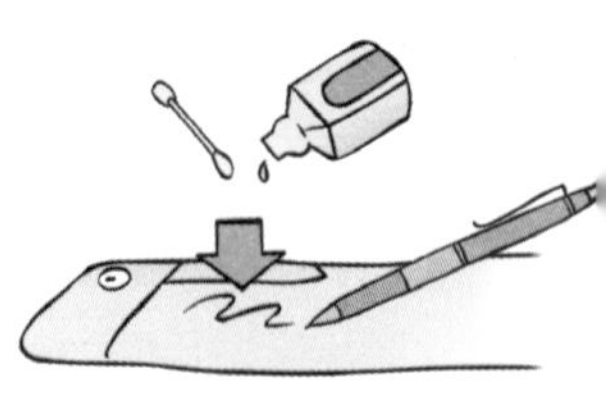

Stubborn stains don't stand a chance – we're swapping smart attack strategies for elbow grease! Check off your rescue team and get down to the business of dissolving, fading and guarding against mishaps before they happen. For general clothes care, look to Garments and Accessories, page 108.

■ Spill first-aid

186. Lift off!

On spotting a spill, get the excess away from the fabric – as much as you can, as fast as possible.

- For solids and semi-solids, don't rub – it'll drive the mess deeper into the fibres.
- Scrape off with a blunt knife or spoon.
- If it's already dried on, use some masking tape to get the surface layer off without applying pressure.
- For liquids, move fast while it's fresh. Dab with a clean white towel or serviette.
- For grease, dust on some talcum powder or cornflour and gently brush away (soft bristles, please!).

187. Float it away!

Once you've got any excess mess out of the way, it's time to lift the soaked-in stuff free of the fabric.

- Use cool running water on all except oil-based stains.
- For oil-based stains, at home, do a spot test clean with white methylated spirit. If it doesn't work, get the stained item to the dry cleaners.

Warning: Warm water will set the stain!

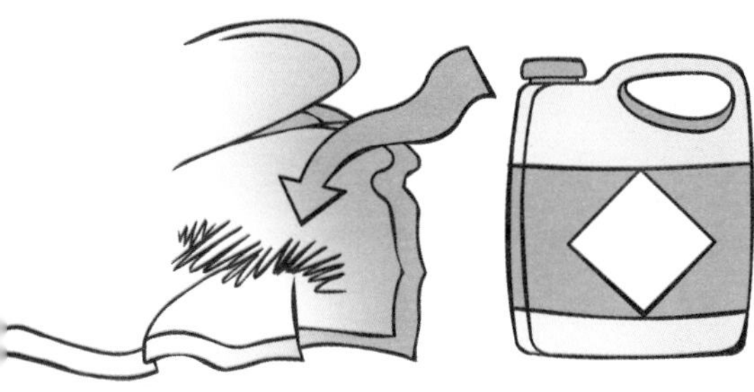

188. Saved by the soda

Baking soda – also a good deodorizer – is brilliant for attacking stains, since it's a mild abrasive and cuts through grease and mineral deposits. Not just your clothes, either – everything from vacuum flasks and casserole dishes to wallpaper and carpets respond well to its stain-busting properties.

- Make into a stiff paste, apply, let dry and brush away.

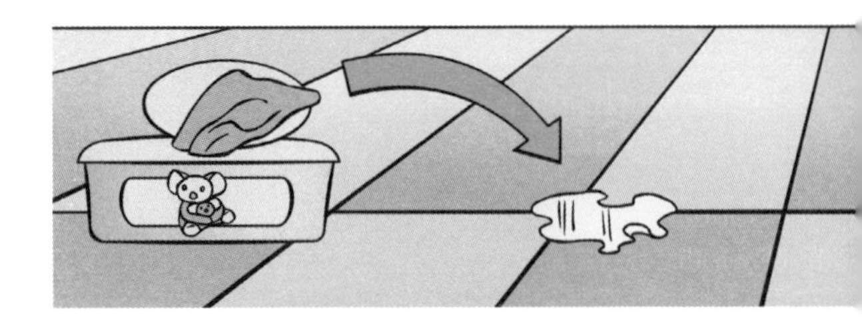

189. Biological warfare

For most protein-based stains – such as egg, milk, blood, gravy – take the biological approach:

- Make a thick paste with a biological (enzyme action) detergent and apply to 'digest' the stain.

Warning: While this works beautifully on cotton, don't subject wool or silk to it – both are protein fibres themselves, and the enzyme might chew into the fabric!

190. Baby wipes for grown-up spills

Even if you no longer have a toddler or infant about the house, an emergency pack of baby wipes is a good idea.

- Use them to mop up spills and stains. Any slight residues should be gone when you do get round to vacuuming.

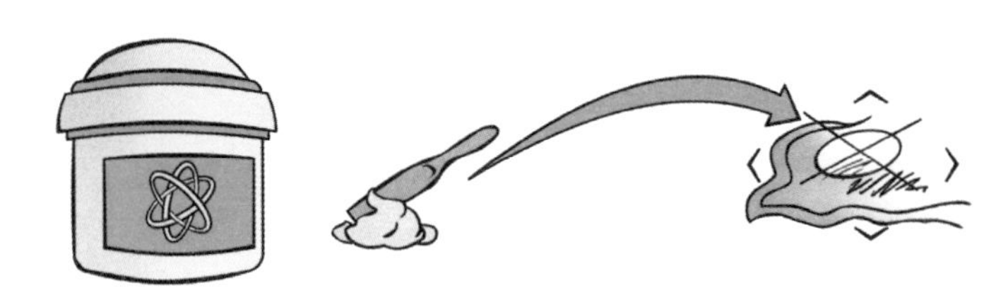

Warning!

191. Wine spills

Up-ending the salt cellar over the red wine spill will only make matters worse, contrary to the old wives' tale! That goes for cola, coffee and tea too – the salt will drive the pigments in and set them in the fabric.

- Sprinkle cornflour over the spill.
- Get table cloths, etc. into the washing machine as soon as possible.

192. Out with oxidation

Not all oxidation (*see Tip 199*) is helpful! Some fruits such as banana and avocado blacken if cut and exposed to air and will do the same if applied to fabric.

- Jump to it with a little washing-up detergent and tepid water as a preliminary treatment.
- Wash at the highest temperature your fabric will stand, using a detergent for delicates.

Rescue efforts against tough 'uns

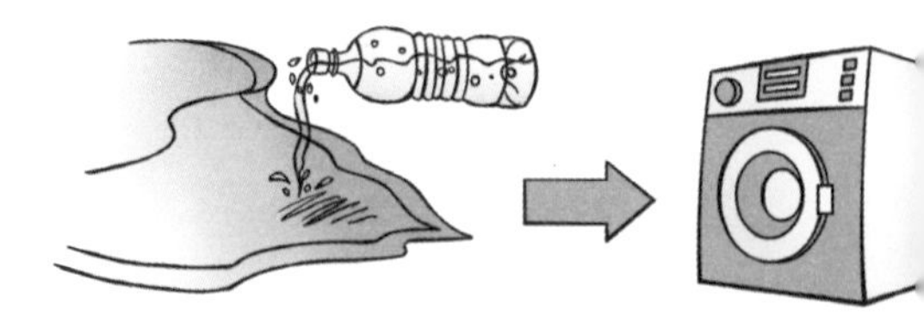

193. Meltaway mess

Candle drips on your tablecloth?

- Gently scrape off what you can with the blunt side of a palette knife.
- Bundle the cloth into a freezer-safe bag and chill for a couple of hours – the remaining wax will become brittle, so it'll come off more readily.
- For what's left over, lay an old absorbent towel on the ironing board. Place a brown paper bag on it, place your tablecloth on top and another towel on top of that. Run a medium-hot iron constantly over the top towel. The wax should transfer to the paper.

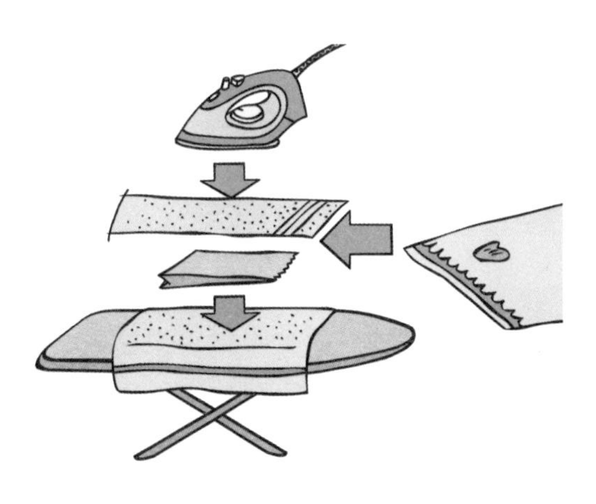

194. Bubbles to the rescue

Always keep an extra bottle of soda water in the fridge for emergency action on spills.

Red wine, greasy gravy, curry… all fizz up to the surface, letting you perform major rescue operations on most fabrics, from wool carpets to silk shirts.

- Use to dilute the stain and prevent setting when you can't get it properly cleaned at once; launder or otherwise treat as appropriate as soon as you can, however.

195. Food stained foodsavers?

Not all plastic storage containers respond well to the dishwasher or even to running water. Sometimes, heat worsens food stains! Try these fixes:

- Rub with a little baking soda paste.
- Scrub with a lemon half dipped in salt.
- Fill with water, add a spoonful of vinegar and leave overnight.
- Use an enzyme-based detergent. Afterwards, rinse thoroughly with a squeeze of lemon juice.
- If nothing else works, put the container in full sun – some edible pigments, such as turmeric, are light sensitive (*see Tip 200*). Wash well.

196. Gum freeze

It may be disgusting, but you must get rid of chewing gum stuck to your hard surfaces.

- Freeze with an icepack until brittle, then scrape off gently and carefully with the blunt side of a knife.

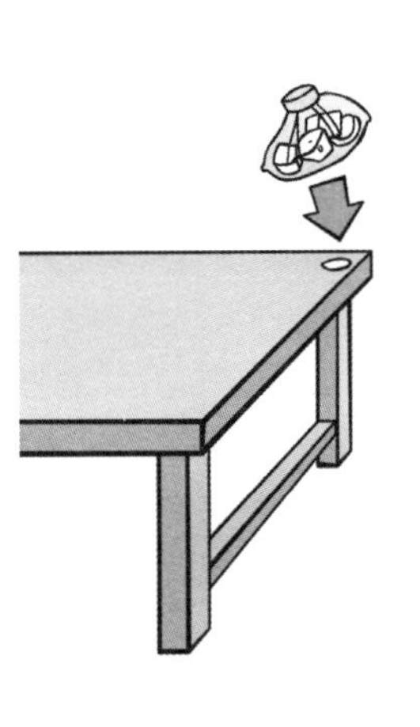

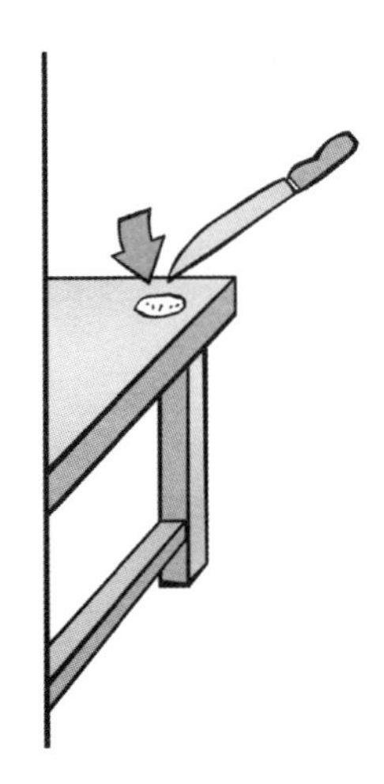

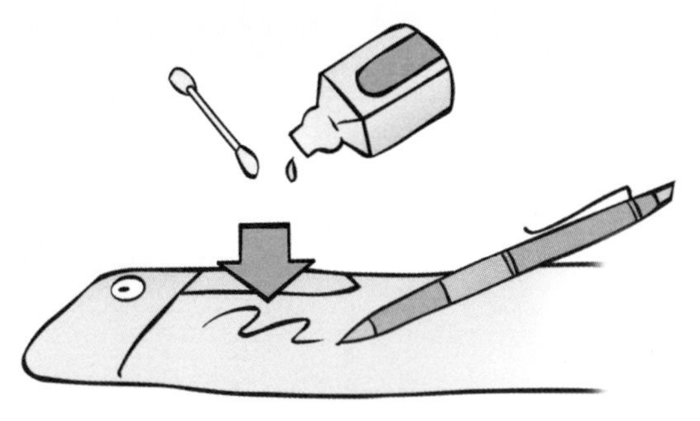

197. Biro buster

A quick-fix for ballpoint ink on fabric:

- First test for colour fastness on a discreet area.
- Lay the garment flat on an old towel or teacloth.
- Spot-treat the stain with repeated applications of eau de cologne – either with a cotton bud or a natural pump spray bottle – working from the outside to the inside of the mark.
- Wash immediately after removing the ink.

198. Tea in bed

Ah, the joys of breakfast in bed! But they quickly fade when you end up with a spilt cuppa that ruins your snowy duvet.

- Working quickly, mop up any excess and remove the outer cover of the duvet.
- Now pinch and lift the stitched casing away from the filling, and try to tie off the stained area with a rubber band to isolate it.
- Sponge with cold water, taking care to keep the filling away from the water.
- If necessary, rub away any remaining faint marks with mild detergent.

Last resorts

199. Fade away...

If stain removal hasn't worked for cottons with a non-protein stain – try some bleach as a last resort.

- Use an oxidizing bleach if there's any colour in the fabric at all; chlorine bleach is only for pure white cotton fabric.

200. Sun power

Many chutneys and spicy Asian pickles are preserved by turmeric, which is a difficult stain to shift. However, it is photo-sensitive, so it should fade in the sun.

- After you've washed and dry-cleaned (the solvent will help shift most of the pigment), hang on the line for several days.

Warning: This won't work so well on synthetics or animal fibres – in fact, hot sun may not be a great idea for those in the first place.

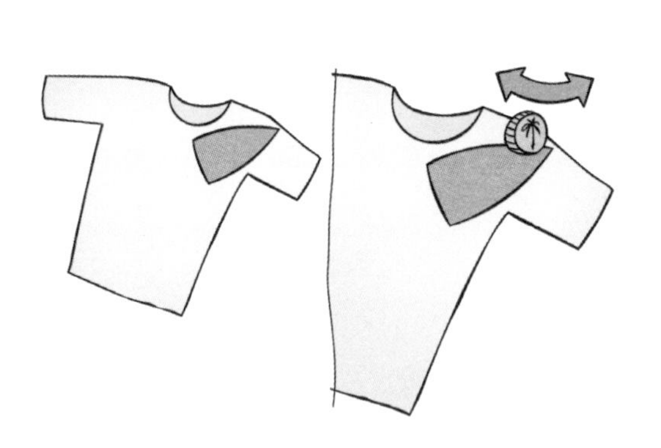

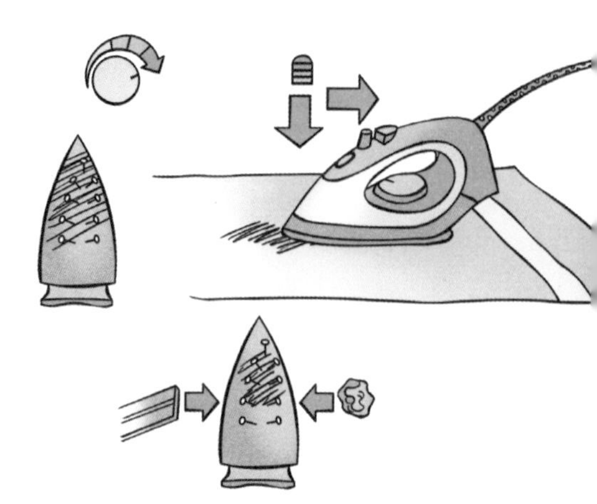

201. Scorched!

If you've managed to scorch a cotton garment, help is at hand.

- Gently rub the mark with the edge of a coin with a 'ribbed' texture along its 'rim'. This will often brush out the scorched fibres and expose the undamaged thread.
- Rinse well, and perhaps use a scented linen spray to counter the smell.

It's difficult, often impossible, to rescue scorched silks and synthetics as the fibres are easily damaged – even if you get the mark off, the fabric is unlikely to retain its strength.

202. Smeared soleplate

A too-hot iron has melted your blouse beyond rescue – and smeared it on the soleplate!

- Heat the iron to its highest setting, gliding it over an old cotton towel.
- Press hard to 'wipe' off the smears.
- Unplug the iron, let it cool slightly and, taking care not to touch the plate with your hand, use a scrunched-up wad of tissue paper to rub away any remaining marks.
- For an uncoated soleplate (not non-stick), a small ball of foil can usually shift stubborn debris.
- Once cool, clean with water to remove lint or foil residues.

Prevention is half the battle

203. Light white on white

White tablecloths?

- Don't even think of burning a coloured candle without placing something under it to catch the drips.

Most of the wax may be possible to take off with an iron (*see Tip 193*), but the dye that gave it colour is going to be rather more stubborn!

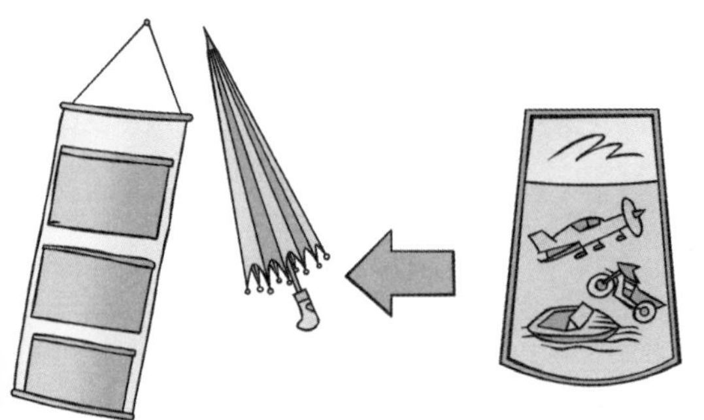

204. Clear plastic

Ordinary household cleaners can cloud transparent flexible plastic – the kind used for hanging pockets and see-through umbrellas.

- Use the polish used on the plastic windshields of convertibles – available from motor factories.

Garments and Accessories

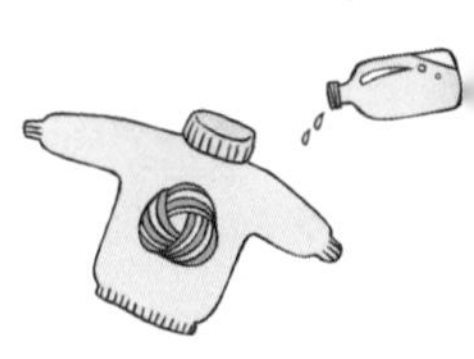

Take the load off! From selecting the washload to fixing a runaway dye and washing up the machine, we're making washday a breeze! The folding, ironing and mending too. And also spruce up the rest of your wardrobe – coddle your accessories (we've got special tips for leather too).

■ A load of laundry

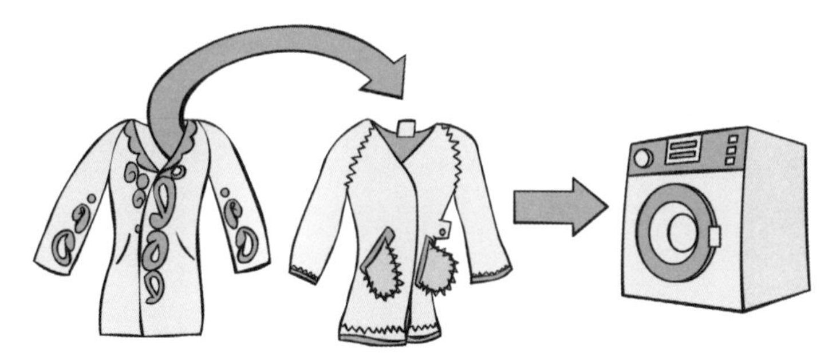

205. In reverse for washing

Some garments are best turned inside out before washing.

- Corduroy, velvet, devoré and other textured fabrics should be washed smooth side out.
- Anything with a raised or rubber print, or surface glitter, should also be washed inside out.
- This also holds for tufted knits – you don't want the loops to snag on a button or hook in the wash.
- For the same reason, turn embroidery inside out – provided the back is neat, of course. (If it isn't, try a gentle handwash or dry clean.)

206. Softest woollies

To keep your fine woollens really soft and shapely:

- Always handwash with pure soap solution (the kind intended for woollens and delicates) in cool water.
- Do *not* soak! Just swish around to loosen dirt, then knead gently.
- Rinse thoroughly till the water runs clear.
- Add a few drops of glycerine to the last rinse as a softener.
- Never squeeze or wring – roll up in a towel to get rid of excess water, then dry flat in shade.

207. Do not soften!

You may be tempted to maintain the softness of your precious cashmere garments.

- Never add fabric softeners, or you'll end up with a freshly felted garment!

208. Shades of silk

Printed silk fabric – as opposed to yarn-dyed silk – is particularly prone to fading and losing dye. That's because silk isn't very porous, and doesn't hold dye too deeply even when immersed.

- Always reverse printed silk garments before washing them.
- Ideally, dry-clean rather than wash.
- Always cool iron on the reverse, after making sure the dye doesn't transfer; test an unobtrusive corner on white fabric to check.

209. Salt and vinegar fix

Those beautiful vegetable-dyed garments are works of art. Treat them with care.

- Before the first wash – ideally, before your first wear – soak them in half a bucket of water to which 2 tablespoons of salt or white vinegar has been added.
- Rinse and drip-dry, inside out, in the shade.
- Turn the garment inside out for all subsequent washing, drying and ironing as well.

210. Sink for smalls

Underwear, especially anything with lace panels or underwiring, is best hand washed.

- Soak overnight in cool to lukewarm water, with a mild detergent.
- Hand wash in the morning, rinsing thoroughly and rubbing folds together gently to get the dirt out.
- Be careful not to twist underwired elements.
- Wring by scrunching in your hand; do not wring moulded or underwired garments.
- Hang bras upside-down by the baseband rather than the straps; if very lightweight, you could hang over a rod, supported by the centre-front panel.

211. Washing the machine

Once a month, clean out the washing machine:

- Remove and clean the filters.
- Replace mesh if need be – just sew on the same size of fine nylon mesh.
- Run the machine on a short wash with some vinegar to neutralize any detergent or mineral deposits.

■ Pressed to please

212. Do not split

Dry-clean all the parts of a suit – skirt, jacket and trousers, or jacket, waistcoat and trousers – together.

- The solvents can affect the dye a little, and it usually isn't noticeable – until held up against the same fabric. Cleaning them all together means they'll match and will wear evenly, too.
- If you have a blouse or shirt that tones in, a favourite scarf or tie that matches, consider cleaning it at the same time.

213. Pull, then press

Smaller items made in absorbent fabrics can get pulled out of shape along the hem bindings when washed.

- Before ironing, ideally while they are still damp, tug them back into shape.
- First take hold of diagonally opposite corners and pull taut, gently, especially with lace or silk!
- Gently stretch from top to bottom: starting at the hem, hold along the sides (hands opposite each other) and pull gently.
- Keep walking your hands up the opposite sides until you reach the top.
- Stretch lengthways the same way.

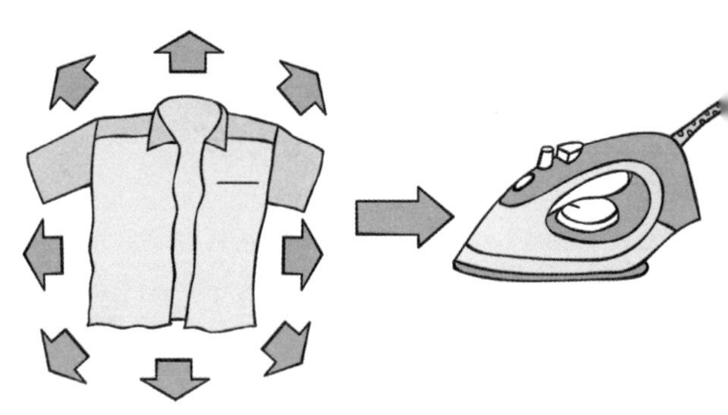

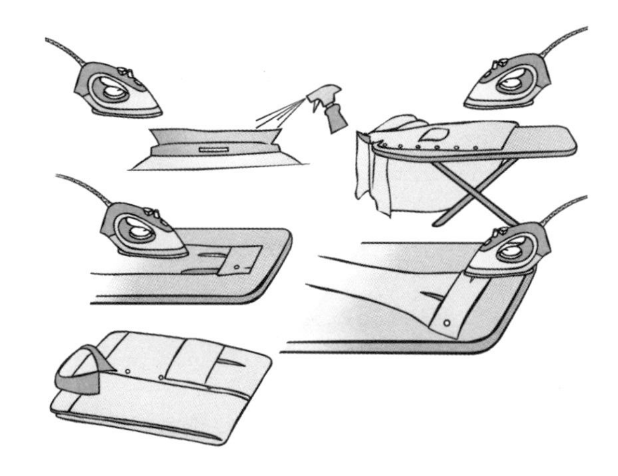

214. Trousers pressed

Not easy to iron, a pair of trousers.

- Straighten out (for in-seam pockets, turn out) and iron pockets.
- For a lightweight fabric, do up the fly and button down the waistband and pockets.
- Pull trousers over the board's narrow end. Iron the waistband, front pleats and yoke (back and front).
- Then iron the hems.
- Lay the trousers down the centre, with in-seams together and centred between front and back creases.
- Fold back the top trouser leg and iron the inside of the lower one, then the outside.
- Repeat with the other leg.

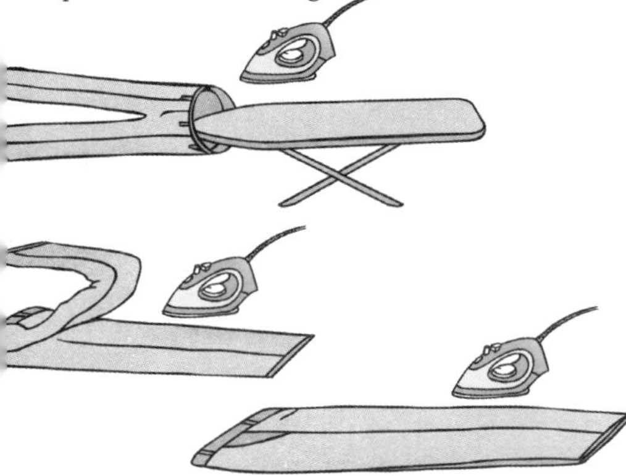

215. Crisp shirts

Make swift work of shirts.

- Iron damp cotton and linen, or spritz to dampen.
- Do the collar first – inside, then outside. Work inwards from the points.
- Draw the shirt over the ironing board one side at a time to iron the front, back, shoulders and yoke.
- Iron the sleeves. Do the cuffs opened out flat first, avoiding the buttons; button up and press from cuff to shoulder, with the opening upwards.
- Flip over and iron, cuff opening downwards.
- Press the fronts, then the back.
- Button up the front and neaten creases.

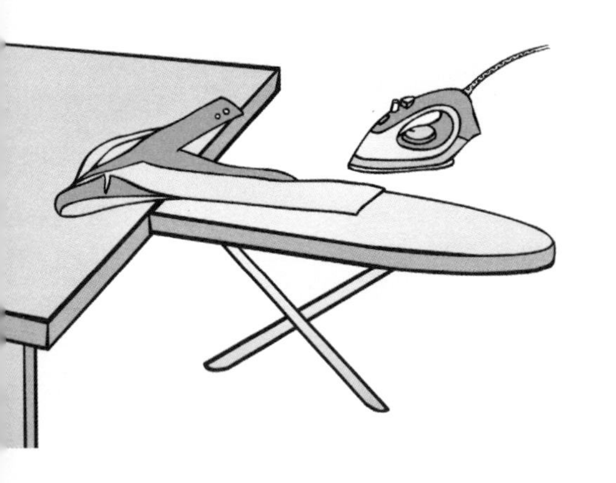

216. Perpendicular pressing

Avoid having one end of a garment trailing in the dust while you tackle the other side!

- Place an ironing board at right angles to your folding table or worktop.
- Let any surplus lap onto the table rather than dangle off.
- This will also prevent garments pulling out of shape or sliding off when, say, the heavy yoked waistband pulls on trousers while you iron the leg hems.
- It also prevents you accidentally standing on longer garments that trail off!

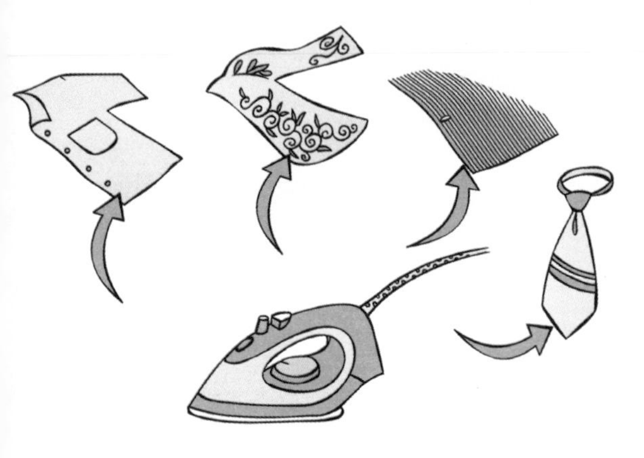

217. Iron inside!

Some garments should be ironed only on the reverse:

- Dark-dyed cottons – ironing on the right side can leave shiny marks!
- Embroidery – it will stand proud if ironed on the wrong side over a towel.
- Corduroy and velvet – otherwise the pile will flatten.
- Ties – otherwise the forked hem and seams will show up.

218. Don't press it!

Never be tempted to iron clothes in need of washing or dry cleaning to get 'just one more wear' out of them! Heat will set the dirt.

- Clothes could, in an emergency, be steamed with a handheld steamer or hung behind the bathroom door while you take a hot shower.

219. Do not iron!

Yes, the garment care label says you can iron that shirt – but you need to avoid the fiddly bits (or at least treat them with caution).

- Never iron over buttons or piping inserts – you'll leave a shine on the fabric on the other side!
- Avoid the velvet bits – those need to be steamed with a handheld device instead.
- Iron only on the reverse of embroidery and appliquéd or printed motifs.
- Iron on the wrong side first for collars, cuffs and pockets to prevent unsightly wrinkles.

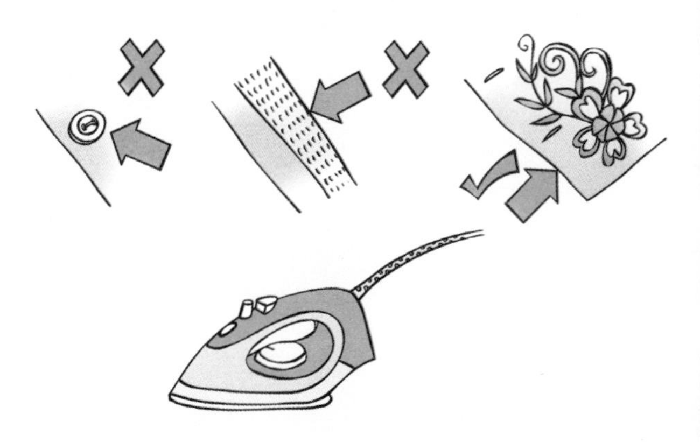

220. Look at the lining!

Always check the lining before you start pressing a jacket. The fabric may require a hot iron (cotton or linen); but if the lining is silk or a synthetic, you'll need to switch to a cool setting.

- Hang the garment outside a hot shower to steam out any wrinkles first, since those are difficult to shift, particularly from linen.
- Don't be tempted to steam iron the garment, though! It's too hot for the lining fabric. At most, use a cool water spray to dampen the fabric as you press.

221. Press and release

Gliding the iron over well-tailored formal wear could ruin the lapels and sleeves, and make suiting material shiny.

- Start with a slightly damp garment, or moisten a clean folded sheet.
- Add an extra layer of padding if needed.
- Lay the damp sheet (dry if the garment is damp) over the garment.
- Now use a 'press-and-release' action to iron the garment. Don't glide – just press down long enough to raise a puff of steam, then lift and move to the next area.
- Don't worry about covering every last inch.

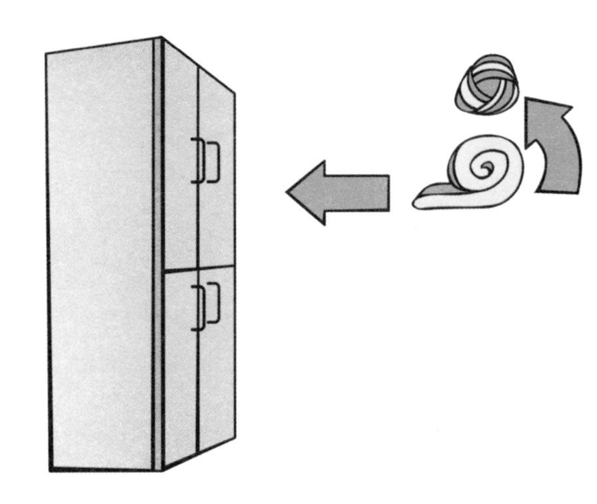

222. Button protection

The smallest graze from an iron heated for cotton or linen will melt those plastic buttons out of shape.

- Protect them by placing a thimble over them one at a time as you work on pressing the placket.

223. No-wrinkle woollies!

Natural wool fabrics bring yet another advantage to your winter wardrobe (besides warmth) – of the natural fibres, they are the least prone to wrinkling!

- Just roll up and put away for the summer.
- Air on unpacking next year and any creases should vanish!

Warning: If you have a problem with moths, take the usual moth-protection precautions before packing away woollies (*see Tips 314 and 315*).

Mending and altering

224. Hemline help

Shortening a garment?

- Measure the depth of the existing hem.
- Leave the same amount of fabric to fold over. Duplicating the old hem means the garment should still drape and hang the same way.
- Press flat.

Lengthening?

- Try to duplicate the original hem depth.
- Press out the old hem fold after you've finished and press the new hem flat.
- If the old crease refuses to disappear, one option may be to add a small line of machine embroidery or a bit of trim to hide it.

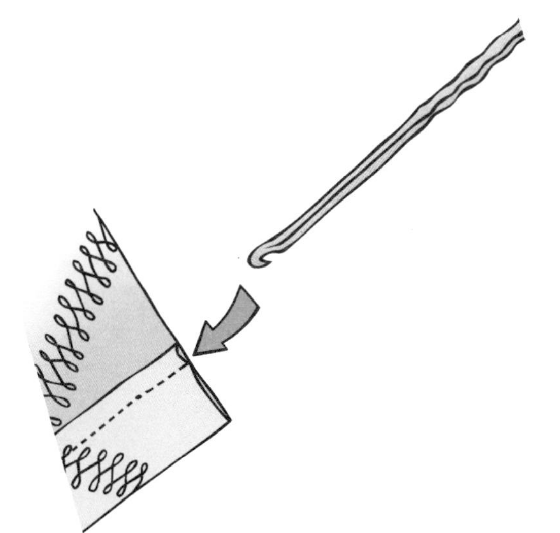

225. Un-sew a fine seam

Need to take apart a garment seam that's sewn tight?

- A very fine crochet hook helps take out the finest stitches without gouging the fabric. And it's safer than a needle held backwards or scissors that may rip the cloth!

226. Cord for cords

Sewing buttons onto denim, corduroy or velvet can be a bit of a pain with an ordinary needle and thread.

- Try using a carpet needle threaded with dental floss instead.
- Add a drop of clear nail varnish to anchor threads more securely.

As a bonus, clear floss matches most buttons!

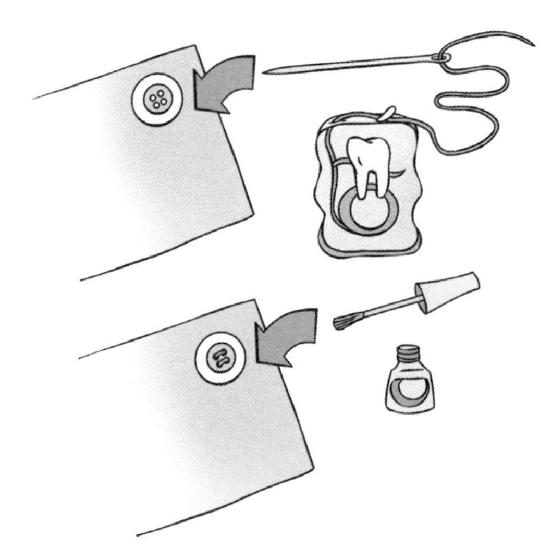

227. Shanks for smoothness

Tight closures can distort the fabric around button attachment points. You can add a shank to flat sew-on buttons.

- Take a couple of loose stitches to position the button.
- Slide a cocktail stick under the button and through the stitches.
- Make tight stitches to secure the button, 6 up-and-down stitches per hole.
- Remove the cocktail stick.
- Wind the thread repeatedly around the loose threads between the fabric and the button, taking a half-knot at each winding.
- Secure the thread to the fabric with a couple of backstitches, knot and snip.

Note: A button shank is a loop of metal, plastic or fabric on the underside of some buttons. A shank will stop stress occuring to fabrics between the button and the garment.

Special care, nips and tucks

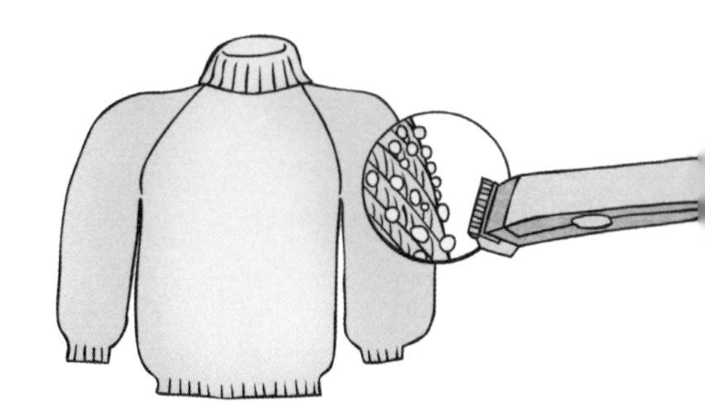

228. 'Old lace'

Lace fabrics are too delicate for some stain treatments. It might be best to think laterally if you find a spot.

- Dye it! Don't worry – it needn't be as drastic as that sounds. Just steep in cold, strained tea for 10–15 minutes and wash to get that creamy 'old lace' colour throughout – that should camouflage all but the darkest marks.

And it still looks like the heirloom it probably is, only more so!

229. Proof against pilling

You can't completely protect clothes against pilling as they're subjected to friction – fold against fold, surface against skin, against each other in the machine.

- Minimize pilling by choosing clothing that's not too tight and by turning inside out for the wash.
- If not heavily soiled, opt for a gentle 'delicates' cycle to minimize agitation.

Already got the bobbles? An electric shaver or trimmer applied gently against fabric held taut should get rid of most of it. Be careful though – you don't want to take off surface fibre and thin the fabric!

230. The garment manicure

Got fraying threads around a zip seam that constantly get caught in the teeth?

- Coat them with clear nail varnish to help them lie flat.

This also works for loose threads poking out of a textured weave or embroidered fabric.

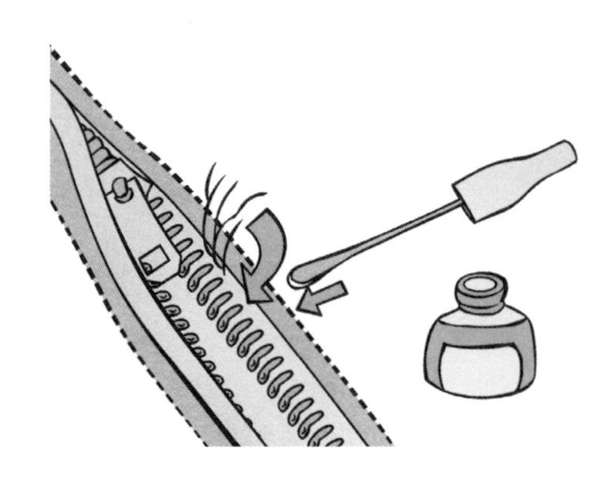

231. Clean, smooth zip-up

With a little care, zips will stay rust- and snag-free.

- Free zips of tufts of yarn or thread as well as dirt and sticky debris that can clog teeth regularly. A quick scrub with an old toothbrush dipped in detergent should do it.
- Rinse well and dry unzipped. (Normally, you should always zip up before washing.)
- After drying, slide a white candle along the zip teeth to coat lightly with wax.
- Zip up and unzip a couple of times to distribute the wax evenly and loosen any clumps.

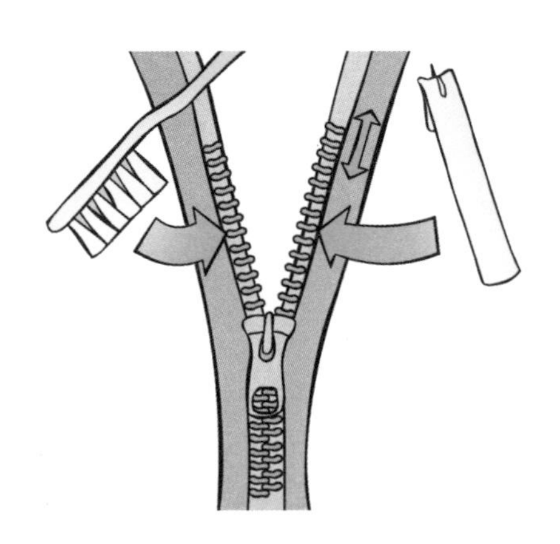

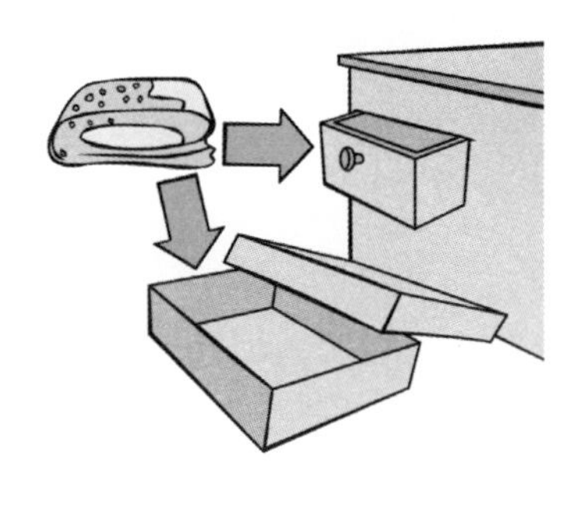

232. Keep your beads off the hangers

Keep your fine beaded eveningwear in good shape. Hanging can distort the fabric and it will no longer drape well.

- Fold flat in drawers or boxes as appropriate.

233. Acid-free wrapping

White cottons and linens as well as vintage fabrics and leather deserve an acid-free stuffing and protective layer. Acid-free tissue and boxes can be specially bought for the purpose, or:

- Cut up your old washed-out sheets for stuffing and use your old pillowcases for protective casing.
- Use any unbleached natural fibre.

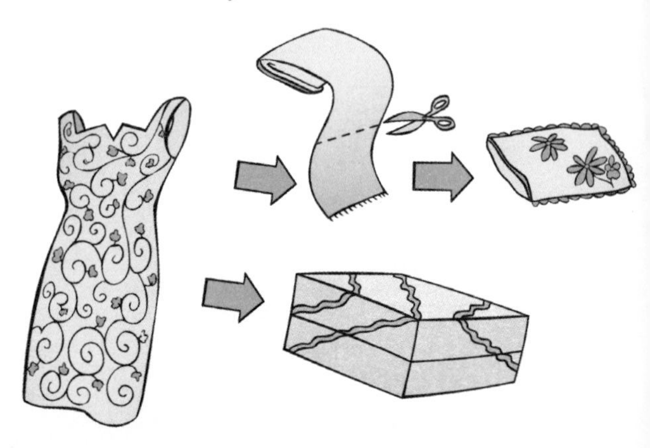

234. Fold-free heirlooms

Crease lines aren't the only problem; finer aged fabrics could wear and weaken at the creases.

- Don't fold antique brocade, heirloom lace or fine silk.
- Roll them up instead and place in a pillowcase (*see Tip 233*).
- If you must fold, refold every few weeks so crease lines don't set in.

■ Love your leathers

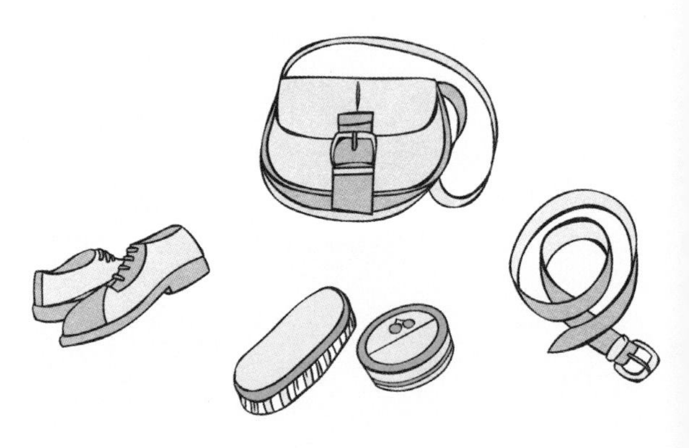

235. Polish is not just for shoes!

You look after your shoes, but what about your leather bags and belts?

- Use cream conditioner or neutral polish on your leather bags and belts to give them extra protection against cracks, scuffs and rain spots.

236. Kid glove treatment

For unlined leather gloves, the easiest and quickest clean-up is to put them on and then wash your hands:

- Wash up quickly with cool water and mild soap, using soap to rub away any little spots and stains.
- Rinse clear, remove the gloves and wrap in a towel to blot excess water.
- Smooth away any creases and dry flat on a fresh towel.

Warning: Lined gloves need a professional drycleaner's help.

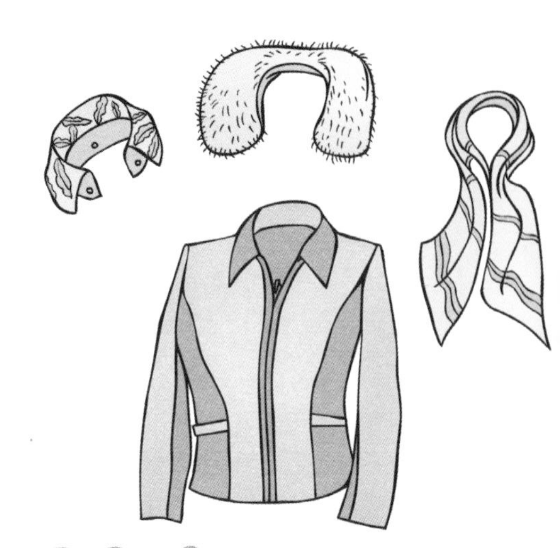

237. Collar that leather coat

A good leather coat, with regular conditioning (using leather cream) and professional cleaning, could last you a lifetime.

However, the collars tend to get grubby long before the rest of the garment needs attention – and it's expensive to send it for full-on care that often!

- Try a detachable (button-on) washable collar in a fun or fancy fabric – faux fur or a paisley weave (machine-washable) never fail to look festive.
- Or drape a chic scarf along the neckline to shield the collar from skin oils and perspiration.

238. Rescue for scuffed leather

A small scrape need not spell the end of your favourite knee-highs.

- Try camouflaging the scratched spot with a matching shoe polish or a little indelible ink (check on an inner seam, such as on the back of a collar, to see that solvents in it don't make the leather dye bleed!).

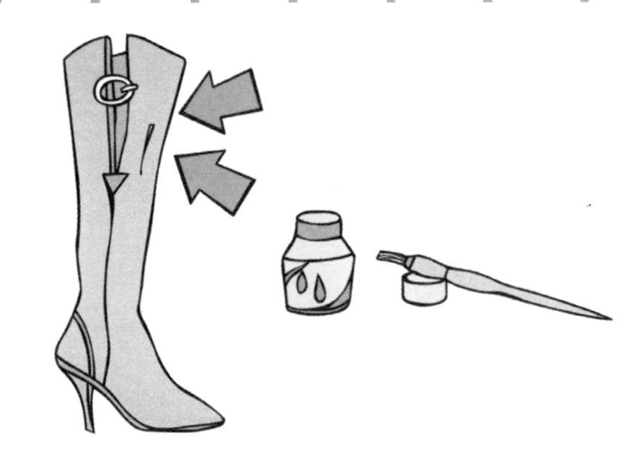

239. Salt off!

Salt stains can retire leather boots and shoes long before they're old.

- Use a solution of equal parts white vinegar and water to clean as soon as you possibly can.
- Let dry before reconditioning with leather cream.

240. Second soles for special shoes

Get a thin rubber sole and heel cover attached to those high heels and expensive evening shoes.

- They are kinder to your feet.
- They'll save you wearing through the thin soles of a sandal.
- They'll help you avoid skids and falls by providing better traction than smooth leather or synthetic soles.

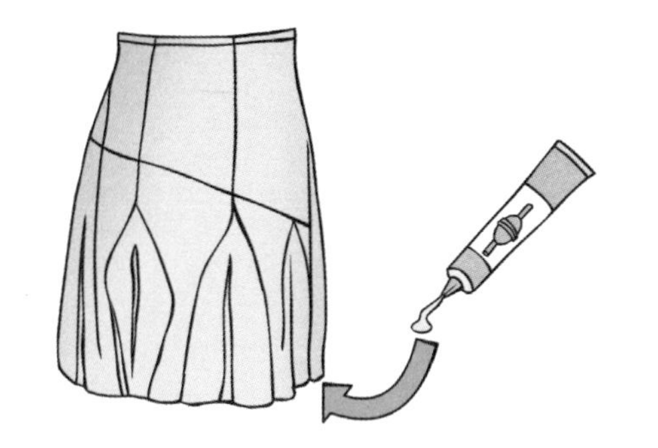

241. Hem raw hide

If your not-too-precious leather skirt is looking a bit tatty around the edges:

- Refinish or tidy up the hem with a dab of shoe glue.

Warning: Do not use on synthetic leather substitute, though – the solvents in one could release harmful gases from the other!

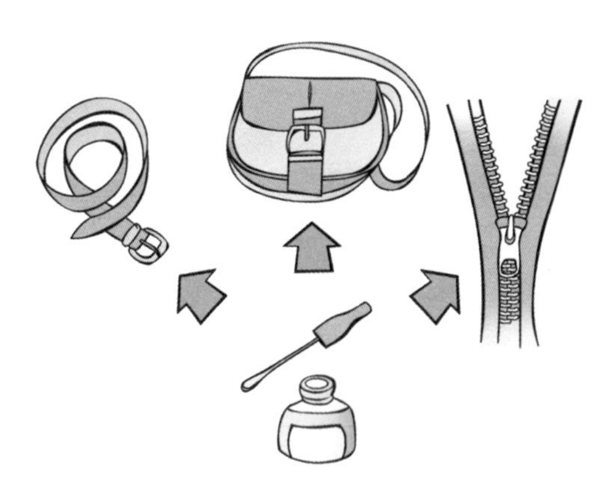

242. Metal enamel

Rivets, buckles, zipper tabs and other metal hardware on bags and belts can rust and tarnish quite quickly.

- Apply a coat of clear nail polish before using or wearing.

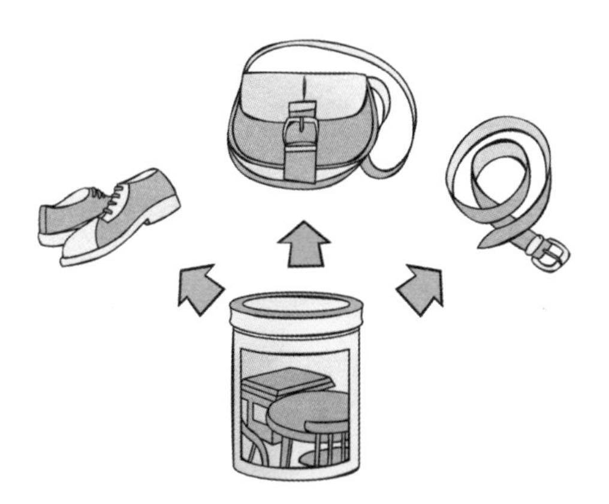

243. Wood wax for leather?

You don't have to invest in several tins of matching shoe polish for your entire footwear wardrobe.

- Use neutral furniture polish instead.

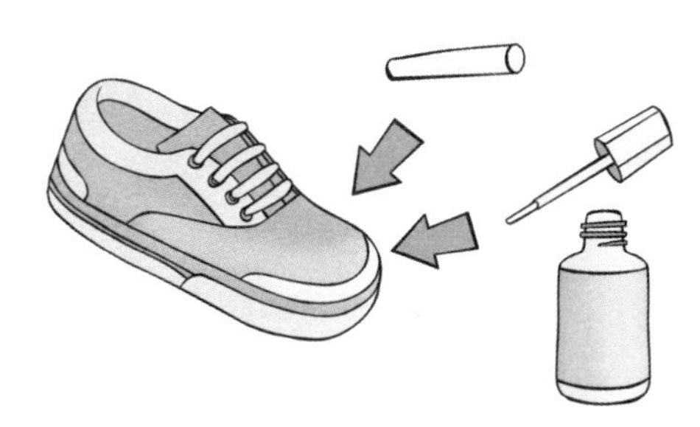

244. Feed your footwear

Similarly, don't despair if the supermarket shelves run out of leather cream.

- A few drops of unscented bath oil or baby oil will be a fine substitute.
- Use kitchen paper to absorb any excess before buffing.
- At a pinch, you could use any edible oil. But don't make a habit of it or the shoes will start smelling rancid!

245. Sporty smart

White footwear is an activewear classic. But dirt shows so easily. Try one of these tricks to smarten up between washes:

- Rub on white chalk for light soiling left after brushing away dirt from canvas shoes.
- A little white correction fluid will take care of small stains, even quite dark ones.

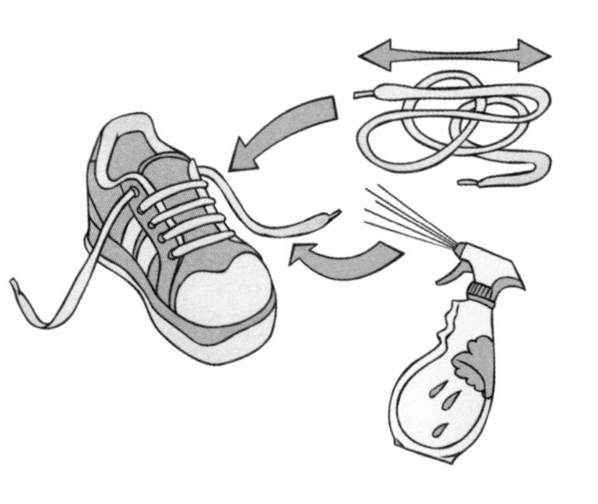

246. Loose laces?

If your shoelaces – or your children's – are forever coming undone, you have two choices:

- Switch to elastic laces – the knots on these tend to tighten with stretching!
- Dampen shoelaces slightly, stretch out and tie – the knot will tighten as the laces dry out.

247. Sweet feet

Banish the smell from those stinky trainers:

- Pour potpourri into socks and pop them in the shoes to absorb moisture while they deodorize.
- Add a few drops of any essential oil.
- Use deodorant on the soles of your feet and in-between the toes.
- Dust your toes with arrowroot powder or cornflour mixed with a good pinch of baking soda and a few drops of essential oil or perfume.
- Rub your feet with an alum crystal.

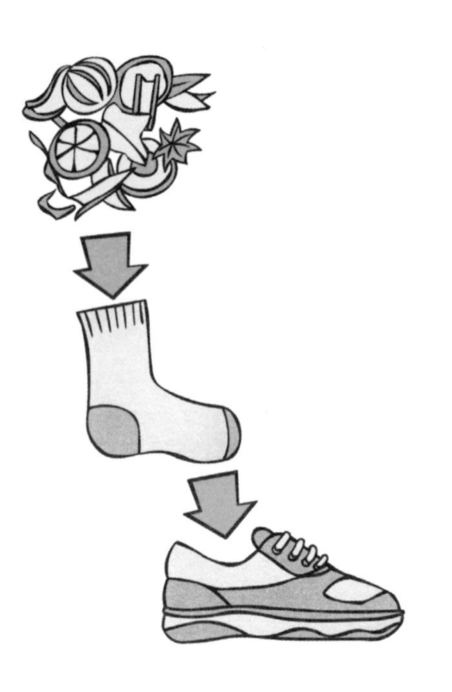

248. Spirit away the tar

Been walking down a melting tarred road?

- Blot the soles of your shoes with a wad of newspaper dipped in methylated spirits to shift the sticky stuff.

249. Soap on a belt

For leather bags and belts that really do need a thorough clean, you have two choices:

- For the really good stuff, you should ideally get it to a professional.
- For hardier, everyday accessories (satchels or cowboy boots, say), use saddle soap. Dab on with a moist cloth to clean the leather, then wipe dry and buff.

This is useful for leather luggage and sofas as well.

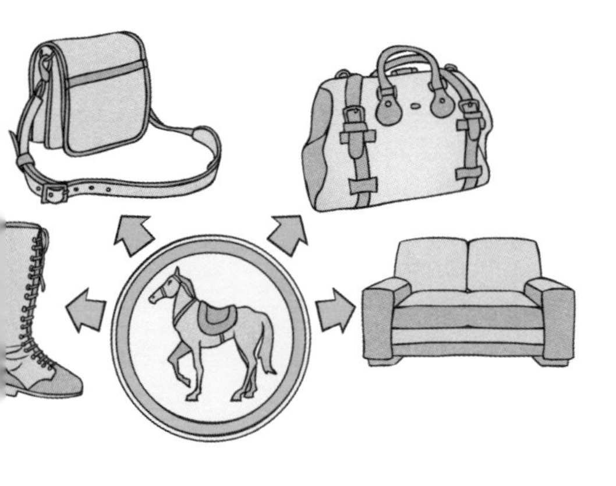

250. For seats, for bags

Synthetic bags that can't be washed in the machine need a different care regime from leather.

- Use a specialist product for cleaning car seats.
- Alternatively, remove any marks with a cleansing wipe and dry; then mist with hairspray and buff.
- For non-washable fabric bags, a baby wipe may help clean up stubborn grime. But first try a brush-down with talcum powder or cornflour, unless there is intricate surface embellishment.

Furniture and Furnishings

Now lavish some TLC on the rest of your possessions! The furniture comes first; furnishings follow suit. Take care of your bed and it will take care of you, we say. And get down on the floor too.

■ Tables and chairs, chests of drawers

251. Spread the wear

There's always a favourite seat in the house, and it can end up looking tired and battered long before its mates have succumbed to wear and tear.

- From time to time, switch the chairs and covers of identical chairs around so that they wear evenly.
- Similarly, turn pillows and cushions, carpets and mattresses over and around regularly.
- Do the same with identical curtains hung on windows facing different directions – that way the southern or western sun won't fade one set faster.

252. Grime busters

Like shirt collars, your favourite sofa can attract a lot of grime along the top as people lounge back happily! And that's especially hard on leather. The Victorians invented antimacassars to deal with the problem, and there are a few measures you can take, too.

- Add a decorative throw across the back.
- Make a little fitted cover in a dark velvet or satiny fabric.
- Go Victorian and add a lace-edged white cloth over the headrest.

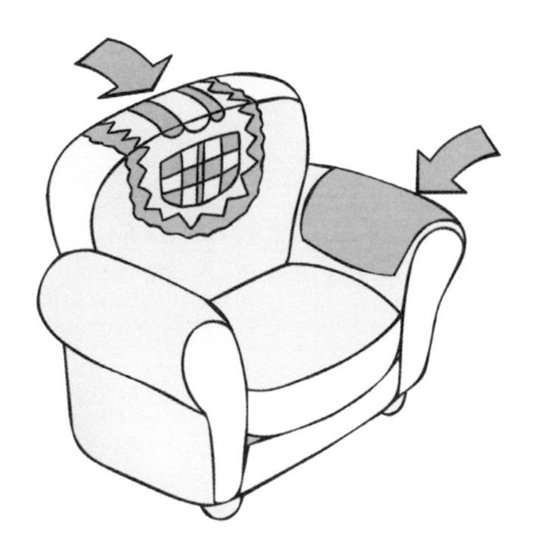

253. Soap for your sofa?

The advantage of cane or rattan furniture is that it doesn't mind a soapy scrub.

- Give cane furniture a bath in warm water and soap in the summer.
- Rinse well with water.
- Leave to dry in the sun.
- Refinish with clear varnish – this will add years to the life of the furniture and make dusting easier.

Warning: Be careful about giving the same treatment to plastic or vinyl — detergents can discolour them!

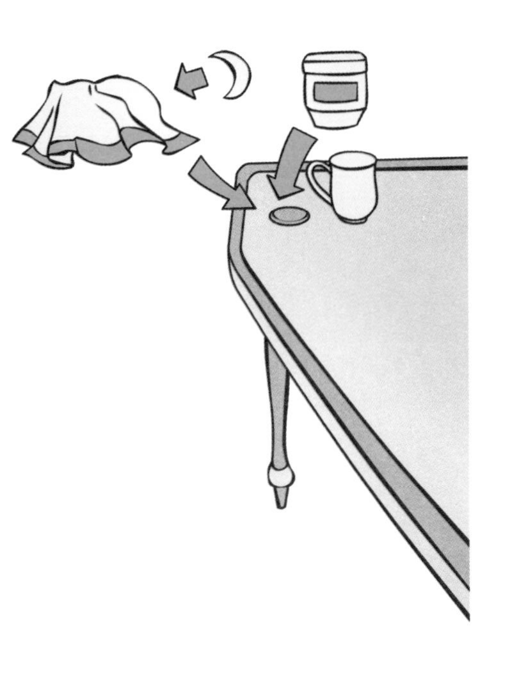

254. Banish those rings

Discoloured rings from coffee mugs or condensation from glasses can ruin a wooden surface.

- Apply a thin layer of petroleum jelly over the ring.
- Leave overnight.
- Next day, wipe off and buff briskly with a cloth.
- If the surface still feels greasy, a quick swipe with a vinegar and water solution can help. Dry well.
- If there are still some leftover marks, try a dot of white toothpaste on a baby toothbrush.
- Then rub beeswax along the grain to condition and season.
- Any residual discolouration could be treated with a matching shoe polish!

255. Oil – good for wood

If your wooden furniture is treated with a pigmented wood stain rather than varnish or paint, it could do with a little extra TLC.

- Protect it with an oil rub every so often – use a little olive oil on a soft cloth. After wiping away the residue, buff with a damp cloth.
- Use a dry cloth to sponge off any excess oil.
- Repeat every season.

256. Lemon for varnish

Varnished wood can also benefit from a little extra care from time to time.

- Substitute the olive oil in *Tip 255* with a dab of lemon oil diluted in olive oil, and apply every other month to retain the shine.

257. Smooth sliding

There's nothing more likely to damage your heirloom furniture than drawers that stick all the time.

- Rub a candle stub along the sliders.
- Give the top edge of the drawers a coat of clear varnish (nail varnish is good) in case there are snags in the wooden surface and the drawer fits too tightly in the frame.

Household linens, soft furnishing, upholstery

258. White is right

White may seem completely impractical for soft furnishings, but it's actually an extremely sensible choice.

- Just make sure the covers are loose and washable.
- Cotton or canvas is ideal – white becomes even whiter when dried in the sun.
- You can bleach white cotton and linen if stain-busting doesn't work.

259. Separate the towels

Luxurious deep-pile towels are such a bathtime pleasure! However, that same fluff that dries you in a jiffy also gets all over the lint of your washing machine – and all over other clothes.

- Avoid washing towels with other garments.
- If you must, choose colours that are identical.
- Certain fabrics pick up lint more than others – keep corduroy, velvet, plush, velour, fleece and looser knits (such as piqué) clear of the towels!
- Terry towelling itself is lint-loving! Don't even dream about washing dissimilar colours of towels together.

260. Hang curtains while wet

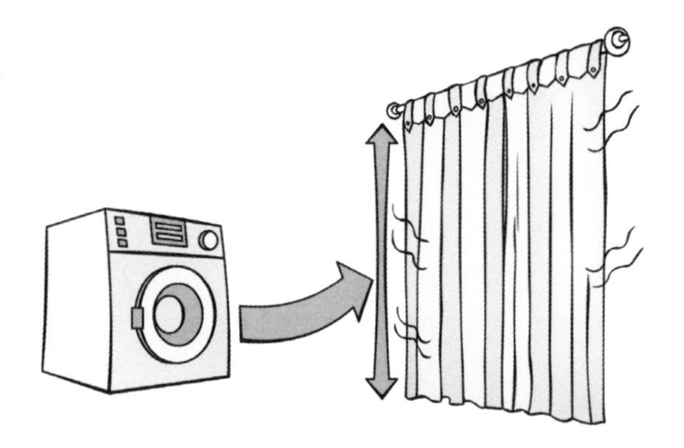

Don't dry washable curtains completely before you return them to the window.

- Spin dry at a low speed rather than tumble drying.
- If drip-drying, wait till there are no more drips but the fabric still feels damp.
- Clean the pelmet, rails and window.
- Hang up the curtains while still damp – the damp weight will pull them down, straightening out any creases and kinks.

261. Freeze those dust mites!

You know all about the amazing durability of dust mites and their debris (*see Tip 321*). But what about the sheets you can't hot-wash?

- Pop them into a plastic bag and put them in the freezer overnight after laundering.

It may not destroy all the mites, perhaps, and certainly won't get rid of the eggs and debris. But it'll at least slow down the population explosion and bring the numbers down!

This is also a good tactic for dealing with moth larvae.

262. Fold before drying

Just washed the sheets? Don't tumble-dry, as this will set the creases, and you'll spend more time ironing!

- Shake out and fold the sheet neatly into a smaller rectangle before you hang it out to dry.
- This will make the sheet quicker to iron – just whip it off the line and lay on the board.
- If you smooth out the hems nicely and give the sheet a sharp snap while folding, you may not even need to iron!

263. Bonus pressing

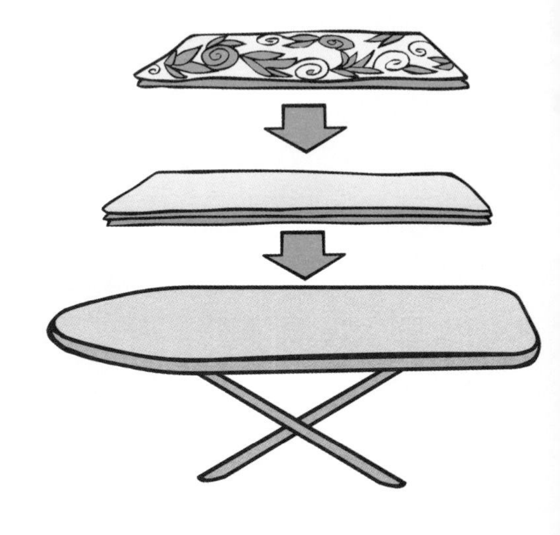

When ironing garments with buttons, corded details or raised textures, it's a good idea to have some extra padding under the items (*and see Tip 222*).

- Lay folded sheets on your ironing board before ironing the decorated items.

The bonus is pressed sheets that needed no extra work!

264. Dripping duvets!

Drying machine-washable, anti-allergy duvets can be a bit of a job. Here are a few options:

- Roll in a bath sheet or heavy bedspread and drape across a large metal drying rack – over the two topmost bars that are furthest apart – pulling more of the surface flat.
- Dry flat on a large, pale-coloured picnic blanket or bath sheet.
- Drape across the backs of two chairs, placed back to back about 1 m/3 feet apart. Use only plastic or rattan chairs, not wood or metal!

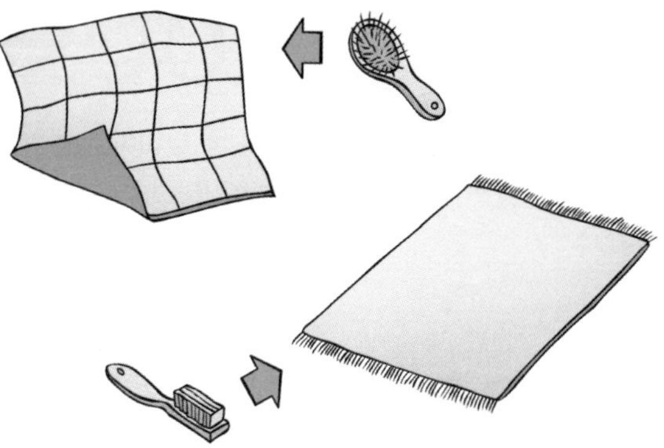

265. Shaggy blankets

Dry-cleaning can flatten the tufts of a shaggy rug, throw or blanket. You can brush them back gently to fluff up again.

- Don't use a brush with nylon bristles, and certainly not wire. Even plastic can damage the pile or tear out fine fibres.
- Get hold of a hairbrush with rubber bristles set in a wooden handle for best results.
- For hardier cotton shag, use a suede brush.

266. Don't fold the (electric) blanket!

You could damage the wires inside and cause a short-circuit.

- Store it under the mattress so it stays flat (only if the bed has a box base – slatted bases are not suitable).
- If you don't have any space in summer, roll up the blanket loosely – do NOT fold! Store in a spacious, uncluttered storage box.
- Check carefully before using it again. Holding it up against strong light or shining a torch through from the wrong side should help you spot any signs of damage.

267. Don't wash the blanket!

Again, it's the electric blanket we mean. It won't like to get wet, and neither will you!

- Should a spill happen, unplug at once.
- Mop up as much liquid as you can and let dry thoroughly.
- Sprinkle a little talcum powder on any stain left behind while it dries.
- Once quite dry, brush away the talcum powder.
- If you still have a visible mark, take it to the servicing agent, who may be able to help. Do NOT try to clean it yourself or have it dry-cleaned!

268. Quilts in the air

A quilt or duvet with a natural filling should be professionally cleaned. However, the thick wadding can retain solvents – you don't want to inhale or have them taint other things in the cupboard.

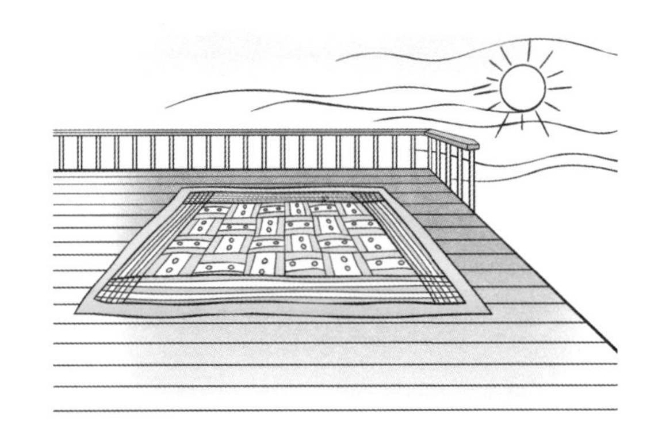

- After cleaning, unfold and air quilts and duvets to get rid of trapped volatiles.
- Hanging them over the back of a chair by the window will do. Turn once to expose both sides to fresh air and sunshine.
- If you have a deck, spread the quilt on a picnic blanket – take in after an hour.

269. Bed maintenance

Vacuuming the mattress?

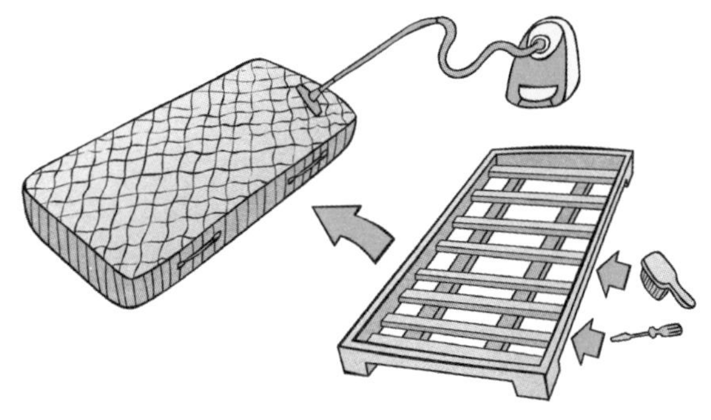

- Take it off the bed to do it on the floor.
- This will give you a chance to clean the bed base.
- While you're at it, check the mesh and screws, if any – get the drill at once if you find the screws need tightening; if the mesh seems warped, see if you can turn it over while you order a replacement.

270. Don't wash, just dry

Washing won't do the natural fillings in your pillows any favour.

- Either have them professionally dry-cleaned (if the manufacturer's label advises it) or just air them frequently in natural light.
- If they can take the heat, it's a good idea to pop them in the tumble-dryer for a few minutes to freshen and fluff them up.
- If the casing seems greasy (it will absorb some skin oils, despite the pillowcase), try sprinkling with talcum powder and brushing it out after a couple of hours.
- Protect the pillow as much as possible by placing a pillow protector under the pillowcase.

271. No foam in the water!

You might think synthetic foam cushions and pillows could do with a nice soapy wash. However, foam is not the most stable material and will soon crumble under the assault of water and detergent.

- Give them a sponge bath with a little soapy water, then with clean water to rinse away the detergent.
- Wrap in a towel and squeeze to get the moisture out.
- Dry in the shade.

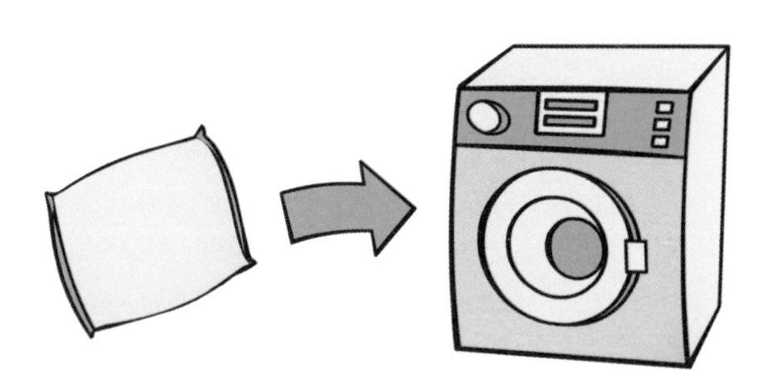

272. Roll up the rug

Putting rugs, mats and carpets into storage?

- Roll up with the pile or shag side facing outwards.
- Never fold rugs and carpets.
- Place in a box made of acid-free paper or in a drawstring bag (cut from an old well-washed sheet) placed inside a chest or closet.
- Unless space is truly at a premium, avoid keeping the roll standing up.

273. Give blinds a bath

The easiest way to clean synthetic blinds is in the bath.

- Fill the bath with hand-hot water and a cup of washing-up liquid.
- Dip the blinds in and rinse well – empty the bath and re-fill with clean water as often as necessary.
- Hang them back up to dry, with folded sheets or large beach towels rolled up beneath to catch drips; change the sheets/towels often, wringing them out and drying to replace again.

Décor and accessories

274. Bread for blinds?

For the weekly dusting, use a few crusty slices of bread to mop up the dust from blinds if you don't want to get out the vacuum cleaner. You could use a paintbrush too, but that just redistributes the dust.

- Hold the bread with the crust facing into your palm and press the softer edge into the top slats.
- Wipe along from left to right, then move down and repeat.
- If you go gently, this works well for paper blinds and split-cane weaves too.

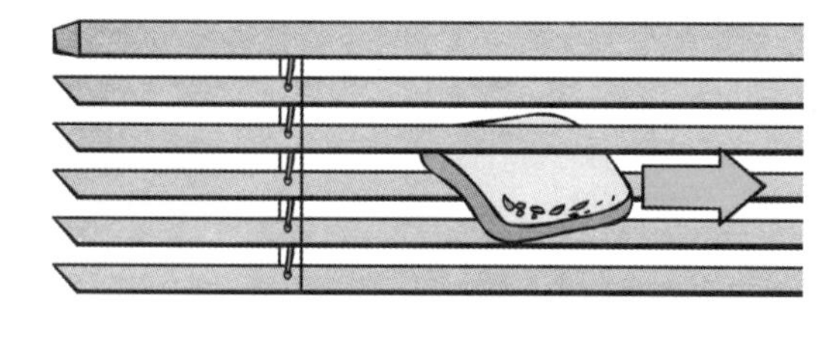

275. Knobs, sills, knockers

The best way to clean door furniture is with a proprietary polish for brass or chrome. However, those aren't kind to wood or paint!

- Before you begin, apply masking tape to the gloss paint around the metal strip up to an inch on each side.
- Now polish away, dry and strip off the masking tape carefully.
- On a matte or distressed finish, masking tape may lift paint, so consider using a coat of petroleum jelly instead.
- Protect window frames in the same way when washing windows.

276. Bread basket

Once again, it's stale bread to the rescue – of woven baskets.

- Wad up a thick slice of bread, moistening with a spritz of water, if necessary.
- Press into the weave of baskets, changing around often, to lift out dust.

This means you won't have to subject the cane or rattan to moisture too frequently.

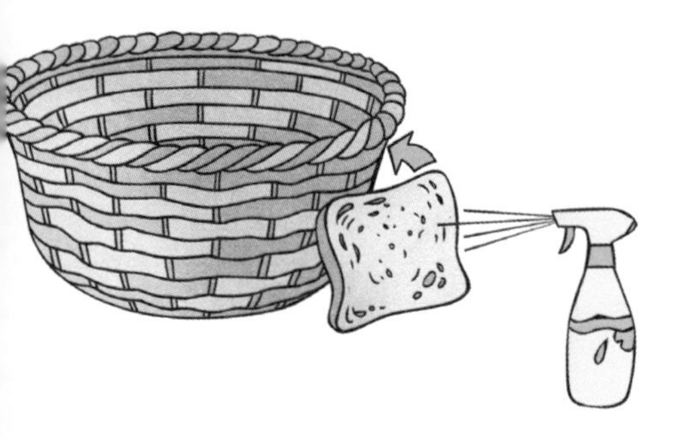

■ Down on the floor

277. Linseed for unsealed wood

Unsealed and unwaxed floorboards call for the care that only linseed oil can give.

- Moisten a rag with oil and dab onto the floorboards until it sinks in.
- Buff to a shine.
- Damp-mop daily to maintain.
- Repeat the 'oil feed' twice a year – you probably won't need to do much more than swab lightly if the boards were well impregnated the first time.
- If you prefer, add a few drops of lemon oil for a nice aroma.

278. Slippers for vinyl stains

Got a stain on your vinyl floor tiles?

- Moondance across it in your slippers (or any soft-rubber soled shoes) to 'erase'!

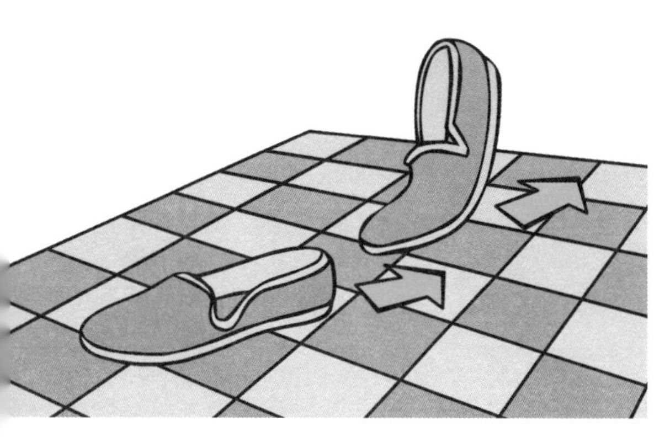

279. Top up the polish

Varnished wooden floorboards need a daily damp mop to prevent dust from scratching the finish.

- A fortnightly addition of a few drops of furniture polish to the mopping water will renew the surface treatment.

Do It Yourself

Doing It Yourself needn't be a task, nor a minefield. Navigate and stock your workshop or workroom with our bright ideas – from powering up and sorting your hobby stuff, to minor household repairs and easers, to smart projects for your home and garden and wardrobes that call for mere minutes!

Workshop basics

280. Power down!

Electricity is potentially life threatening. When working with electricity:

- NEVER work on a live circuit.
- Always test with a voltage tester: it looks like a screwdriver but lights up if the wire is live.
- If the tester lights up although you've turned off the switch, the circuit breaker may be faulty. Switch off the mains power.
- Never pull out a plug by the cord! Always hold the plug firmly and pull gently. Never touch the prongs while doing so, either with your hands or an instrument.

If you ever have any doubt about what to do, get professional advice first!

281. Hang it all!

You don't need a fancy, niche-for-every-last-screw toolbox to keep DIY equipment sorted.

- Fix a large section of grating or length of strong wire fencing along your garage wall, and hang it all off it!
- You can use S-hooks, bulldog clips to hold flat objects (like sandpaper) in place, small metal flowerpots or sand buckets to hold nuts and bolts, and perhaps some strong magnets to attach awkward shapes like hard hats and keep pairs of gloves together (*see Tip 282*).

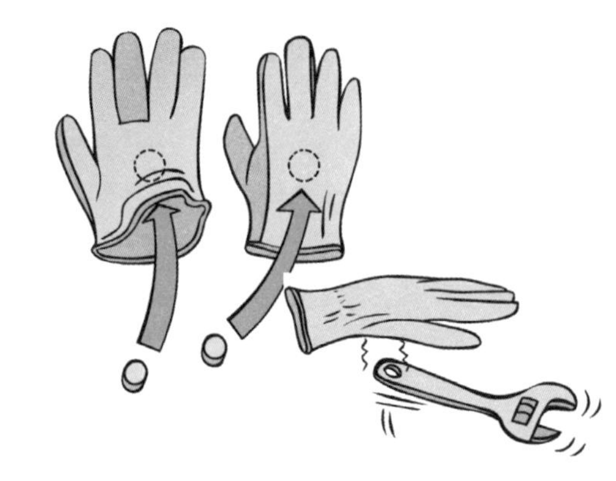

282. Get a firmer grip on gloves

Missing one of a pair of gloves? Prone to having tools flip out of your hands? Here's a stick-together solution for you!

Get a set of small round magnets – like those used on magnetic boards or the fridge door.

- Attach one to the inside of each of your work gloves, in the palm.

So when you put them away, they'll hang together, and when you handle a tool with an iron core, they'll hang on to that too. Plus, has clearing up a spilled box of nails ever been so easy?

Repairs and household maintenance

283. Stop that drip, quick!

Leaking taps waste gallons of water yet are usually easy to fix – especially the old-fashioned sort. They usually just need to have their washers replaced.

- Keep an assortment of washers in different sizes and thicknesses in your repair kit.

The more modern ones have ceramic washers or O rings instead. The first type shouldn't need replacing unless you have a faulty product (in which case the manufacturer should replace it). The second is better left to the manufacturer's service staff, since you'll probably have to order the exact parts to fit your fixtures anyway.

284. Painted wood, clean glass

Getting a little paint on the window panes while doing the frame or sill may seem inevitable.

- Mask the sill with tape before you start painting

Try this for splatters already there:

- Dip a sponge or rag in warm vinegar and hold over the stain to soften it.
- Now scrape the paint away with a sharp-bladed razor or craft knife.
- Rinse and wipe the window.

285. Smooth locks and silent hinges

Got a lock that sticks or a hinge that keeps creaking? Try this for a no-mess solution.

- Rub the offending hinge or the 'sticky' key with a graphite pencil.
- Now open and close the door (or wiggle the key in the lock) several times to distribute the graphite.

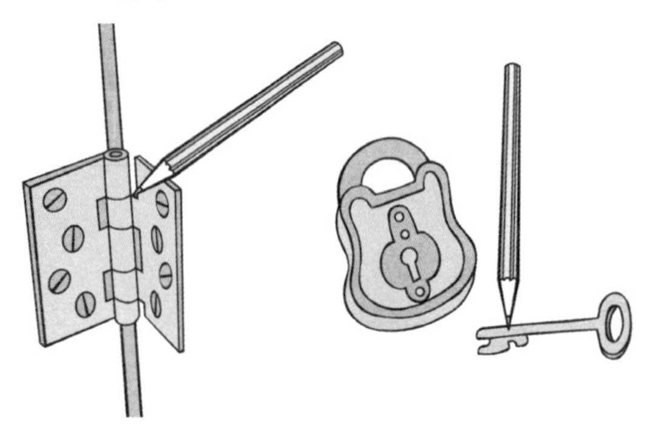

286. Vase with a 'vent'!

Your favourite vase sprung a leak?

Use a little food colouring to help seal the weak spot, then rinse clean.

- Let dry and dribble a little wax from a melting candle to seal – preferably from the inside.
- Alternatively, paint the crack on the wrong side with thickened nail enamel or acrylic paint.

287. Tangled jewellery?

Untangling the bling collection is always a problem for teenage girls; and every mother's nightmare. Reduce the confusion with a Hollywood greenroom-style mirror.

Make it big, possibly floor-length, and they won't keep popping into your walk-in wardrobe!

- Now chuck the strip lights and screw in an odd collection of assorted knobs – mix it up for extra funkiness.

Hang all the bits and bobs on those knobs for instant access. Tangle sorted!

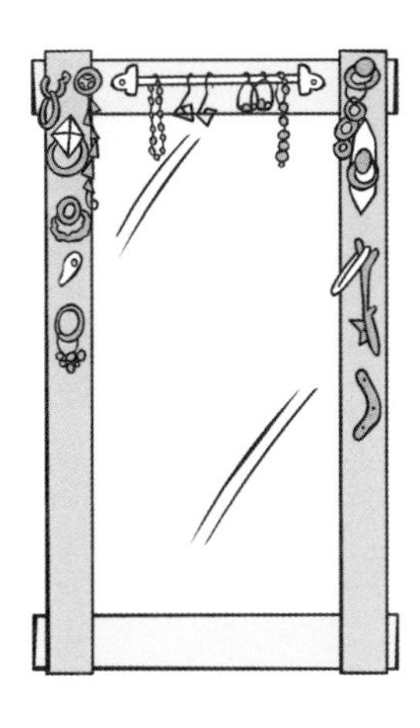

288. Curb your herbs

Unless your kitchen garden sits in pots on the window sill, the more invasive herbs – such as mint – can quickly overrun their allotted beds.

Push sections of plastic builder's pipes into the soil to a depth of 7–10 cm/3–4 inches, and use them as 'planters'.

The open-ended cylinders give your herbs the benefits of being bedded rather than potted, yet keep them in their places!

289. Chalk marked

With some blackboard paint, almost anything becomes easier to label.

- Recycle ice lolly sticks as plant tags.
- Turn the skirting boards in the nursery into one long toddler-high drawing easel.
- On folding garden chairs, paint neat rectangles in which to scrawl guests' names to indicate the seating plan!
- Paint on paper or metal for rewriteable labels for boxes and jars (slip the label behind clear film so it won't rub off with regular handling).
- Scrawl a 'Busy' message on your home office or workshop door!

■ Aesthetic extras

290. Fairy glow

Make your own magical string of fairy lights!

- Cut out circles 15–18 cm/6–7 inches in diameter from white and pastel card.
- Remove a 'quarter wedge' from each and make the wings – fold over, draw on a feathery edge (*see illustration*) and cut out.
- Roll the three-quarter circles into cones and snip off the pointed end.
- Sew on wings with small running stitches or use glue.
- Remove bulbs from your string of lights, push holders through each cone and screw the bulb back!

Warning: Don't try this with incandescent bulbs which might get hot and start a fire!

291. Ribbon-pleated light

Use a spool of fire-retardent satin ribbon to give a plain paper or fabric lampshade a pleated silk look.

- Using fabric glue, tack one end of the ribbon to an inside rim of the lampshade.
- When dry, wind the ribbon taut around and through the frame, overlapping the bands to look like pleats.
- When you've finished, fix the end in place the same way.
- For extra security, attach two lines of fabric tape along the inner top and bottom rims with glue to hold the ribbon in place.

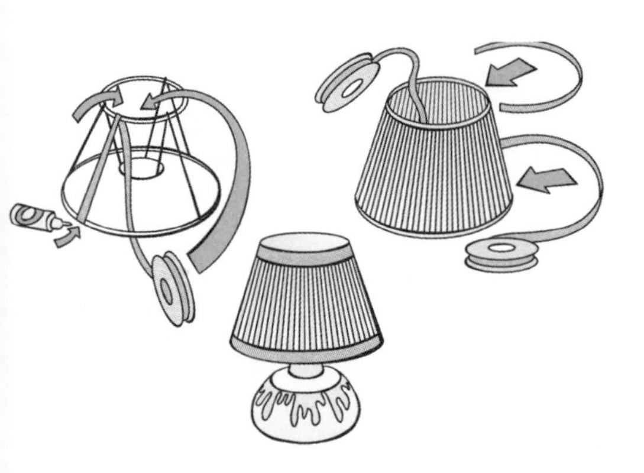

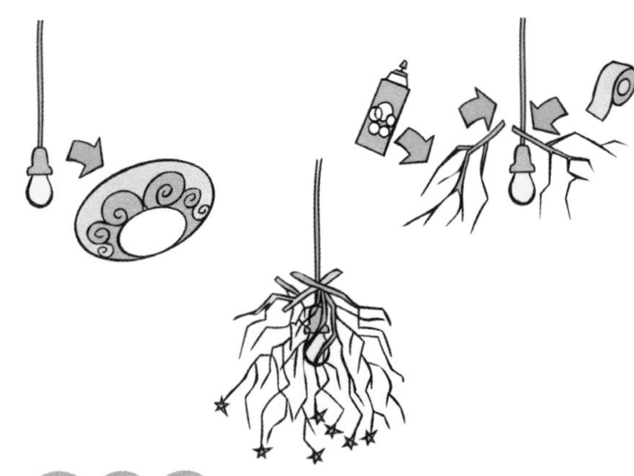

292. Natural chandelier

Make your own chandelier with dried twigs from the garden or local park.

- Remove the shade of your pendant lamp, making sure the socket can still hold the light bulb securely.
- Spray-paint the twigs silver.
- When dry, cluster around the light bulb and tie onto the pendant cord with metallic parcel tape.
- If you like, you can even dangle paper or tinsel stars or frost with fake snow.

Warning: Don't try this with incandescent bulbs which might get hot and start a fire!

293. Light up, do!

Metal cigar tubes are perfect for making outdoor candles.

- Run in a wick (available at craft shops) to the bottom.
- Keeping the wick centred, fill the tube with wax granules (also from the craft shop).
- You can add a few drops of essential oil.
- Don't fill right to the top. Leave a 2.5 cm/1 inch gap and add scrunched-up paper to fill the space so that the wax and wick don't shift.
- Before lighting, remove the paper and anchor the tube a couple of inches deep into sand or soil.
- Never leave unattended!

294. Framed by the pane

An old window shutter or cabinet door with multiple panes can be easily converted into a picture frame for those happy family photos!

- Cut out a piece of glossy cardboard the same size as the door or shutter.
- Measure and mark the positions of the window panes on the cardboard.
- Centre a photograph in each pane and stick to the board base – use non-permanent adhesive or photo corners to remove easily.
- Carefully nail the cardboard to the back of the door/shutter frame and hang.
- Leave the doorknob on for a quirky touch!

295. Busy daisies

Brighten up a plain surface or piece of fabric by stamping with a row of flowers. You'll need fresh flowers for this – a daisy type, such as gerbera, will work best.

- Mix fabric or acrylic paint to a spreadable consistency with thinner (not water) in a saucer and press the flower into it face down.
- Blot the flower on a sheet of brown paper to remove excess paint, then begin stamping, holding the flower by the stalk.
- You should get 2 to 3 impressions per dip.

As a bonus, the brown paper will look good enough to save as handmade wrapping paper!

296. Candle in a tin

It's easy to make a perforated 'shade' for outdoor candles if you have some old tin cans to hand.

- Get a sturdy hole punch for metals.
- Remove any label on the tin, clean well, and use a can opener to remove the top and bottom, giving you an open cylinder.
- Carefully punch through the can wall at random to perforate.
- Add a light coat of clear varnish or car wax to prevent rust.
- Slip over your candle to use!

297. Paper for your drawers

This is a pep-up plan for that tired-looking but serviceable chest of drawers.

- Get some wallpaper to match your décor.
- Unscrew the drawer handles.
- Using double-sided sticky tape, position some wallpaper to fit the drawer fronts, not including the frame. Mark the size for each drawer on the wallpaper in light pencil.
- Remove the drawers, sand all the surfaces and paint the frame in a coordinating colour.
- When dry, paste the sections of wallpaper onto the drawer fronts.
- Seal the drawers and frame with a coat of clear varnish.

Pest Control

You don't want to be annoyed by buzzing insects, but you don't want to poison your own environment either! Here are safe, swift and effective ways to stall the creepy-crawlies' takeover agenda – and vanquish the weeds too. Banish them all from your garden, as well as from the pantry and cupboards and library...

Weapons and armour

298. Open with caution!

Fill a tight-shutting aluminium box with:

- Mousetraps
- A non-toxic insecticide safe to use in food preparation and dining areas
- A botanical garden insecticide
- A small bottle of lemon grass essential oil (keep two bottles – diluted in alcohol and vegetable oil – ready for use) and some citronella candles or incense
- A spray bottle filled with a weak solution of one part detergent or glycerine in two or three parts water
- A big box of borax
- Antiseptic wipes and disinfectant ; kitchen paper
- Rubber gloves – disinfect with bleach solution after use

Flying menaces

299. Flies stop here!

A strong-smelling set of herbs in your window box can deter all but the most persistent housefly – provided your kitchen is hygienic (therefore not too attractive!).

- Growing pots of mint or basil (especially the more intensely aromatic Thai basil) is especially effective.
- A small bay tree near the door will look pleasingly Mediterranean and provide an aroma unattractive to most insects but lovely in cooking.
- Trim the herbs regularly, or rub a few leaves between your fingers as you open the windows or door to release the aromatic oils.

300. Spritz and swat!

The simplest anti-insect measures can be the best.

- Spray insects with detergent/glycerine spray (*also see Tip 301*).
- Have a fly swat handy (or even a rolled up newspaper or magazine).

The mildly sticky solution hangs on to insect wings and weighs down creepy-crawly legs, making them less of a fast-moving target. Now swat them!

Warning: Never attack hornets, bees and wasps in this way – they may turn on you!

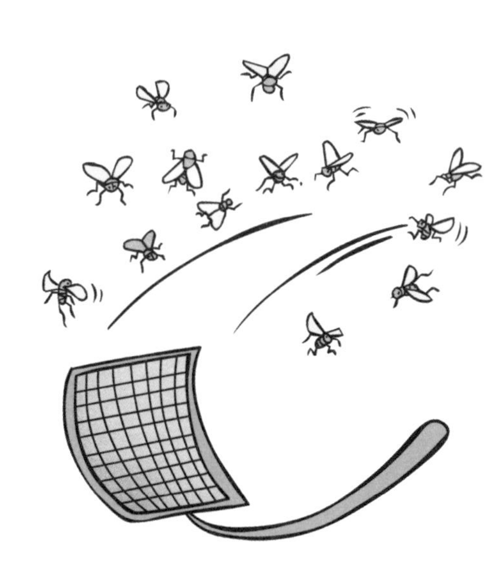

301. Lacquer the mosquitoes!

You may be bothered with mosquitoes during a hot summer or when on holiday in warmer climes.

- When you see mosquitoes, spray the air with hair spray – it stiffens their wings and drops them.
- Swing the can around to cover a wide area quickly.
- Now swat!

302. Lemon grass mosquito wash

Lemon grass keeps mosquitoes at bay – most of these annoying buzzers seem to hate the lovely aroma!

- Add a few drops to your mopping water.
- Dab some on your cleaning cloths and sponges.
- Use the oil to wipe down wooden benches, window and door frames.

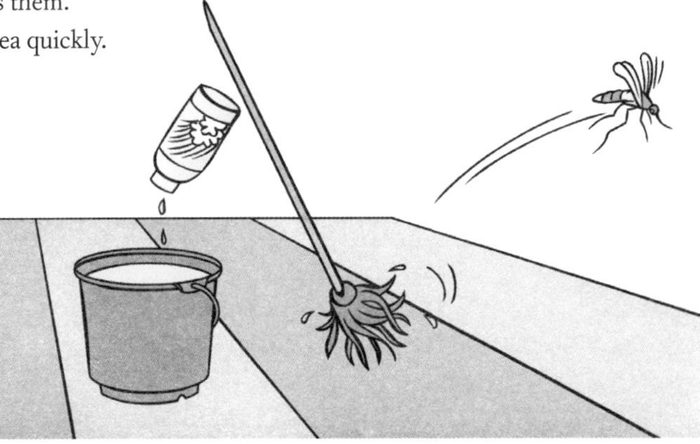

303. Swipe away bee stings

Swiping a bee provokes it to defend itself with a stinging attack! (Should you spot an entire swarm or hive, run!) If you have been stung:

- Don't squeeze; you'll drive the venom deeper (see that sac pulsing on the end of the sting?).
- Fish out your credit card and scrape at an angle to drive the sting out without squeezing.
- Dab on a solution of baking soda to ease the sting.

304. Wasp sting soother

Wasps and hornets, unlike bees, won't leave the stinger behind.

- Soothe with a dribble of lemon juice or vinegar to neutralize the venom – or get hold of an anaesthetic spray.

305. Maddened by midges?

Eucalyptus oil can keep most insects at bay. (It also takes care of lingering cooking smells, as most of us humans find it refreshing rather than repelling!)

- After you've finished cooking a barbecue supper and are just about to sit down to eat, throw a few eucalyptus twigs on the barbie before you grab your plate.

306. Get rid of wasps

As soon as you spot a wasps' nest:

- Place uncovered jars of sugar-water (half honey or sugar and half water) near the nest.
- The wasps love the sweet syrup so much, they'll die to get at it!

307. The bug-free barbecue

Ah, glorious summer, with its alfresco dinners and barbies! Beautiful – if only the buzzing cloud of insects would steer clear...

Make citronella your signature scent for the outdoors, on camping trips and even the back garden.

- The scented candles add elegance to your table.
- Garden torches and tealight holders 'planted' in pots help keep the swarms away from the vegetation they love to hide in.
- If you can stand the stronger smell, burn citronella-scented incense (coils or cones, or whatever's convenient) – the smoke acts as double deterrent.
- Burn a few coils or cones under the table to protect ankles from nips!

■ Creepy-crawlies

308. Infested with silverfish?

These insects love starch, endangering your library especially. They also attack photographs, cardboard packaging, textiles, papier mâché and toiletries with starchy fillers.

- In a pet- and child-free home, bait 'traps' with flour and borax. This should do the trick!
- Add packets of silica gel, as silverfish thrive on humidity.
- Decant packaged foods into tight-lidded plastic containers.

309. Give those ants their marching orders

Borax to the rescue again.

- Follow them home. Now you can feed them to death.
- Mix sugar or coarse cereal (such as polenta or oatmeal) with borax.
- Leave spoonfuls of these near the entrance to ant homes. The insects will carry the grain back in with them, maximizing your chances of getting the whole colony – something spraying insecticides doesn't do.

Warning: Make sure children can't get at the borax-tainted bits.

310. Roach attack!

In the event that you come across pests on holiday, borax will be your best friend again.

- Make a stiffish paste of flour, sugar and borax.
- Leave near cracks, crannies, drains and under cabinets.
- Place a saucer of water nearby if there isn't a source of water close.

The cockroaches will eat the bait and get thirsty, then they'll drink water, swell up and explode!

■ Rodents (and other storecupboard thieves)

311. Your pantry is bugged!

Any evidence of mothlike insects, weevils or white maggots in cereal grains, dried pulses and flours? Unfortunately, there's no way back for infested foods.

- Throw out any jar with a hint of movement, 'floury' bits at the bottom or 'tunnels' pockmarking the surface of flours.
- Empty the cupboards.
- Wash *everything* in hot soapy water – containers and shelves.
- Dry everything in the sun if possible.
- Spray non-toxic insecticide into every crack and crevice.
- Dispense with all loose lids and paper packages.
- Decant foodstuff into sealed transparent jars.

312. Rats!

Rats are a real health hazard and you must keep them at bay at all costs.

Cleanliness and tidiness are the only answers.

- No stray crumbs and spills, no dirty dishes in the sink, no uncovered food or bins.
- Dispense with clutter – full wastepaper baskets, mattresses that leak stuffing, old rags, soiled dishcloths, smelly mops.
- Plaster any cracks and crevices in the walls.
- Wrap tape around pipes where they meet walls.
- Set traps near vents and ventilators.
- Use wire mesh screens on windows and doors.
- Seal gaps under doors with felt (saves on heating too).

■ Wardrobe raiders!

313. Mouse attack!

Baiting the mousetrap?

- Wash your hands with vinegar to eliminate any odour and don rubber gloves – mice have a good sense of smell, and will avoid anything that smells odd, such as humans!
- A blob of peanut butter or a stiff ball of porridge is a better bet than the traditional cheese – mice are carb-loving rodents, which is why they like the farmer's fields!

314. Save your silks (and cashmere)

Dry cleaning's kind to delicate fabrics and should kill any moth eggs hiding in there. Clean everything before putting away for a season. Even woollies marked safe for a cold machine wash are better off being dry cleaned.

- Moths are attracted to food smells and perspiration, so long gaps between deep cleans means trouble.
- Upholstery and carpets need a seasonal steam-clean.
- All garments that can take a hot wash should get one before being put in storage – with plenty of mothballs.
- Freezing works well, too – seal clean garments in a re-sealable bag and place in the freezer for at least four hours.

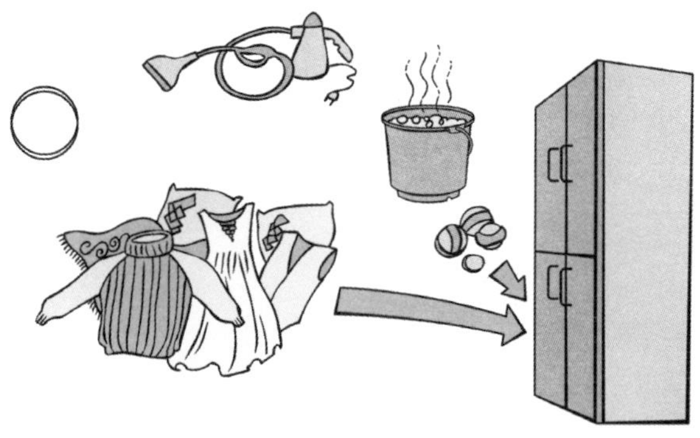

315. Clothes safe in the chest

Storing winter clothes in a cedar or camphor chest provides great protection from munching insects.

- Use fine sandpaper lightly on the inside to refresh the aroma.
- If using other woods, dab camphor or cedar essential oil (diluted with vegetable oil) down the sides. Repeat as the scent wears off.
- Leave the used cotton balls in your drawers to protect smaller garments.
- Small muslin sachets with chips of cedar or camphor wood help, as does dried lavender.
- Once the chips (or lavender buds) seem to be losing their smell, burn them on your log fire, if you have one.

■ Outdoor patrol

316. Feed the birds to save your garden

Not only might you save your precious buds and blooms, inviting a feathered flock means natural insect control!

- Many birds like to supplement their seed snack with a protein-rich caterpillar or a juicy gnat.
- Others will make straight for the insect course, if you give them a shady playground and some water.
- The birdfeeder and birdbath needn't be fancy – strings of popcorn and a sturdy shallow basin or an old trough will work well. Change the water daily though, to avoid it turning into an insect-breeding ground.

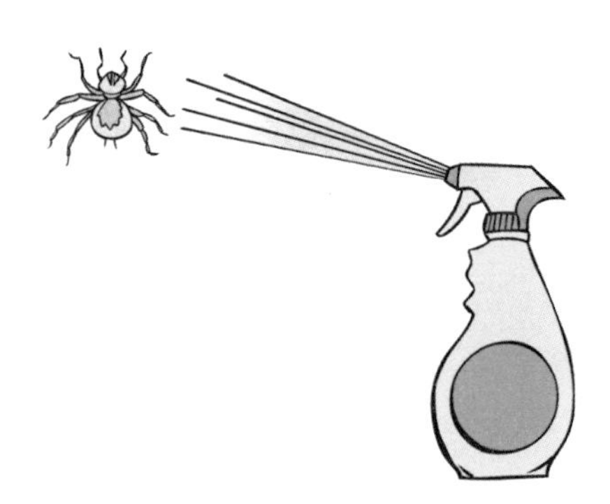

318. Shell the snails!

Mount a shell attack on garden slugs and snails.

- Strew crushed seashells, fine gravel or coarse sand over the soil in flowerpots, window boxes and small beds to deter soft-bellied snails and slugs, which love to feast on your tomato leaves.

317. Shower away spiders

They may give you the heebie-jeebies, but most garden spiders are your allies against insect pests.

- If they do bother you, spritz water from a spray bottle to send them scurrying.
- If they're building cobwebs in the kitchen and it's hygiene you're worried about, persistent removal usually persuades them to choose another location.

319. Plant-type pests

Don't use a chemical cocktail of weed killers, if you can possibly help it.

- For weeds coming up between paving stones or through cracks and crevices, just scald with some boiling salted water.
- For weeds in flower pots and beds, mulching is your best bet – it saves you water (and watering time) too.

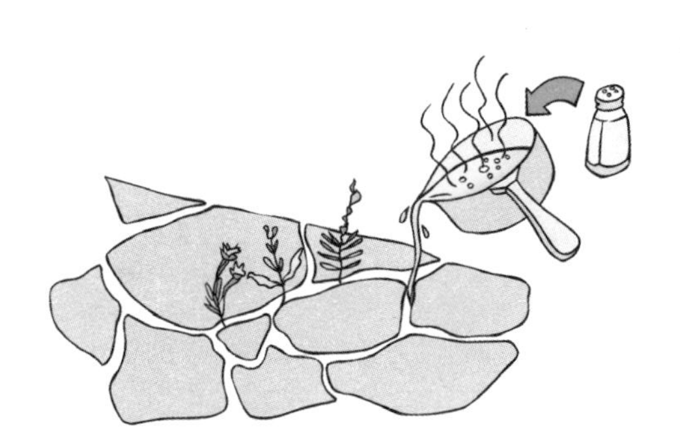

In bed with the bugs!

321. Give those mites the brush-off!

- To kill the mites and remove residual allergens, wash bedlinen at temperatures above 60°C/140°F.
- Cold or warm water will swill out the allergy-causing bits, but won't kill mites that cling on.
- Dry cleaning can kill mites, but the dead bodies will stay – and continue to irritate every time you breathe them in.
- If your bedding can't stand a really hot wash, dry cleaning and then washing may help.
- Hypoallergenic covers and synthetic fillers will help.
- Keep your pet out of the bedroom.

320. Pet peeves

Fleas and ticks, like many other insects, are repelled to some extent by strong smells. The trick is choosing products that are safe for your pet as well.

- Consider adding brewer's yeast and garlic to your pet's food.
- Strew your pet's basket, bed or sleeping area with rosemary, eucalyptus or rue leaves, or fennel seeds.

Pet Care

Because your pets are as entitled to a safe, comfy home as you are, we have tips that help you settle in a new addition, treat every species (canine, feline, avian and rodent) right, and pet-proof your home to boot!

■ New among us

322. One at a time

If you've got a pet, try to plan any pregnancies for when the pet is grown-up and secure.

- During your pregnancy, playing with a baby doll and going through cuddling motions will help you spot any signs of jealousy.
- Mark the bedroom and nursery off-limits.
- Be loving and attentive to your pet.
- Have a child over often so it gets used to small people.

Preferably wait until your child settles in school before getting a pet. Start small – a fish, a bird or a rabbit make good first pets.

323. Home, new home

Playing with a new young pet immediately upon arrival can be rather unsettling for it.

- Set up bedding, litter (for a kitten), food and water bowls in a quiet, warm corner.
- Put your pet there first – offer company, talking in a low, soothing voice.
- Let it explore in its own time but keep an eye out.
- A ticking clock tucked in the blanket and a warm water bottle at bedtime will help.
- Try to bring a familiar piece of comfort from the kitten's or pup's first home.

324. Your pet and your pre-school

Learning the rules early means growing up together is safe and fun.

- Teach the children – by example and advice – to wash their hands after playing with their pets or handling the pet's food dishes or toys.
- Supervise playtime together and ban the pet from the nursery until your child is at least five.
- Teach children that it hurts to have tails, ears and whiskers tugged. (Compare it to their hair being tugged.)
- Let them help with brushing coats, putting out food and filling water bowls.

325. Cardboard comfort

Don't invest in a fancy wicker basket just yet!

- Wait until your cat or puppy is fully house-trained and past the teething stage.
- Until then, a warm bed of old clean throws and clothing in a cardboard box is easiest to replace in case of accidents, or when it gets soiled or worn.
- When you do choose a permanent bed, washability should be your main consideration.

326. Well groomed!

Establish a grooming schedule.

- Start early.
- Designate a quiet spot, where your pet can stand up on a wide bench or table.
- Get it used to standing still. Praise and pet continuously.
- Help it get used to examination. Pick up the paws, look in the ears, open its mouth and touch its teeth.
- Brush its back in short sessions, speaking soothingly throughout.
- Go on to its legs, neck, head, belly and chest.
- Never punish during grooming.
- Never threaten a pet with a grooming tool.

327. Learning through play

Cats and dogs learn through play. So let your pet learn its place in the family from playing!

- Young cats love to play predator.
- Young dogs interpret 'winning' as a move up in the pecking order. Never lose a game of tug of war.
- Teach it to 'drop it' or 'let go' before it gets too big for you to beat at the game!
- Never encourage wrestling matches with your pup.
- With dogs, make sure all toys are 'handed' back to you at the end of play to establish dominance.

328. All together now

Pets get bored if left on their own and love it if you play with them.

- Cats love hunting – favourite prey includes fabric or paper butterflies tied to (non-fraying) ribbons, or catnip mice.
- Dogs and cats love balls – roll a small ball on the carpet for kitty or puppy to chase!
- Adult cats and dogs enjoy retrieving – even scrunched up paper (avoid newsprint). However, it should be too big for your pet to swallow!
- Puppies can get quickly bored with an 'old toy'.

329. Home alone

Emergencies can occur which mean you have to leave your pet.

- Have someone trusted look in on a young pup a couple of hours after you leave and perhaps take it out for a quick walk.
- Secure it in a large barred crate with safe toys and perhaps a rawhide chew.
- Play the radio softly in the next room – the sound of voices helps young dogs feel secure.
- Pet and praise when locking and letting it out.
- But avoid melodramatic drawn-out goodbyes and excited arrivals.

330. Net over cot

Babies and young animals can transfer germs and parasites to each other, overloading their delicate immune systems.

- If you have a young pup or kitten, fit a net over your baby's pram and cot. After all, the warm, soft spaces are very tempting for pets to curl up in!

■ Pet safety

331. Keep safe

A pet has the same safety needs as a toddler.

- Use a sturdy child gate at doors, windows and stairways you don't want it to have access to.
- Restrain it repeatedly to cure attempts to climb or jump out.
- Wire fencing isn't really the best bet; it has 'give', which can allow a dog or cat to burrow or slip under it.
- If you take your pet out in the car and it is too big to crate, invest in a harness that clips on to seatbelts.

332. Clamp up the cables

Teething pups will chew anything rubbery and curious kittens love trailing ropes, which is dangerous if they choose electrical wiring.

- Make sure all cables are either enclosed or clamped well above reach of a pet.
- Any that you can't enclose or move higher, you need to enclose in rigid plastic casing.
- If you can find nothing else, use rigid corrugated pipes – fang-resistant metal or sturdy plastic.
- Train your pets to avoid adopting these for chews and toys – this may save your garden hose and tyres later!

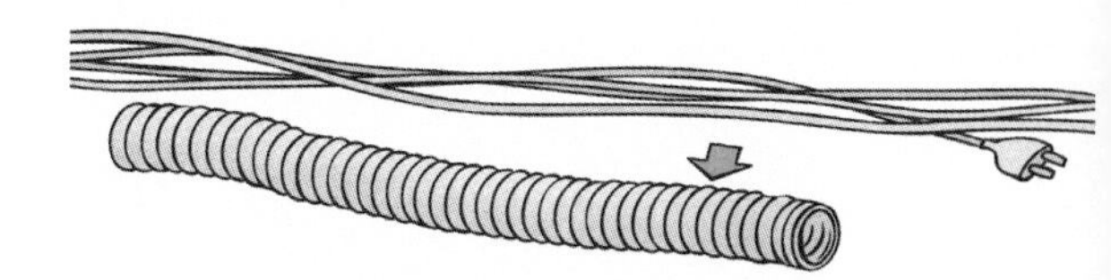

333. Play it safe with solids and substances

Your sewing basket or craft kit could turn lethal.

- Plastic or metal bits can kill if swallowed. So can larger objects that splinter under attack.
- Glue, varnish and paint stripper fumes are dangerous. Whenever you use these, shut your pet out of the room! Allow them back in only after the room has been well ventilated and supplies put away.
- Beware cigarette butts.
- Concentrated detergents or washing up liquids are unsafe.
- Beware small batteries, which can choke and poison.
- Tinsel and sewing thread can cut a cat's intestines!

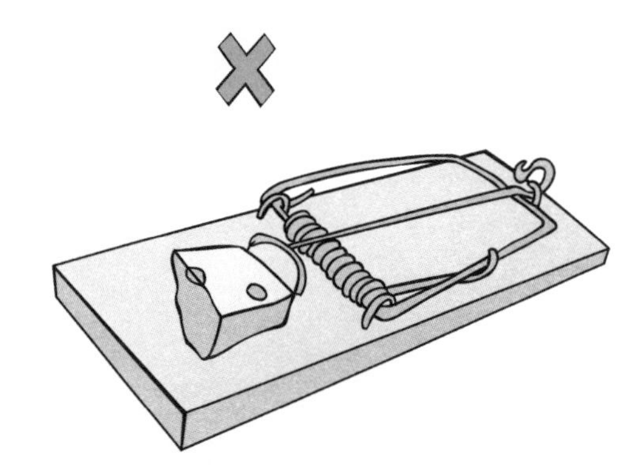

334. Save the trap

Avoid putting down rodent traps and baits while your pets are at home.

- If you've got a cat or terrier-type dog (one of the ratter breeds), don't even think about using poison in mousetraps! If they catch a poisoned rodent, your pets could get poisoned.
- Do not use spring-loaded mousetraps in which a paw, tail tip or whisker could get caught!
- If you have an infestation, either leave your pet in a temporary home or take a family holiday while the pest control people do their job.

335. Lick alert!

Cats and dogs lick themselves clean. If they've got toxic chemicals on their coat, this is dangerous.

- Avoid using chemicals in the garden. Even after using 'natural' solutions, keep your pet indoors.
- Certain plant oils are toxic to pets. Avoid using these on surfaces they inhabit.
- Keep your workshop and workroom off-limits.
- Never use solvents to clean a spill off a pet's fur! Take them to the vet immediately.
- If your pet accidentally gets a splash of a chemical, wrap them in a towel and take them to the vet immediately.

336. Poisonous plants

Some common houseplants are poisonous:

- Lilies and other plants that grow from bulbs – daffodils, crocus, hyacinth, iris and narcissus
- Ivy, holly, mistletoe and poinsettia
- Rhododendron
- Cyclamen
- Foxglove
- Hydrangea
- Laburnum
- Lantana
- Rhubarb
- Taro (elephant's ear)
- Wisteria
- Yew
- Certain types of sage, verbena
- Fruiting trees and stones or seeds of apples, pears, cherries, aubergines, tomatoes, apricot, peaches and plums.

Just part of a leaf of some plants can be dangerous! Check with your local garden centre and your vet. Don't grow or use them in floral arrangements.

337. Quick! Make it sick!

If you spot your pooch swallowing something poisonous or toxic, try to get it to throw up.

- Give your dog some salt – one teaspoon for smaller breeds, two for larger ones should do it.
- However, if you didn't catch it in the act, don't waste time. Get to a vet immediately with a sample of the substance or its packaging.
- Even if it did throw up at once, you should still see the vet. Call immediately after making the dog sick.

338. (B)right on the road

Accidents happen, but you can take precautions. Make your pet visible by dotting its collar with reflective stickers or patches.

- If unavailable at your pet shop, check a sports shop. Bands or reflective tape can be cut into spots and used.
- Dot the collar with patches at 2.5 cm/1 inch intervals or, if using tape or cutting from a reflective fabric jacket, wrap fabric all round.
- Use fabric glue and let dry for a day.
- Watch out for adhesive allergies when you put the collar back on. If there are any, repeat the process with a needle and thread.

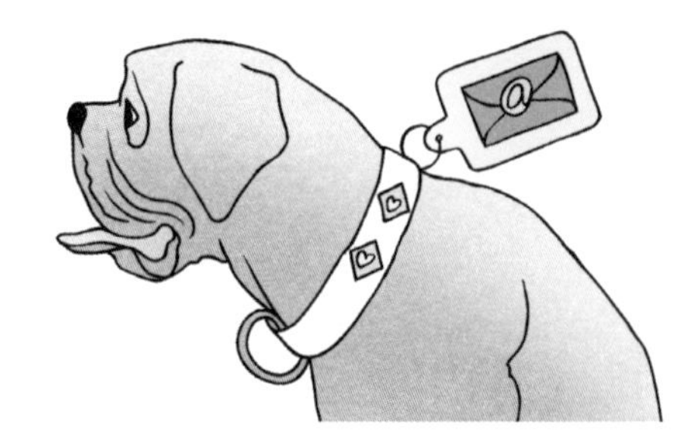

339. Fence in close

Fences and railings keep your pets home and safe.

- Check regularly for loose boards and bent rails; also banister rails and those bordering balconies and terraces.
- With a new pet, especially diminutive breeds, your fencing and railings should be higher than their shoulders.
- Ensure that the gap won't be a very tight fit for their heads or paws – you don't want them to get stuck.

340. Dog@mail.net

Putting your contact information on the back of your pet's tag or collar is the standard safeguard for a pup or tomcat prone to playful straying. However, you may feel that including your telephone number may compromise your privacy.

- Get your pet his own email address or a profile on a social networking site! Put that on the reverse of its dog tag. It helps more than an address if you're moving house or travel often.

General care

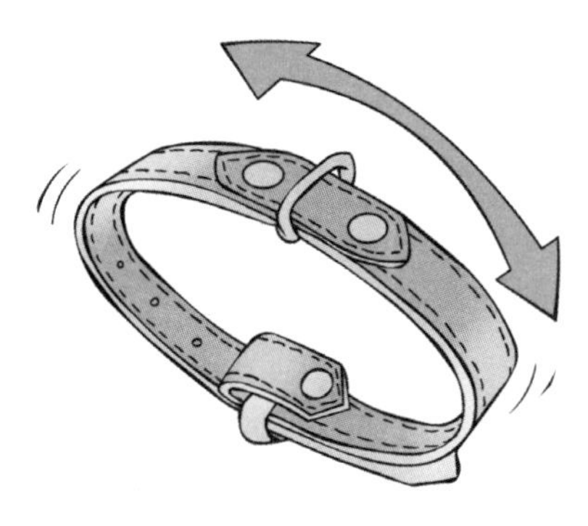

341. Soft collar

Pet collars can irritate and may damage fur around the throat.

- Minimize damage and discomfort by choosing a soft material – the softest leather; or a fabric one padded or lined on the inside.
- For greater safety, choose one with a little stretch or add an elastic insert. Should your pet get caught in a hedge, it can still pull free.
- Adjust the collar so that your pet can pull free of the collar in an emergency.

342. Cuddly beds

A household pet's bed calls for even more care than your own – especially since it can't clean it.

- Hot-wash and disinfect bedding every week for dogs and cats.
- For small caged pets, such as hamsters, clean out the cage and change the bedding material daily or every other day (this depends on how many occupants there are).
- Make sure bedding is dry – if there seem to be water spills, change the bedding at once.

343. Pristine pet food

Serve your pet hygienic rations.

- Fix times, place and dish for meals.
- Remove the food bowl after an hour (earlier if they're finished) and wash – separately.
- Disinfect their eating area.
- Bin leftovers separately.
- If possible, fit a separate sink in the utility room for your pet's things; if not, use the sink in the garden shed.
- Clean water bowls twice a day and refill several times.
- For caged birds, change the water daily.
- Ensure seeds, cereals or nuts for rodents and birds aren't rancid.

344. Keep the weight down

Obesity can precipitate a whole host of diseases – from hip problems in a dog to fatality in smaller mammals such as gerbils.

- Make sure active species get enough exercise.
- Never skip the dog's walk.
- Hamsters need their treadmills for exercise.
- Smaller rodents such as gerbils should be fed a varied diet, with not too many of the oily seeds they love. Give them plenty of green stuff and vegetables, as well as hay for fibre.

345. Flea attack!

Whenever you groom your pet:

- Lay down some newspaper and have your pet stand on it.
- Before disposing of the paper in the outside bin, dab at the debris with dampened tissue – any reddish specks indicate flea droppings!
- If you see either fleas or their droppings, it's time for treatment – for your pet (keep proprietary products out of children's reach) and upholstery. Carpets can harbour flea eggs for years before they hatch!
- Hot-wash pet bedding regularly through the treatment, and replace when you've run the course.

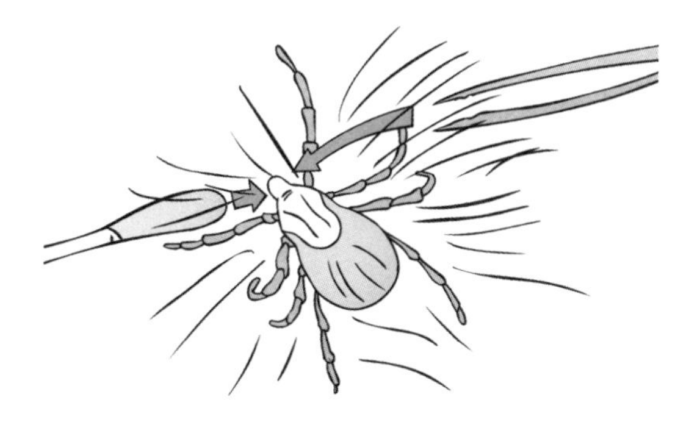

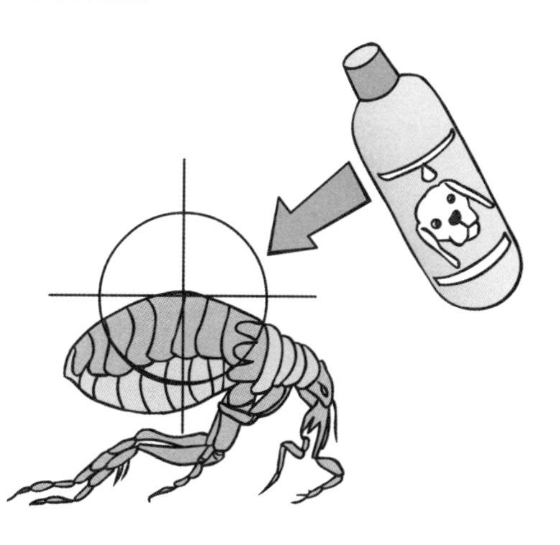

346. Tweeze those ticks!

Turn surgeon for your pet.

- Get a pair of long-nosed pointed tweezers and a bottle of rubbing alcohol.
- Keep your tweezers in your right hand; if your pet's jumpy, get someone to hold it.
- Use a cotton bud, in your left hand, to dab a good drop of the alcohol on the tick's head.
- Quickly grip the tick by its head and pull off.
- With a magnifying glass, check that the jaws are out. Should you suspect you've left one behind, visit the vet as soon as possible.

347. Popping pills

- Put the pill inside a pellet of a favourite food.
- Open its mouth and drop the pill on to the back of the tongue.
- Stroke its throat to encourage swallowing.
- If it licks its nose, the medicine went down!
- Offer water immediately afterwards.
- Deliver liquid medication in a dropper or bottle – open its mouth, press the dropper's mouth against its cheek (outside the teeth) and hold the muzzle closed before squeezing.

348. Pet hair problems?

To enjoy canine or feline companionship, be prepared to deal with pet hair.

- Brush furry coats regularly.
- Comb carefully – if it hurts, they'll avoid it. Cut away snarls rather than tug.
- If your dog lounges on the sofa, get a throw that can be washed in hot water.
- To get hair off upholstery in a hurry, use a piece of synthetic carpeting – brush to generate static in the pile, then pull over the surface, moistening lightly with water and run over again gently.
- Don't have carpets or rugs in pet-accessible areas – hard flooring is the best option.

■ Canine companions

350. House happy

Dogs need house training.

- Puppies squat slightly even to urinate. Pick it up (hands behind forelegs from the back) and put it where it should do its business.
- Cover its entire play area with newspaper – except its bed. It will avoid soiling the bed.
- Put it on the covered area when it is outside its crate.
- Gradually reduce that area.
- Once it is comfortable with a single square of paper, move it slowly to where you want it – even the garden.
- Gradually use less paper till you dispense with it entirely.

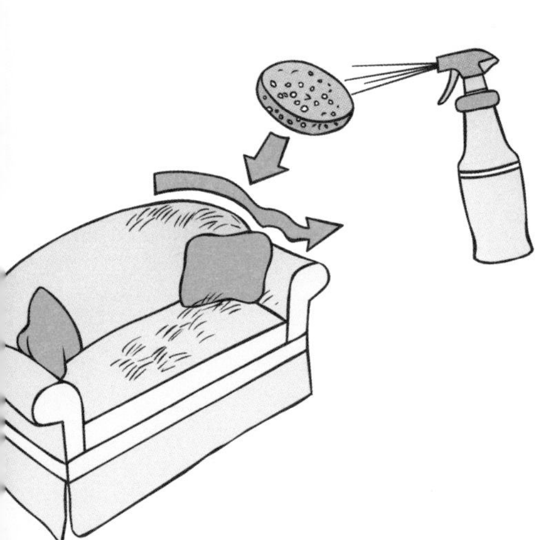

349. Quick fix for fluff

Two quick wipe-ups for pet hair:

- Wrap masking tape around your fingers sticky side out, then 'wipe' over furniture. Change as soon as it gets furry.
- Wring out a damp facial sponge and wipe over the upholstery. The hair will stick to it. Wash the sponge frequently and repeat.

351. Learning curve

Train your pup early.

- If you don't want the adult dog on your bed, don't put the pup there!
- A pup may cry at night but don't sit up with it! Keep its bed somewhere it can see or hear the family.
- Don't let your pup teethe on your fingers. It tells it that biting is acceptable!
- Take away unsuitable objects at the teething stage with a firm 'no'.
- Don't let it jump to greet you. Hold its paws and apply gentle pressure on the rump, saying 'Sit' firmly. Then praise it.

352. Lead on!

Teach your pup its name and to wear a collar and lead. Reward it initially.

- Choose an easy name. Use it whenever it comes to you.
- Start calling from further away.
- Put on a soft collar. Offer a treat to distract it. Let it go free, then try the collar again. Do this several times a day in short sessions. Increase collar time gradually.
- Attach a light lead and let it trail. Don't restrain it at first.
- Get it used to you picking up the lead.
- Gradually wind it in.

353. Car barkers!

One easy way to get your dog to stop barking out of car windows is to restrain it with a firm 'No'.

- Put it on a short leash.
- If it continues barking, don't raise your voice.
- Repeat a firm 'No'; pull it below window level.
- Hold it there and ignore it until it stops.
- Praise and pet lightly when it stops; wait a few minutes before giving a second chance. Be prepared to repeat.
- If it hasn't stopped by journey's end, be prepared to start over on the next leg!

354. Who is top dog?

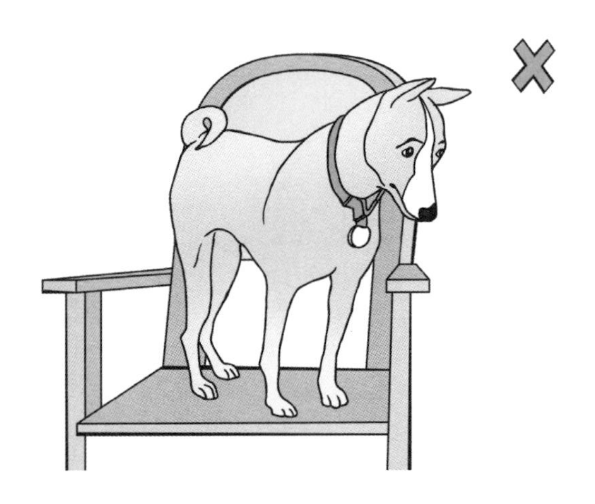

These things can establish obedience from a dog.

- If your children play on the carpet while the pup sits in your chair, its position teaches it that it's dominant! Don't let it sit on sofas and chairs.
- Don't bring your dog food or treats; let it come and get them.
- If it's come to its accustomed place for food, make it wait to be served.
- When it comes to play, you start the game and you stop it.

If all this sounds cruel, it isn't. Dogs are pack animals!

355. Doggie bowl

For your dog, the whole family is its 'pack'. Establish the pecking order kindly and carefully.

- It's best to feed your dog only after the family has eaten.
- Let your child put out its food – the dog will see this small human as its master or mistress.
- Train a pup to sit quietly while the family eats or at least while you serve it.
- Teach it early to wait for your command to begin eating – this prevents impulsive gobbling of anything seemingly edible.
- Never offer table scraps – it encourages begging.

356. Hot under the collar

On a blistering day spare a special thought for your furry friend.

- Walk your dog on grass rather than tarred or paved streets. Avoid standing still for long.
- Never leave your pet in a parked car on a hot day.
- Leave some time between a walk and a feed.
- Snub-nosed and short-muzzled breeds suffer more, especially if they are elderly or overweight.
- You could clip back the fur of long-haired breeds in summer. Don't go so close that the skin shows, or your pet risks sunburn!

357. Dog day at the beach

A day at the beach means taking a few extra precautions.

- Dogs can get overheated quickly. Make sure your pet has a cool, shady place to lie down in.
- Fill its bowl with fresh water first thing. Sea water is not a healthy drink.
- Sea salt isn't kind to your pet's fur. Hose it down or give it a bath in fresh water if it's been in the sea.
- Don't give the dog ice cream! Rather, put a couple of ice cubes in the water bowl.

358. Dog with a bone

A juicy bone isn't necessarily the safest chew.

- Bones can splinter and stick in the mouth or injure the gut. Never give your pet chicken bones (brittle) or slender ones (sharp and prone to splintering).
- Rawhide chews are a good compromise.
- If you must give a bone, choose a really large, sturdy one – preferably hard-baked (available at pet stores).
- If it's teething time or your dog usually eats soft food, a good chew will help strengthen its jaw and clean its teeth. Carrots work as well!

359. The vegetarian dog?

Dogs aren't exclusively carnivorous.

- Your pet needs carbohydrates besides meat. Add rice or bread and vegetables (including starchy ones) to home-mixed food.
- Minus the spices and salt, most vegetables, beans and carbohydrates you eat are fine by your canine!
- Avoid excess sugar and fat.
- Add 'fresh' food to feeds.
- For a primarily vegetarian pet, provide enough whole grains, pulses and seeds along with powdered milk products.
- The occasional egg is a nutritional boost whatever his diet.

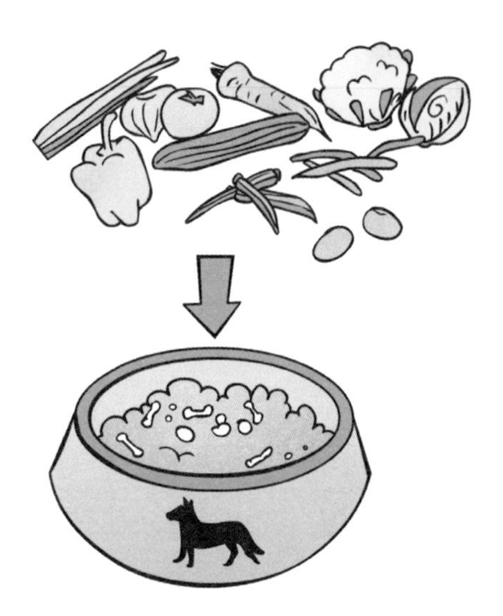

Felines in the family

360. Kitty litter

If you have a cat but no access to a garden, you'll need to have a litter tray.

- Place the tray in a low-traffic spot that is also easy for the cat to access.
- Put the litter box on a large washable rubber mat; change daily (get two).
- Alternatively, stand the box on an opened out and flattened cereal box. Discard daily.
- Wearing gloves, empty the litter at least every other day. Scoop up faeces when you notice any.
- Clean up any 'accidents' at once.
- If you're pregnant, let someone else clean the litter.
- Always wash hands with soap and hot water afterwards, and disinfect the gloves as well.

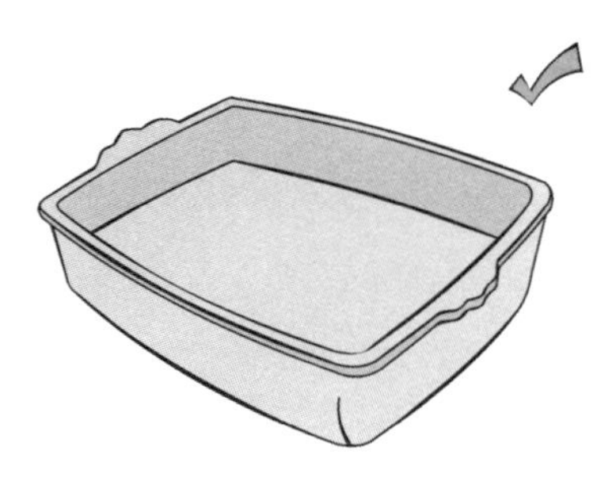

361. Not litter!

Buy a proper, purpose-made product for your cat's litter tray.

- Do not use shredded newspaper, sawdust or wood shavings for litter – first, they aren't easy to collect together for changing and can easily be trekked all over the house; second, the shreds and splints can lodge in paws or in muzzles.

362. Scratching cats

Cats need scratching posts to keep healthy.

- To ensure kitty uses your preferred post, dangle a toy from it when he's a kitten.
- The post should be sturdy and tall.
- An alternative to the post wrapped in sisal rope or textile is a section of sisal carpeting (or similar upholstery) stapled to the skirting board.
- Keep the post near the cat's bed or curl-up spot.
- If the cat has used your furniture for scratching, get it cleaned to remove the scent marking.

363. Knit-free kitty

We all love the traditional image of a kitten playing with a ball of wool or a knitted throw. However:

- Little claws can easily get snagged in knits and be damaged.
- It's also possible for a cat to develop a habit of chewing wool if you keep giving it woollies to play with.
- The fibres, especially now that so many 'wools' are really blends, can collect in and plug up the digestive or respiratory system.

364. Couch kitty

Unlike dogs, cats are better off indoors.

- Typically, cats don't wander except for territorial display or mating. Neutering or spaying helps avoid this and a host of other health problems.
- A cat who isn't used to the outdoors will be happier indoors. Make kitty feel 'at home' from day one.
- Let home be stimulating and secure so the allure of the outdoors is reduced – offer toys and a warm quiet spot.

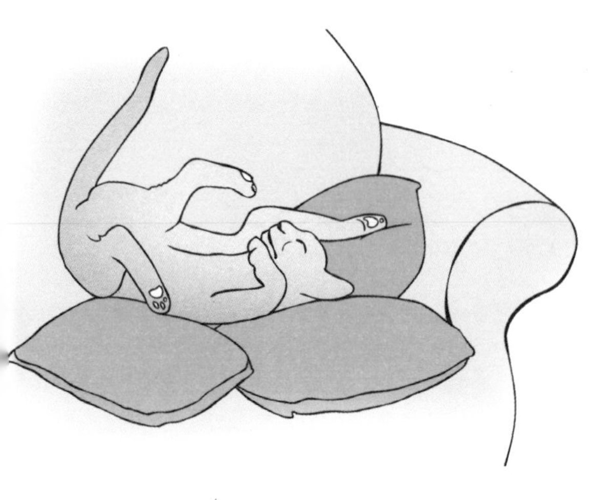

365. Not on my chair!

Rescue your favourite reading corner from your feline friend!

- Place the basket near the radiator or build a window seat over it – the warmth will lure it.
- A cushion filled with catnip should win it over to the sleeping spot of your choice.
- Use a stronger, pungent fragrance in your own spot – mist with a linen spray filled with a spicy or intense floral aroma.
- Push a bag of cloves down the side of the chair.

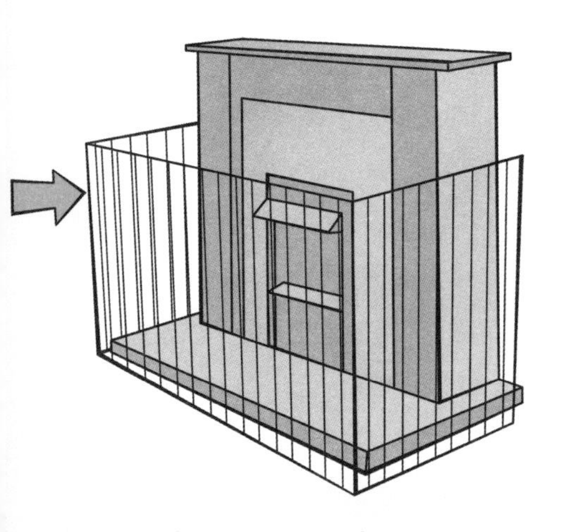

366. Hot spots for cats

Cats' attraction to warmth often draws them towards vibrating machinery!

- Always keep the washing machine and dryer closed when not in use. Do check for errant felines before filling!
- Do not encourage cats in the kitchen.
- In the hearth, always use a sturdy fireguard and keep any small unstable objects well clear.
- The boiler or heater is tempting, but if it's in a basement (for instance) a build-up of carbon monoxide is possible. Keep the door shut at all times to keep your cat out and have the heater serviced regularly to keep emissions down.

367. Tumbles hurt!

Yes, we know the old saying, but a startled cat may not always land on its feet. And anything could scare kitty off balance.

- Keep windows and doors leading to terraces and balconies shut.
- If your home has narrow ledges near the roof, add railings (to guard against falls) or roofing tiles (so they can't walk there to begin with).
- Make sure you have cat flaps in both the front and back doors.

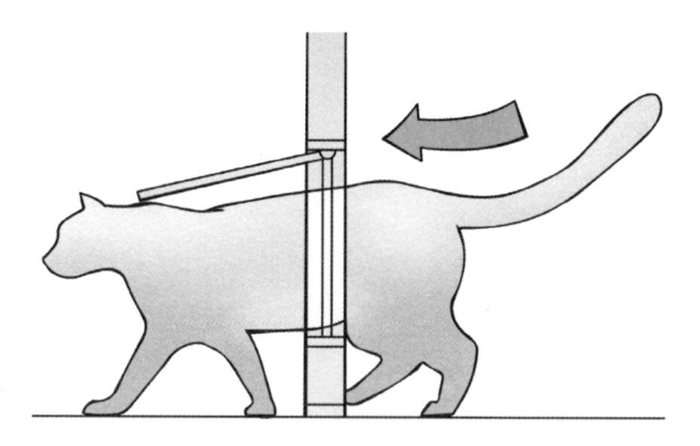

368. Cat in a flap

Teach your kitten to use the cat flap.

- Try when it is in a playful, calm mood, just before a meal.
- Place its favourite food on the other side; hold the flap open to let it see it.
- Encourage it to go through with a gentle push.
- Let the flap drop. Wait a bit before opening it and calling it back in.
- Repeat by pushing it through without actually holding up the flap.
- Holding the flap slightly open, let it return on its own.
- Now try it without food.

369. Home for tea

For cats, the pack mentality doesn't apply. However, food can still be used as an excellent behaviour modifier.

- With cats that are prone to wandering, set a schedule of feeding later at night to encourage it to come home.
- A delicious 'free meal' at the end of the day is often all the incentive a cat needs to regard a house as 'home'.

Rabbits and other rodents

370. Bunny litter?

Like a cat, a rabbit can be trained to use a litter tray. However, it doesn't come naturally (like it does to kittens).

- Choose a low-sided tray for easy access.
- Early on, put the litter tray inside a pen with the bunny. Confine it to the pen until it is quite used to using the tray.
- By way of introduction, scoop some of its droppings onto the litter (as a hint!) and put bunny in the tray to do its business.

371. Gnawing rodents

Rodents' front teeth keep growing – in natural circumstances they would get filed by gnawing constantly. This may not happen with a pet given prepared foods.

- Provide something in the cage for them to gnaw.
- Crusts of bread toasted in the oven or a sturdy twig from a fruit tree are good ideas.
- When picking up your rodent, allow it to sniff your fingers first. Never make a sudden grab, as rodents have poor sight.
- Get rats, mice and gerbils used to your scent by hand-feeding them a treat occasionally.

372. Hay for bunny

Bunnies need more than carrots.

- Make sure they always have ready access to grass and/or hay – for essential fibre.
- The tougher texture of hay makes it a good chew too – encouraging your rabbit to choose it over, say, a chair leg or the carpet for a nibble!
- If the hutch is outdoors, make it a moveable one you can shift around the lawn – that way bunny can nibble while using the rabbit run, and the grass can grow back when he is moved.

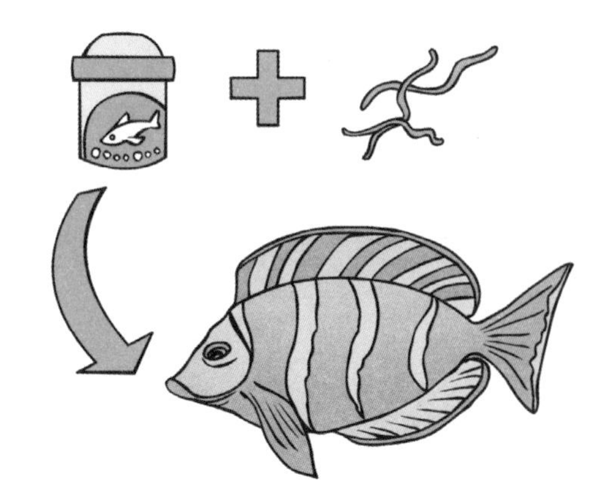

373. Less fresh!

While fresh food is good, watch out.

- Introduce fresh foods to rodents gradually. A sharp change in diet can affect their health.
- Rabbits and guinea pigs consuming their droppings for nutrients is normal.
- Ask what your new pet has been used to and replicate that diet for the first two weeks. Introduce new foods gradually.
- For larger mammals, mix the new food in small amounts with the old initially.

With some fish too, little fresh food and excessive pellets result in constipation. A few juicy worms will help.

Piscean pals

374. Fresher for fish

Whiffy water is a common problem with fish tanks.

- You'll need to clean the aquarium a little less often if you add a few charcoal pellets along with the gravel at the bottom.
- From time to time, recharge the charcoal by removing, washing well in a little vinegar-water, rinsing thoroughly and drying in the oven. (That will get those trapped whiffs out and ready the porous surface to absorb them again.)
- Of course, make sure the pellets are too large for your largest-mouthed fish to swallow!

Feathered friends

375. Mirror half

Caged birds will get very lonely – restless, even depressed – if single.

- Until you find a friend, attach a large enough mirror (securely!) to the cage's side.
- Some birds' mating rituals include offering food to a prospective mate (budgerigars and lovebirds). A solitary male may offer food to its reflection! This will pass and does no harm.
- However, most smaller species, which tend to be social creatures – finches, canaries – will need friends if they are to be well adjusted.
- A companion encourages songbirds to be vocal.

Bringing Up Baby

You need special safeguards to make your home child-friendly: precautions to take when you learn of the new arrival; playground rules for indoors and outdoors; travel tips and teething troubles sorted; shopping advice and daily routines to make sure your little one's secure.

■ Safety locked

376. Three, four, lock the door...

Some doors should always stay locked with children at home, keeping locks and keys out of their reach as far as possible:

- Cabinets and cupboards, all drawers and filing units.
- Storage for cleaning supplies, medicines, pet supplies, gardening equipment, matches, lighters, knives, razors and other sharp or heavy tools.
- The garage, basement and loft.
- Doors to the garden or terrace, especially if you have a pond or pool.
- Heavy-lidded trunks and chests.
- Sewing kits, toolboxes, craft supplies.
- The toilet lid – yes, such a product does exist!

377. Special equipment

You're right to be suspicious of 'must-have' gimmicks. However, there are a few bits of safety equipment you should invest in:

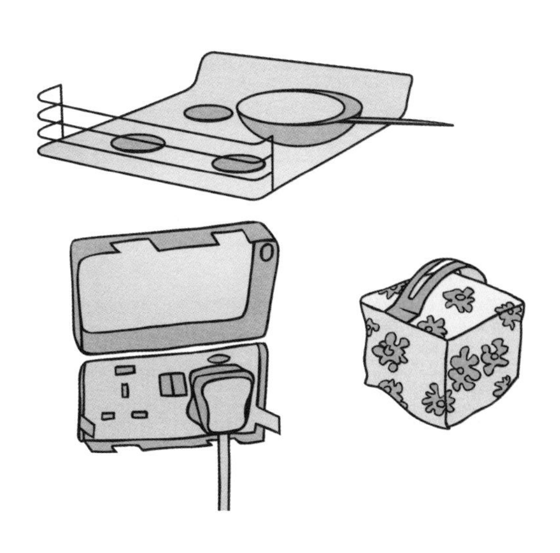

- A hob guard for the kitchen.
- Socket covers.
- Childproof catches for low cabinet doors.
- Sturdy doorstops that don't have removable parts (to avoid finger-in-hinge accidents).
- Fireguards for fireplaces and wood-burning stoves.
- A sturdy, well-padded playpen that's not likely to topple if a toddler throws his or her weight at one side.

378. Gate those steps

Fit safety gates at all danger spots:

- At the top and the bottom of stairs until you're confident the child can climb up and down sturdily.
- In the doorways of dangerous rooms – the kitchen, bathroom and home office.
- At the bottom of low or French windows, especially in upstairs rooms.

379. Danger – water!

Any container that's large enough for a small child to fall into presents a danger. If a small child falls into a large barrel with even a few centimetres/inches of water, he or she could drown.

- Any barrels, buckets or drums that can hold more than about 10 litres/2½ gallons of water should be stowed out of reach or banished entirely.
- Keep all large containers empty, and turn them over for good measure.
- Use a chain and lock on any larger containers in use – water butts, water storage tanks, etc.

380. No-lock loos

With young children at home, you don't want bathroom lock-ins.

- Install locks that can be opened with a key from the outside.
- If you have very young children (under six years of age), instead of locking the door, use hotel-style doorknob tags.
- Help children cut out and colour cardboard door tags announcing: 'Occupied!' or 'I'm inside!' Let the whole family get into the habit of using these – even if adults are using the locks, they should still use the tags so that children see it as a non-discriminatory family rule and adopt it readily.

381. Ring that bell

Children love chimes. Make this your excuse to:

- Place a loud wind chime near every door so it clangs every time the door is opened even a crack.
- Add strings of bells to windows as well – large sleigh-bell type Christmas ornaments are perfect, or a noisy rattle will do.
- This way, you can hear curious fingers opening up exit routes and avert danger.
- Of course, these are additional measures. Your first stop is fitting bolts on every door and window – and using them.

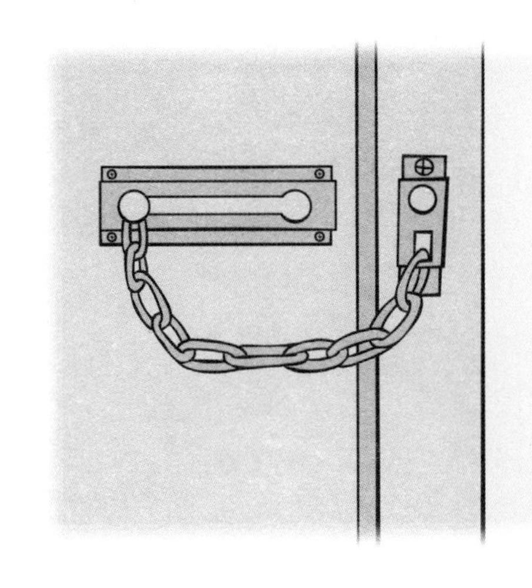

382. Safely shut

Not everything can be locked. For all those other doors and drawers, there are safer shutting options.

- A magnetic clasp on drawers and cabinet doors won't keep out a determined toddler; but if sturdy enough it will prevent younger infants from crawling right in.
- Use rubber stops at the tops of cabinet and cupboard doors to prevent doors shutting on tender fingers.
- Alternatively, for doors you don't want the baby going through in the first place, a short chain near the top is best.

383. Low locks

Sometimes door handles are too low to keep out your toddler.

- Install door knob safety covers, designed to allow an adult to open the door but keep it shut against children trying to turn the knob.
- Fit internal safety catches, which have to be lifted and released to open the door, in cabinets that can't be locked.
- For double-door cabinets, the half with the inner lip (as opposed to the door with the overlap, which you must open first to free the second 'inner' door) should have a bolt at the top.

384. Childproof? Think child resistant!

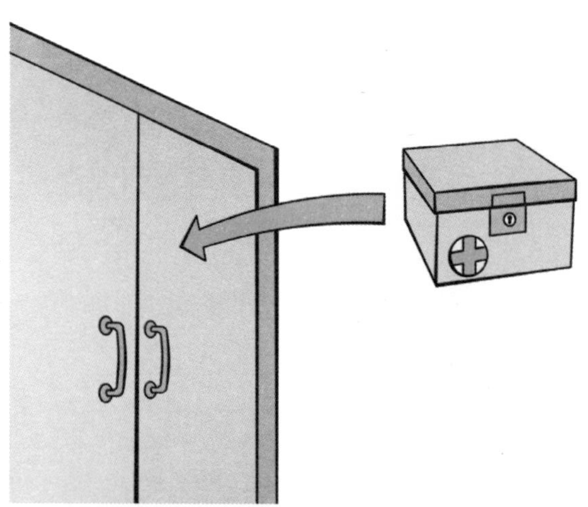

Believe it – there is no device so ingenious as to be completely childproof!

- You must double- and triple-layer the protections.
- You cannot relax your vigilance just because you have installed safety devices.
- Keep even childproof medicine bottles locked up – a child can learn to open them, or even manage to crack them accidentally!
- Even if the cabinets are locked, put sharp objects, matches and lighters, and cleaning supplies on higher shelves.
- Don't just close the stair gate, shut the door to the nursery as well.

■ Electrical safeguards

385. Flexes away

A child can strangle itself with a trailing flex or pull down dangerous electrical appliances with dangling cords.

- Lock away the iron when not in use.
- Never leave a hot iron unattended – if you are interrupted while ironing, unplug and place the iron on a high shelf with its soleplate to the wall. The ironing board is not a safe place to keep an unattended iron!
- Get short spiral flexes (like the ones on telephones) for all your appliances so they can't dangle or trail.
- Use a wiring tube to hide computers and home entertainment system flexes – looks neater, too.

386. Light of your lives

Keep lighting baby-friendly.

- Recessed lighting is best: avoid lamps that can topple, flexes that can cause havoc, or jutting parts to tug on.
- With a small child, brighter ambient light allows you to spot spills and hazardous objects early!
- If the living room or nursery doesn't have enough daylight, consider adding a skylight, if possible.
- Choose nightlights that are cool to the touch and place them beyond the child's reach.

■ Fire alert! (& other alarms)

387. Light the way

Consider using photo cells or occupancy sensors for light fittings in children's rooms.

- It teaches them about conserving energy.
- It also means that entering a room 'in the dark' holds fewer frightening possibilities.
- Plus, it means the light will turn off even if they forget to switch it off, saving electricity.

388. Firewatch!

Keeping open flames to a minimum (even outside the kitchen) is common sense with an inquisitive infant around.

- Avoid lighting candles for ambience.
- If at all possible, avoid having an open fire.
- If you have an open fire or a wood-burning stove, use a sturdy fireguard.
- This is your best excuse for not smoking – a lighted cigarette tip entrances your baby, who is very likely to make a grab for it just when you are distracted. Big ouch!

389. Alarm call

Install alarms for safety.

- Install alarms on doors to dangerous areas – back garden, basement, loft, utility room, cleaning cupboard, toolshed, garage, roof/ terrace and pool.
- Use a chime that rings by your headboard with the switch near the child's bed, which he or she can use if they feel frightened or unwell at night.
- Install smoke alarms everywhere, including cellars, lofts and sheds.
- Put a sticker on the most accessible window in your child's room so that in case of a fire, rescuers know where the child sleeps.

390. Hot water!

With a young child in the house, you need to watch out for overheated water from the pipes as well.

- Turn the heater thermostat low enough that water is never hotter than 50°C/120°F. If your heater doesn't come with this feature, you can usually get a plumber to install a device to make this possible.
- Don't allow toddlers to turn on hot taps unsupervised – remind them red is for 'danger'!

391. *All about baby*

Update the list of emergency numbers by your phone (*also see Tips 23 and 24*) once you have a baby.

- Add your baby's weight to the list – it is an important factor in determining safe dosages for small children; update regularly.
- Give a copy to your babysitter and point out the location of the medicine cabinet and its keys.
- If your baby has any known allergies or drug sensitivities, jot those down on the emergency list as well.

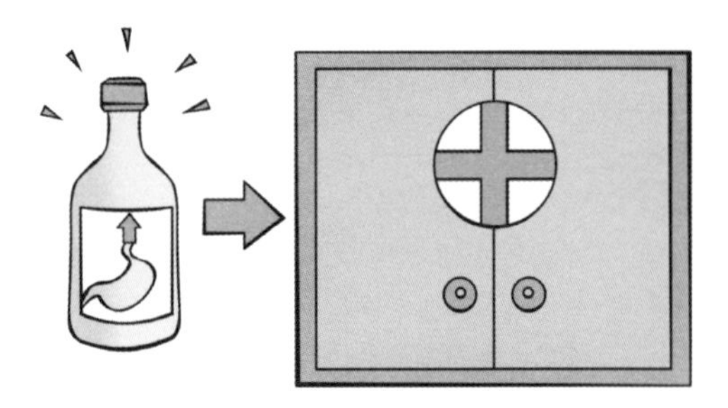

392. *Bitter brew*

With a young child at home, an emetic is an essential addition to your medicine cabinet. Ask your pharmacist to recommend one suitable for young children.

- If your child has ingested something harmful, this will make him or her throw up.
- However, check with the hospital first to ascertain a safe dosage.
- If you know what has been ingested, let the hospital know – you shouldn't make a child throw up if a corrosive substance has been swallowed for instance, and it is useless in case of fast-acting toxins, so let the nurse guide you.
- Even after the child has thrown up, take them for a check-up.

393. Soft landings

The surest way to spot danger at baby height is to 'be a baby'. Do this before baby comes home! After the arrival you will not have time or energy for this.

- Get down on all fours (or get Dad to do it) and crawl all over the house.
- Before your due date, deal with enticing nooks; delicious-looking non-edibles; sharp corners and edges; electrical fittings and so forth.
- Put covers in electrical sockets.
- Add rubber corners and bumpers to sharp edges.
- Remove loose mats wherever possible.

394. Free-fall flooring

Since your baby will spend most of his or her first years at floor level, you may as well start making it child-friendly.

- Fix loose tiles or flagstones, repair cracks and crevices.
- Cold, hard floors – tile or stone – need a soft covering. Wood is not as hard on hands and knees, nor as cold.
- Wall-to-wall carpets will need frequent vacuuming and shampoos.
- For carpeting, choose darker colours – brown and grey are best, or dark blue, red or green – and make sure it's washable.
- Lots of floor cushions are a good idea.

395. Trusty tables

Once you have a young child at home, it's time to clear the tabletops.

- Tabletops will inevitably get tugged and bring everything on the table crashing down. Put away your ornaments for now.
- Don't put the tablecloth or mats on the table until immediately before the meal; remove as soon as the plates are cleared.
- Get rid of the paperweights and stationery items (from pens to staplers and clips). Give them new homes in boxes placed out of reach.

396. Low life

Now that the pretty knick-knacks have moved up high, what can you keep on those lower shelves and surfaces?

- Keep the low tables empty for the baby's changing mat and nappy bag.
- Put the toy baskets on the shelves.
- Near floor level is ideal for the throws, rugs and pillows that will help ensure a soft landing when your little one goes exploring.

397. Furniture fix

No furniture is entirely childproof.

- Keep furniture minimal in the early years. Apart from the hard knocks, it also obstructs your view so you won't know at once when your child gets up to mischief!
- Ideally, all furniture should be too heavy to pull over, and padded to avoid scrapes and bruises.
- Make sure lighter furniture is really light – too light to seriously injure or trap a child if it falls. Choose plastic, or light aluminium and cane.
- Check that lighter furniture isn't brittle – avoid glass insets or wood that is prone to splintering.

398. Storage safer

Baby can challenge your versatile storage!

- Make sure heavy-lidded baskets and solid chests are securely locked. Those that aren't must have a lightweight lid and perforations for ventilation should an infant manage to get trapped inside.
- Stacked furniture – tall modular bookcases or a stack of graduated trunks – should all be reorganized.

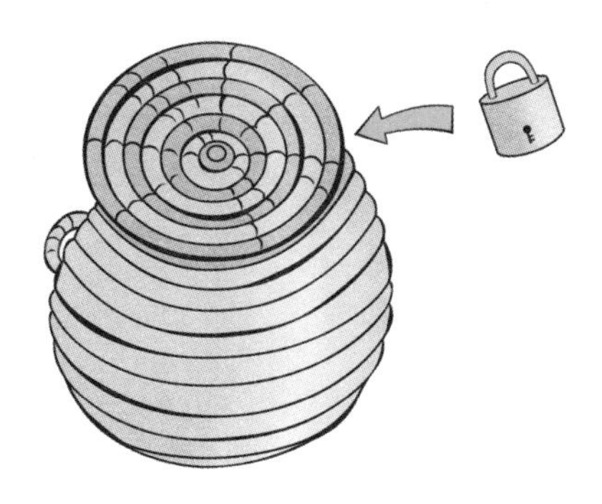

399. Screw it safe

For children's rooms, stand-alone furniture that you can adapt is the most versatile solution. However, all but the sturdiest can be pulled over by a determined tot.

- Keep all standing furniture safe by drilling through the back wall and screwing it to the wall behind.
- Holes in the walls can be filled up with putty when you remove the furniture – a small price to pay for your child's safety.

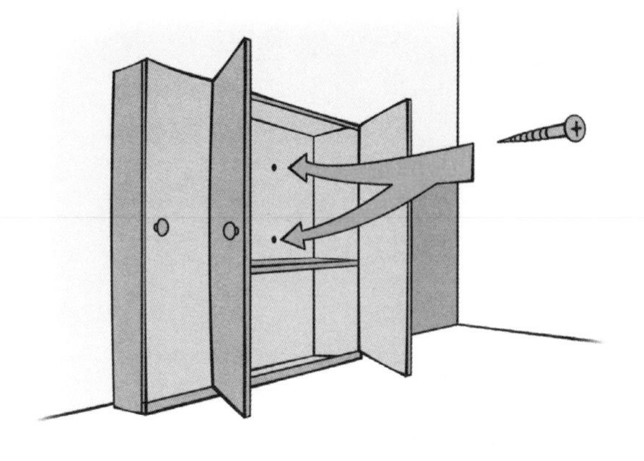

400. Window on their world

For the children's room, traditional window hangings are fraught with unpleasant possibilities.

- Curtains and blinds get stained and soiled, and can be brought crashing down – pelmet, rods and all – by a persistent toddler. So keep them short and washable.
- Avoid curtain ties and blinds with cords that dangle or can be pulled free.
- Use a fixed screen for privacy, which also lets in diffused morning light, rather than curtains or blinds, until your children are older.
- Also consider fixing an 'etched' pane on the window to provide adequate privacy for now.

401. Period pitfalls

Certain features of period homes enhance their value, but can be hazardous. Some things you can't change. For others, there are solutions.

- Many older homes used lead paint. Paint over with latex; watch for children teething on banisters, railings and window sills.
- Fix netting behind any railings with hooked shapes or wide gaps.
- Make sure the wiring is earthed!
- Replace brittle glass with tempered glass – in doors, windows and shower enclosures.
- Block up unused fireplaces and laundry chutes; lock up the dumb-waiter.
- Be vigilant about collapsible grilles in lifts and dumb-waiters.

402. Glow in the dark

For those living with chronic conditions such as asthma or epilepsy, sudden attacks that call for quick relief are nothing new. When the patient is a child, though, finding their medication or an alert alarm that rings in your room can be difficult in the dark.

- Use a fluorescent sticker on the child's inhaler bottle or outline the alarm switch with fluorescent paint.
- Make sure it gets enough light during the day to recharge.
- Check that it's glowing bright before turning the lights off at night.
- Use fluorescent stickers on the nursery ceiling, to outline doorways (nursery, bathroom, your bedroom) and skirting boards along corridors.

403. Canny kitchen craft

Yes, we know it's impractical to completely ban the baby from the kitchen.

- Select a 'safe cabinet' near ground level for toys or empty plastic storage containers with no small parts. That's for baby, and the rest belong to Mum and Dad.
- Put a label on it so the baby knows it's his or hers, and the others are not.
- As your child gets a little older, you might want to let the little one stack his or her 'junior chef' toys in there.

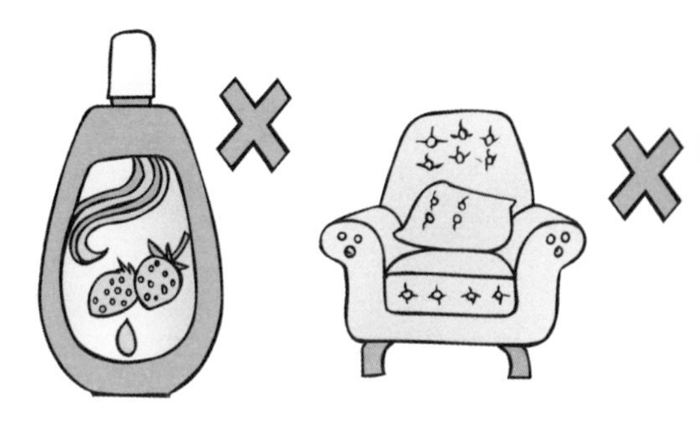

404. Hidden hazards

With a small child, even seemingly safe substances and objects can present dangers.

- Keep all medicines and toiletries out of a child's reach, especially if jumbo-sized. Certain herbs and spices, mouthwash, deodorant, shampoo and meat tenderizers can cause serious harm if ingested in large enough quantities.
- Avoid buying toiletries that are food-flavoured until the child is old enough to know the difference between edible-smelling and edible! Yes, we mean that chocolate-scented body wash and the strawberry-'flavour' baby shampoo.
- Avoid beaded or sequinned furnishings and buttons (on cushions or pillowcases).

405. Good gardening

Some extra safety tips for the garden when you have a small child in the family:

- Make sure you don't have any poisonous plants here or inside the house – your local hospital and garden centre can both advise.
- Consider removing plants that attract bees.
- Otherwise move them and make that part of the garden off-limits – put them near the water butt, compost heap and tool shed, all clustered together to contain the danger.
- Don't allow under-fives to play in the garden unsupervised.
- Avoid having laddered fencing or garden gates, as they can encourage a child to climb – vertical boards or railings are best.

406. Perilous plants

Not all houseplants are safe if baby decides to have a chew!

- Many common indoor plants – such as philodendron and other members of the arum family – contain oxalates in the leaves, which can result in a painful mouthful!
- It's always best to check with your doctor whether any of your plants are especially unsafe.
- In any event, it's best to keep plants out of reach – not just the leaves, the soil too.
- However, make certain too that houseplants aren't on a shelf of such a height that a persistent toddler will pull the planter down on himself or herself!

■ Play it safe

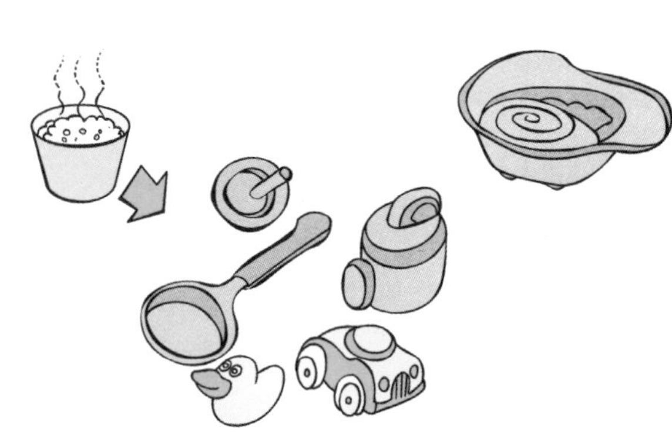

407. Play clean

Toys always find their way into a toddler's mouth. Even non-toxic toys are bound to have a host of bacteria and dust. You need to wash toys regularly as well as disinfect surfaces daily.

- Carpets aren't particularly hygienic – a washable rug with non-slip backing that can stand a hot wash is better.
- Wash plastic toys in warm soapy water.
- Wipe wooden toys with a damp cloth moistened with a mild baking soda solution.
- For easier bath times and cleaner toys, give rubber, plastic and washable cuddlies a bath with your child.

408. Soft-toy spruce-up

These are the worst culprits for dust and dirt, and they harbour germs and grime.

- Choose soft toys that can be machine-washed, preferably in hot water. Slip into a mesh laundry bag and use the delicates cycle.
- Non-washable ones can be freshened up with baking soda too – sprinkle through their 'fur' like powder, rub in lightly, leave for half an hour, then brush out.
- Vacuum soft toys gently after cleaning.
- Wipe sticky and slimy non-washable soft toys with a damp cloth dipped in a gentle soap solution.

■ Friendly foods

409. Playground rules

Choose safe play equipment for the garden.

- Don't hang swings using S-hooks – the sharp points can be dangerous if they become detached. Use ring fasteners and check weekly.
- Make sure ropes or chains are strong enough to support an adult.
- Use soft or lightweight swing seats that won't cause injury on impact.
- Anchor play equipment in a sand bed to minimize injury from falls, or make sure the grass is soft and clean. It should extend at least 1.3 m/4 feet from the equipment and be at least a hand-span deep.

410. Best baby food

Bottled foods are convenient, but they contain additives, so are nutritionally diluted.

- Consider feeding your baby a milder version of your traditional cuisine, provided your diet is nutrient-dense.
- It's a good idea to go beyond the popular bottled flavours to more esoteric ones. A baby's taste is very keen.
- If you decide to make your own baby foods, greater control over your baby's diet and lower costs can offset the time and thought.

411. Not so sweet

Avoid adding sweeteners to your baby's food. Sugar will help your child develop a sweet tooth. And there are health implications too.

- Fruit and vegetable purées and cooked grains are naturally tasty. The sugar habit only makes these naturally yummy foods taste 'pale'.
- Never give honey or golden syrup to a baby under 12 months. They may contain bacterial spores that cause botulism, and your baby's immune system isn't strong enough yet.

412. Choke alert!

Many foods are a potential choking hazard for infants under two to three years of age. Even for the two-plus brigade:

- Look out for small foodstuffs that can lodge in the throat – seeds and nuts, raisins, small hard sweets, whole grapes or cherry tomatoes.
- Other foods require proper tooth-tongue coordination to chew before they go down – tough meat chunks (including bacon or ham), popcorn, and sticky peanut butter.
- Encourage your child to take time to chew.

413. Avoid cured meats

Cured meats are high in nitrates, which can cause anaemia in young infants and so are best avoided early on. Nitrates are also naturally found in some vegetables.

- Wait till your baby is nine months old before you start giving nitrate-rich foods.
- Meat products to avoid include cured ham, bacon, sausages and salami.
- Common vegetables to watch out for are beetroot, carrots, green beans and spinach.
- Check with your baby's doctor for a comprehensive guide.

414. Hay fever hints

If your young children seem prone to hay fever, you might want to watch out when serving them certain foods.

- Oats, rye, kiwi fruit, tomatoes, celery, carrots, apples, pears and some spices contain compounds similar to the ones that make pollen so painful for them.
- Watch for any aggravation of symptoms when you wean them on to these foods. It'll save many a sniffle if a reaction is spotted early.

415. Greens are good

It's a misconception that children 'naturally' hate vegetables, especially greens.

- Rethink shopping and cooking strategies. Buy fresh and seasonal. Stir-fry or grill rather than boil.
- Ensure that even adults can't say 'no' to anything you serve. Doubters can take a smaller serving – two spoonfuls for adults and a single spoonful for children under ten.
- Never allow anyone to say 'I hate that stuff!' when it comes to food. Strong words engender strong feelings. Tell children it is impolite. They (and adults as well) can say 'I'm not too fond of it' instead.

416. Tot-friendly temperatures

Babies and toddlers have no idea what piping hot food will do to their tender mouth! It's up to you to prevent pain.

- Always check the temperature of food before feeding your child.
- For children under five, the temptation to reach for what is set before them is overwhelming – so don't even plate the food until it's cool enough for them to eat.
- For babies up to 18 months, it's best to serve foods lukewarm or at room temperature.

417. Hiccup helpline

Can't stop those hiccups? Not all home remedies are old wives' tales, but some will suit your child better than others!

- Hold your breath!
- Eat a piece of dry bread.
- Swallow a spoonful of dry sugar.
- Drink a glass of water.

Try the remedies in the given order, with about 20 minutes between. Once you know what works best, you can go straight for that next time!

418. Ring, ring!

There's a lot of scary stuff a child can get up to while you're answering the door or phone.

- Install cordless phones. With a baby in the house, the fewer cords the better!

A cordless phone also means you can walk with it – which means not sacrificing business or social calls because you have a small child. It also means you can supervise bath time, cook or keep an eye on them as they play in the garden without having to turn your back or go to another room.

419. Blissful bath times

For safe, pleasant bath times:

- Have a store of bath toys to rotate for novelty.
- Put a rubber mat or spare towel in the bottom of the tub for a non-slip surface.
- Then run the water, making sure it's not too hot.
- Never, for even a minute, leave an under-five alone with a filling or filled bath.
- Even with older children, the door should stay unlocked during bath time, and you should stay within easy earshot. Any sudden silences should be viewed with suspicion!

420. Safely penned

Start baby's day by setting up the play pen.

- You don't have to use it all the time – just while you're busy in the kitchen, in the loo, answering the door or on the phone in the next room.
- Have a separate set of playpen toys.
- When you're called to the door or the phone, put your child in the playpen with a favourite toy (if it's handy) before you attend to callers.

421. Overnight easy

Spending a night away from home – whether on holiday or with extended family – can be unsettling for young children.

- Bring along their favourite toy and night-time read.
- Pack a portable nightlight.
- For infants, take along a brand of baby food they know and like.
- If possible, avoid combining a host of strange faces with a strange place in the baby's first couple of nights away from home. Positive early experiences mean less anxiety later. So let the first visit be to grandparents, or a family friend.
- If the child is past toddler stage, explain that the time away from home is just temporary and that you will all be going home again.

422. Motion sickness cures

You don't have to shop for (or cart around) expensive concoctions and concentrates to ward off motion sickness.

- Have some stem ginger, peppermint sweets, gingernut biscuits or peppermint tea handy when you travel. All safe for kids as well!

423. Avoid traveller's tummy

You know not to give tender tummies any water other than bottled in places of questionable sanitation when you go globetrotting *en famille*. But if they brush their teeth with tap water, it's that same contaminated fluid you're risking!

- Get them to use bottled water to rinse their mouths and toothbrushes too, as well as to wash hands when you don't have access to soap or disinfectant.

424. Safe away from home

Here's a list that applies to children of all ages while they are away from home.

- They must know their full home address and telephone number – and your work address and telephone number.
- Younger children should carry cards with all these details, but not their own names.
- Tell them not to accept lifts or gifts from people they don't know very well – not even from casual acquaintances. Ask them to say they cannot do so without your permission.
- Teach them to walk confidently and stay alert on the road.
- Tell them to avoid loitering, especially when they are alone.

Good little habits

425. Easy riders

Make a set of rules for using bikes, roller skates or skateboards. Make sure these rules are followed by all members of the household, young adults no exception.

- Always wear a helmet, and preferably elbow and knee pads as well (especially with skates).
- Don't ride or skate while wearing headphones or while talking on the mobile phone.
- Avoid riding bikes at night, and definitely don't use skates or skateboards unless the pavements are well lit.
- If they must ride after dark, make sure they wear reflective gear and that the equipment itself has reflective stickers.

426. Tidy tots!

If your toddler is old enough to drag Teddy downstairs, he or she is old enough to bring it back to the nursery. Discipline is a habit – like brushing your teeth.

- Start children on the clear-up-before-bed game as soon as they are old enough to cart their clutter around – and it'll become second nature as long as you do it too. (If it's yet another bedtime battle you're afraid of, ask yourself: would you rather do the battles with a knee-high now, or wait for the teenage nagging wars?)

■ In the cupboards

427. Tuck in the quilts

It looks luxurious, a bed with a big quilt overflowing its sides.

- Make sure you tuck it in at the bottom of the bed, though, to prevent it sliding off the bed and onto the floor as the sleeper shifts (or throws it off, especially if your child is a restless sleeper).
- It's good safety practice to keep babies and even toddlers tucked in tight. Indeed, with babies, aim to have all three sides well anchored to prevent any possibility of smothering.

428. Safely stored

Your bedroom, and your child's, may have several little gremlins in them!

- Put away perfume bottles.
- Lock up jewellery – even costume jewellery – lest it pricks or presents a choking hazard.
- Don't leave sequins and beads lying around. These are a choking hazard and are often found up children's noses.

429. Clothes for kids

Think before you buy!

- Buy clothes in stretchy (with 2 per cent Lycra) rather than woven fabrics – it'll mean less ironing and they won't grow out of them all that quickly.
- Avoid ties, buttons and hooks on clothes and footwear. Velcro, zips and large press fasteners are much safer.
- Make sure all sashes and ties are sewn on firmly.
- Avoid clothing decorated with sequins and beads.

430. Mesh is best for bags

For children's toy and laundry bags, avoid suffocation hazards:

- Choose breathable mesh or netting rather than tight weaves and plastic.
- Rather than plain drawstrings, have elastic cords for closure – this will reduce the likelihood of children putting their heads in and pulling the fastening too tight across the throat.
- Check buttons regularly to make sure none are coming loose.
- Velcro closures or open rigid rims are probably the safest choice.

Home Aesthetics

The thoughtful extras that make your house a *beautiful* home range from lights, flowers, aromas to action in the back yard, with art and aesthetics factored into every single step.

■ Flowers & other fragrances

431. Flower foods

Add any of these to the water in your vase to help flowers last longer:

- A small aspirin tablet
- A pinch of baking soda
- A few grains of sugar and a single shake of salt

433. Fitting in the flowers

Too few for your big vase?

- Gently lift them out and ask someone to help you tie them.
- Pop the posy back in the vase.
- Fill the gaps with scrunched up cellophane paper – in toning colours or transparent.
- Some pretty pebbles or marbles help with stability.
- Add water.

For a dressier look, large leaves or feathery ferns can fill the gaps. This arrangement won't last as long because the leaves will start to rot underwater. But it's stunning!

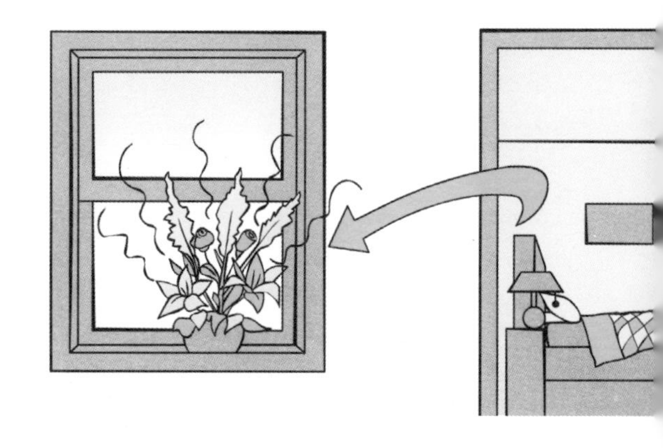

432. Bedhead blooms

You wouldn't wear a heavy spicy perfume in summer, would you?

- Similarly, flowers with a very heady fragrance can become oppressive on a hot night.
- Worse, they start to decay faster in the heat too – definitely not a welcome fragrance!
- If you have any in the house, move them out of your bedroom to another (well-ventilated) room.
- In other rooms, too, try to place them near an open window.

434. Scents or aromas?

At a meal, it's the aroma of your food that should take centre stage.

- Avoid scented candles in strong floral fragrances.
- Avoid using very heady flowers as table decorations – no gardenias to compete with the curry.
- Better options are fruity fragrances – spices or citrus, or herbs such as lemon grass.
- Some flowers are nice for meals if mild – roses, violets, fruit blossoms, and flowers with fragrances suggestive of edible ingredients.
- Foliage such as lemon balm or chocolate geranium adds a novel note.

435. Perked-up potpourri

You've run out of the fragrance refill and your potpourri is smelling like, well, nothing!

- Zap in the microwave for 10 seconds on low heat to revive before guests arrive.

It doesn't last forever, but it's a good temporary fix.

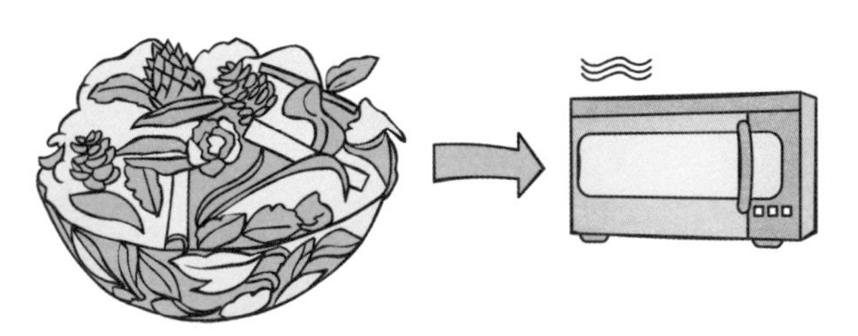

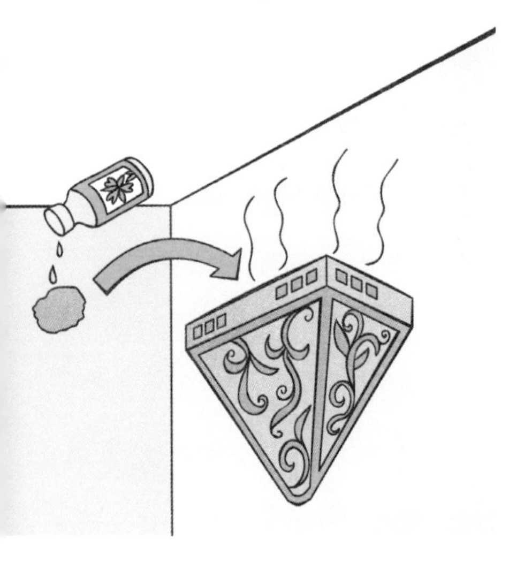

437. Skirted lights

This is an easy way to keep changing your lampshades without actually changing them.

- Make a skirt – a cylinder really – of your fire-retardent chosen fabric to exceed the maximum circumference of the lampshade by an inch.
- Gather the top of the cylinder and sew on a band of elastic, as if sewing the waistband of a skirt.
- Now all you have to do is slip the shade on.
- If you use a washable material, so much the better – just wash whenever it's a bit grubby and replace on the shade.

436. As fragrant as a lightbulb?

It's the simplest diffuser you could have.

- Dab your turned-off and cooled lightbulbs with a few drops of essential oils.
- When you switch on the light, the heat will help the fragrance diffuse into the air!

Warning: Don't apply on a still-warm bulb – especially if you're using an alcohol-based fragrance product.

438. Ring a ring of stars

- Get a wire wreath frame and starburst bows (home-made or those sold at a stationer's) to cover it, plus some smaller starbursts for extra dimension.
- Staple a point of each smaller starburst to a bigger starburst.
- Glue the starbursts to the frame to cover it.
- Staple together the touching points of adjacent stars.
- Make a starry garland in the same way to wind down the centre of your dining table or swag along the banisters.
- If you're making the bows yourself, why not use paper reserved for recycling – cut into inch-wide strips for 'ribbon'?

439. Not your usual pricey print

Customize 'art' to match your room's décor.

- Frame wallpaper and carpet samples identically.
- Line up a trio of toning patterns or similar prints in two or three same-family colours (blue, navy, violet or green, blue, yellow).
- Frame parts of a larger pattern from the same wallpaper.
- One long rectangular frame can add depth to stairwells and narrow corridors.
- Substitute a filled frame for a headboard.
- Try the same with leftover fabrics and a set of embroidery hoops.

440. Winter wonderland

Whatever climate you live in, this arrangement will deck your home for winter.

- Slip a sprig of sturdy evergreen – a conifer twig or an ivy leaf or some holly – into half a dozen clear baubles.
- Stack in a deep clear vase with pine cones.
- For greater height and drama, add an interesting dried branch with pine cones dangled off it like ornaments – secure ribbon or garden twine to the 'stem' of each cone with a loop of wire.

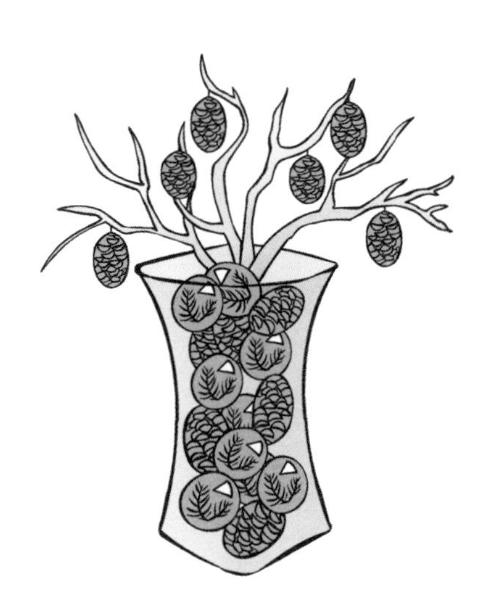

441. Nowhere to go, but up

Small rooms can easily be overpowered by large-scale furniture, unless it's high rather than wide or chunky.

- Height draws the eye up, making you aware of vertical space above eye level.
- It also distracts from the lack of floor space.
- It can mean a great deal of extra storage, which in turn can free up lower surfaces in the room, making it seem more expansive.
- Keep the lines clean and light for best results.

Window dressing!

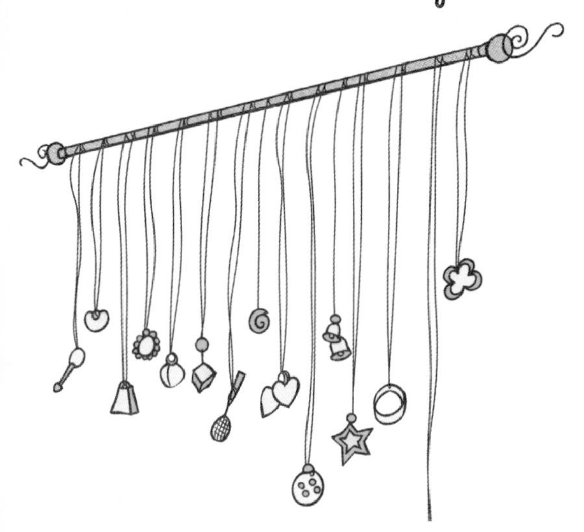

442. String up some trinkets

Neutral, the easiest colour scheme, and white, the most adaptable, can be rather bland, especially in cold or cloudy weather.

- Take out your old boxes of trinkets, key chains, Christmas ornaments, seashells, toys, napkin rings and biscuit cutters.
- Tie different lengths of colourful ribbon to curtain rods and knot a pretty bauble to the end of each.
- Add a ribbon to the back of each chair at your dining table.
- String some baubles from the banisters.

443. Hangings straight

Help curtains close without that annoying crack of light where they come together!

- Attach 2.5 cm/1-inch lengths of Velcro tape along the reverse seam of the curtains, at intervals of about 45 cm/18 inches.
- Make sure they are at the same level on all curtains. No need to keep track of which pair goes together!
- Of course, you need Velcro hooks on one side and Velcro loops on the other to fasten!
- Put the 'loop tape' on the right-hand edge of every curtain and 'hook' tape on the left-hand seam of each.

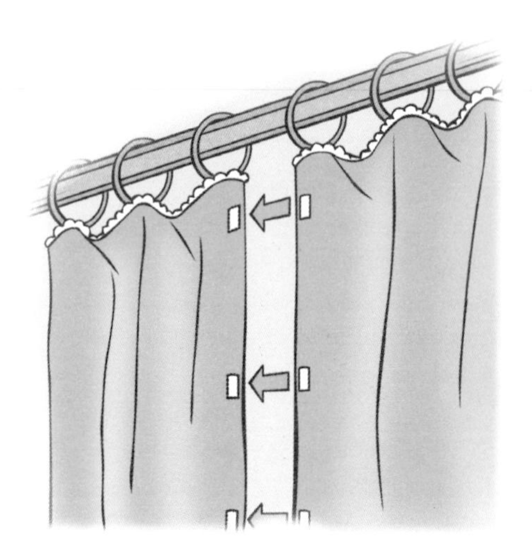

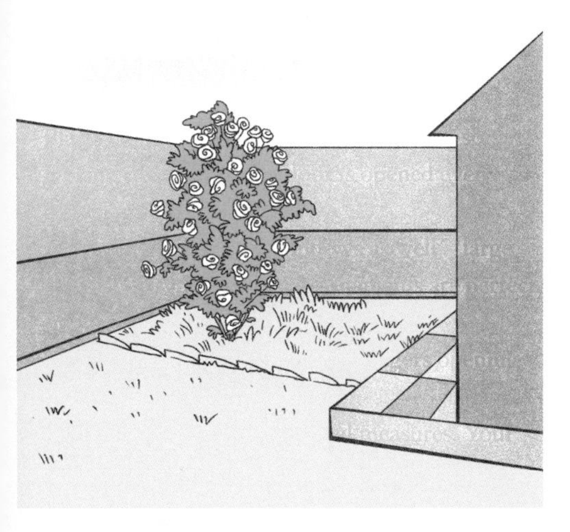

444. White for garden light

How would you brighten up a north-facing room? Let nature come to your rescue.

- Grow some bright white flowers there – choose big massy blooms, whether lilies, lobelias or hydrangeas. The reflection of light works just as well – and is even prettier – if you can trail them up a pale trellis. How about a trailing rose, in *Sleeping Beauty* style?

445. Multi-purpose mulch

Mulching the surface of the soil can prevent loss of water through evaporation. It can also be a decorative accent if you choose some interesting materials. Try:

- Coloured gravel, the kind used in the bottom of aquariums
- Decorative ceramic pebbles
- A cache of old-fashioned glass marbles
- Even a sea of shells (particularly effective with pots painted cornflower blue!)

446. Window box winners

To make it easy to update your window box selection of greenery, plant them with pots!

- Choose containers in a similar material to fit your window box.
- Vary heights and shapes a little for interest, as well as to suit different kinds of plants.
- Fill gaps with garden pebbles, stone chips or gravel for neatness, or hide the evidence with a few trailing vines.

This way, you can put together plants with quite different soil needs, and readily switch plants with every season and on a whim!

447. Indian summer colours

The end of summer and beginning of autumn is when gardens look drab.

- Make the inorganic bits of your garden stand out from the greens and browns.
- White, blue and bluish-purple or pink garden furniture liven up foliage.
- Many flowers and seedheads dry to a lovely sculptural shape. Spray-paint these. Sandwich the stem to be sprayed between the can and a sheet of cardboard or metal to protect the foliage behind. Work in short, light sprays to prevent drips.
- Garden fixtures can add colour too.

448. Amusingly utilitarian

Even a kitchen garden can look bright.

- You can use the foliage and flowers of vegetables if you mix up the planting. Courgettes and pumpkins, runner beans and onions all produce stunning blooms.
- Not all greens are the same; mix hues ranging from bluish to red.
- If the light and soil conditions don't allow you to mix crops in one bed, add a container plant needing similar light but different soil.
- Add a quirky touch with the props and containers. A wind chime of forks and spoons; bread bins for potting; a teapot for herbs.

449. Blooming lawns

Live where the skies open up often?

- Sow a few rain lilies in the lawn. These crocus-like plants react to rain by perking up with pink blossoms overnight – and they flower as long as fresh rainwater falls on them!
- Otherwise, they're no thirstier than lawn grass.
- You don't have to completely supplant the existing ground cover either – just a few clumps will spread rapidly with the seasons, until you have a waving pink carpet to rid you of those rainy-day blues.

Welcome to Our Home

For a home that's not just aesthetic but inviting, we have ideas to spoil your guests silly, whether they're new friends, old pals or little visitors. These easy-to-execute extras cost you hardly any time or effort, but will gild your reputation as a gracious host or hostess with all comers. Statutory warning: put all these tips into play at once, and your guests will feel entirely at home!

House-proud hosting

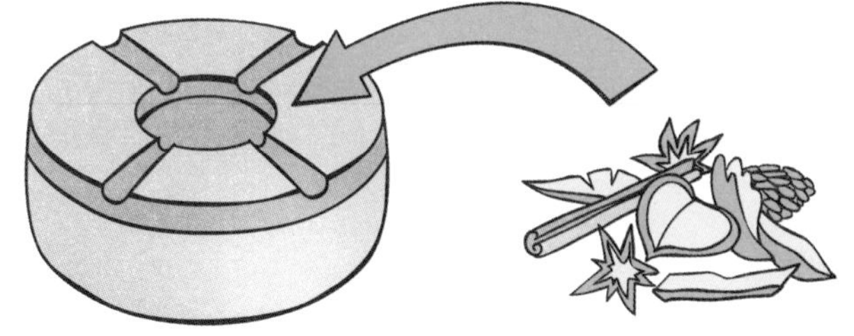

450. Scented smokes, please

Whether you're inviting smokers into your non-smoking home or anti-nicotine neighbours to your cigar-redolent den, the lingering tobacco trail makes for neither good manners nor a good impression.

- To stop the stench at source, put lots of little ashtrays around – but first pour in some scented potpourri! The smouldering butts will tease out more aroma from it.
- Make sure there's a layer of sand or water below so you don't end up with flaming ashtrays!
- Before and after you have guests, leave a couple of saucers of vinegar around to deodorize the living room thoroughly.

451. Fragrant rooms

Greet guests with air that is aromatic and environmentally friendly to boot.

- Pour a few drops of lemon grass oil on balls of cotton and tuck them in corners where they will be out of sight but will still be in contact with the air… elbows of CFL bulbs for instance. This will also help keep out unwanted pests.

Warning: do not place near incandescent light to avoid fire hazard.

452. Floor protectors

A hardwood floor you'd rather not see scuffed, or a white sheepskin rug whose pristine fleece you fear for? Offer your guests some slippers.

- Keep a stack, in drawstring bags, in the hallway.
- Stock children's sizes, plus standard adults sizes for women and men – 12 pairs in four sizes is plenty.
- Avoid cutesy motifs and 'gendered' colours. Stick with a basic carpet slipper pattern, in perhaps bold red, chocolate brown, or nautical navy stripe.
- No pastels – they look grubby quickly.
- Sand the soles to prevent slippery accidents!

453. Raincoats for loan

Live in a shower-prone area?

- Keep a basket of thin roll-up macs by the door for guests and visitors caught out by a minor deluge – the disposable or short-use type made of transparent plastic are fine.

454. Child distractions

It pays to have a quiet distraction on hand when a friend or relation drops in with a fractious toddler in tow.

- Have some favourite children's reads and crayon colouring kits in the cupboard at all times – even in a child-free household.

While the child reads or doodles, it gives you and your guest time to actually catch up!

Stocking the guestroom

455. Just for guests

Keep these supplies in stock for those unexpected overnight guests:

- Soft disposable foam earplugs.
- Adaptor plug – in the dressing-table drawer.
- Bottled water.
- Pocket-size pack of tissues as well as the regular box in the bathroom.
- Selection of guest soaps.
- A pocket-sized torch, plus spare batteries.
- Small card or board game – for jetlagged insomniacs.
- Disposable laundry bags or re-sealable bags for packing soiled garments or carrying wet swimwear or leaky cosmetics.

456. Book supply

A stack of books catering to your house guest's tastes and interests is a thoughtful addition to the guest room.

- A swap shop or secondhand bookshop should offer something for most readers, and should be able to offer advice on subjects you know nothing about. The well-thumbed look is charming too.

457. Entertain at (arm's) length

Constantly keeping the guest company might not be restful for either of you, and disrupts a household with children or pets. There are books by the bed, but if your guest doesn't read much, here are some options:

- You could offer them free use of your den (if it's a usually quiet place).
- In-room entertainment – a portable radio or music system.
- If there's a TV, you can hook up a DVD player with a choice of films.
- For children, a new handheld video game can be pretty enthralling.

Ultra-friendly treats

458. Sleep like a baby

Don't feel that you have to create a 'grown-up' environment for guests – away from home, even the sophisticated city slicker may find a touch of nostalgia relaxing. Use your own childhood mementos or your children's.

- Pin an old patchwork quilt over the headboard or throw it over the armchair.
- Display vintage toys.
- Framed children's drawings or black-and-white prints will give the room a family atmosphere.

459. Beyond basics

Your guests will find your home especially welcoming if you have these in a basket on the dressing table or in the bathroom:

- Hand cream in a gender-neutral fragrance
- New hairbrush of good quality, or a vintage one scrupulously cleaned after every departure
- Scented candles
- Miniature bottle of cologne
- Deodorant wipes, discreetly placed in the bathroom cabinet, perhaps next to the extra loo rolls
- Lip balm
- Sunscreen
- Pair of new socks for wearing to bed or around the house – even airline socks will do
- Spare bathrobe or dressing gown – again, stay gender-neutral

460. Fresh from the oven

Make your guest feel special with a batch of nibbles.

- Bake biscuits with personal appeal – cricket bats for an enthusiast; musical notes for a trombone player or dancer; cat shapes for a feline-friendly grandma; fruit and leaf shapes for a gardener; pound signs for a banker; trees for a happy camper. Write the guest's name on each biscuit in edible ink.

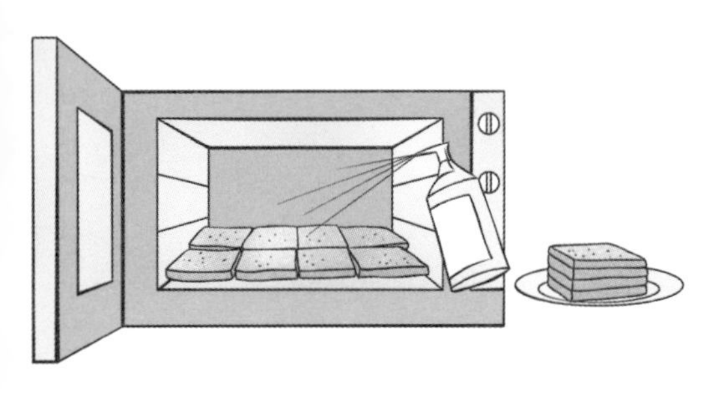

461. Flavoured waters

It costs little or nothing, but can dress up a simple repast and make a guest at your table feel honoured.

- Add a few fresh lemon or cucumber slices to every jug of water in the house.
- For narrow-necked bottles, a few sprigs of mint would be lovely.

462. Elegantly eclectic bookmark

A sprig of fresh rosemary or thyme, a sprig of lavender or a fresh bay leaf can make fragrant bookmarks.

- Offer one with the books you leave in your guest bedroom. The aromas from the crushed foliage will also keep many insects away (*see Tip 299*).

463. Sweet-scented dreams

Finding sleep in unfamiliar surroundings can be difficult. Encourage sweet dreams with a pillow pouch.

- Put a spoonful of dried lavender buds on a square of muslin or organdie.
- Gather the corners together and tie with mauve ribbon, threading through a 'Sweet Dreams' note.
- Sneak into guests' rooms after dinner to leave one on each pillow before they go to bed.

464. Foot refresher

Hold out the promise of a sensory treat for those travel-weary toes, with a home-made 'foot spa' at the bottom of the bed.

- Place a scoop of smooth pebbles in the bottom of a sturdy ceramic basin.
- Nestle in a small vial of essential oil – such as refreshing peppermint or tea tree.
- Slip in a note to 'Add hot water' in the folds of a towel laid on top.
- Lay out fleecy slippers next to it.

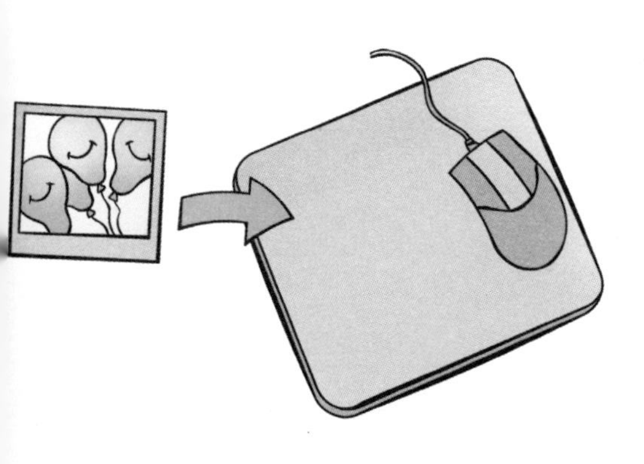

465. Thank-you snaps!

Here's an innovative way to say 'Thanks! I loved it!' or 'Great having you! Come again soon!'

- If it's a gift or dinner you're saying thank you for, send a Polaroid or digital print of you with your present or of the party. Add an appreciative note on the back.
- For a guest, slip into their overnight bag a print of special moments during their stay (maybe on a mouse mat or some coasters?) or the recipe for that jam they loved (use a fancy script on your word processor).

466. Triumph over jet-lag

Keeping up with the clock when travelling far to the east or west of your own time zone can be difficult. Gently lead jet-lagged guests into a new routine:

- If they travelled from the east, organize a few outdoor activities (not too hectic) – maybe tea in the garden – to help them stay awake until dusk.
- If they flew from the west, wake them up with a cuppa by a window – they need sunshine, ideally half an hour of it.
- Synchronize activities with daylight to reset their body clock.

467. Guest goodies

Maybe your guest is an early riser, or has a body clock that's still in a different time zone.

- Put a small electric kettle, a mug, a selection of teas and coffee, sugar, pods of UHT milk and a teaspoon on the dresser.
- Offer an assortment of zingy waker-uppers as well as soothing bedtime teas – mint, chamomile and Earl Grey are a good basic team.
- Replenish regularly.
- But don't forget to offer your guest tea with the rest of the family as well, and make them a fresh cup if you find they have risen late.

468. Travel guide

Send first-time guests a route map and your address.

- You can post them a hand-drawn one with all the landmarks marked in.
- Or send a clear local map (the same one likely to be found at the airport) with the route and address marked in.
- Scan a copy and send it to them by email as well.
- Include your phone number, in case they get lost!

It's a Wrap

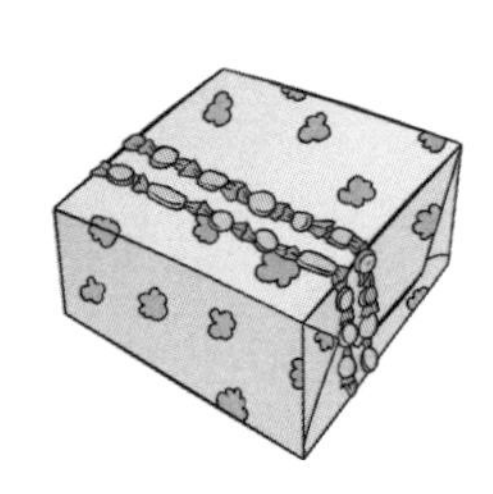

For special seasons and momentous occasions, as well as for everyday perker-uppers, a thoughtful gift given with extra care will make someone's day – and elevate you to the super-Santa club! Which means you'll never be out of ideas for the perfect present again...

■ Quick, clever present-ing

469. Gift-wrapped

Don't bother tying bows!

- Wrap your gift.
- Add a piece of double-sided sticky tape underneath.
- Secure one end of the ribbon to it.
- Wrap the ribbon around the gift like a sash – go round at least three times with each new band slightly overlapping the previous one.
- Tuck in the free end, securing to the piece of sticky tape.
- Add a small accent – a chopstick stuck into the ribbon 'obi'; a bauble threaded or hooked through; a feather or flower (silk or fresh); a bold leaf or sprig of a hardy herb (such as rosemary).

470. Petit parcel

These clever wrappings are for ribbon-phobes:

- Lay your gift diagonally on a square of wrapping paper or fabric. Gather the corners to the centre; seal with a sticker.
- Twist one or both ends of the paper closed (pop it into the cardboard core of a loo roll first if it's an awkward shape).
- Put it in a box and secure with an elastic ponytail ring with an appropriate accent.
- Got a pretty jam jar? Shred coloured paper or foil to fill the jar and hide the gift. Stick on a clever label.

471. Plain made posh

No wrapping paper or ribbon?

- Use computer stationery, baking parchment, greaseproof paper, or newspaper. Add a simple rubber stamp – monogram the recipient's initials or choose a paisley design.
- To a well-washed foil container, add an ice-cream stick 'tag'; write on plain paper, fold into a fan and stick on.
- Secure the top of a small flowerpot with foil, paper or clingfilm. Put a sticker label on top.
- For a small gift, try a well-rinsed yogurt carton with an upside-down muffin case for a lid, secured with tape or a rubber band.

472. No-wrap presents

A pretty present may not need wrapping. Just tie a big bow around:

- A special stuffed toy
- Elegantly bound books, a tin of chocolate or soap, or some exquisite bed linen

However, don't do this if you're bringing the present to a big party, or if the recipient may set it aside and not open it immediately.

473. Pretty knots all in a row

Make knots rather than bows for an interesting package.

- Use stiff, slim (5-mm/¼-inch) cord and tie the bow all the way through, pulling the loops through into a knot.
- Now repeat several times (4–5 at least) so you have several knots in a row.
- Shift the ribbons close together so that the knots are lined up against each other.
- Trim the ribbon ends to equal lengths and straighten so that they look like pleats.

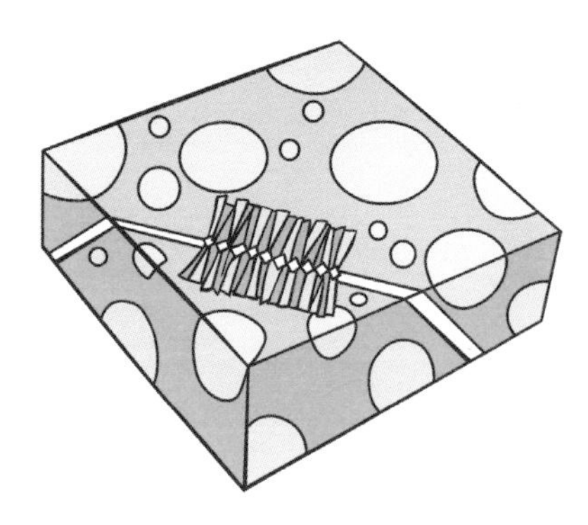

474. Trendy ties

Left loop too long, right loop too droopy... Forget ribbons!

- Wrap cigars or special tobacco in a bright paper bag tied with a pipe cleaner in a contrasting colour!
- Wrap a book in plain paper. Use a leather thong as the tie. Slip on letter beads to spell the recipient's name, knotting at either end to hold the word together.
- Wrap a box of truffles or miniature art with plain white paper, securing with a decorative buckle.
- Hold a soft fabric parcel together with an elasticated bead bracelet or looped necklace.

475. Sweet grip

Make your own garland of sweets to dress up your gifts.

- You'll need a bag of wrapped sweets and a stapler.
- Staple the wings of.the wrappers of each sweet to another. Continue until you have the necessary length.
- This string can replace the handle of a gift bag.
- You can wrap a long chain three times around a boxed gift. Staple the last 'link' to the one below.
- You can even use these as party decoration – up the stairs, along pelmets or window sills, and down the centre of the dining table.

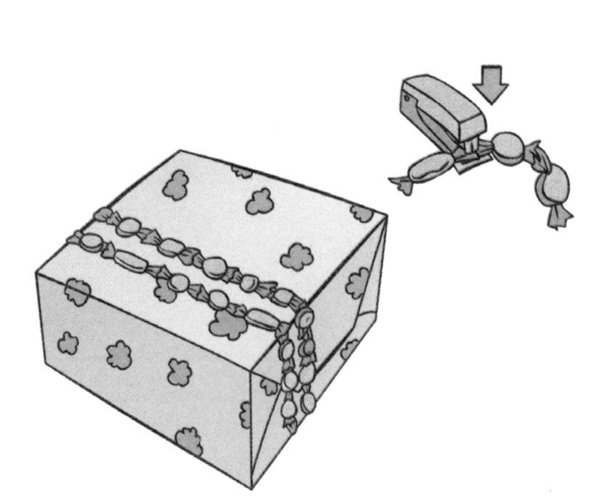

476. Wine wrappers

Everyone likes a good wine. Here are some ways to wrap it:

- Use a length of no-sew felt to make a drawstring bag. Edge with a quick, bold blanket stitch in contrasting wool. Use a length of ribbon, braid or tassel to tie.
- Or wrap the bottle in crushed colourful tissue and slip it into a net bag.
- Or sit it in a large square of net fabric, gather up the edges at the top and tie with ribbon at the neck.
- Add a gift tag cut in the shape of a chalice.

477. The label's the thing...

Giving a great vintage? Don't hide the label.

- Girdle the neck with a small wreath of herbs or evergreens.
- Tie a plain ribbon knot in a festive colour – red, gold or silver. Add a couple of bells or baubles to the ends of the ribbon.
- For a spicy red to pep up a curry, make a 'skirt' of bay leaves and dried chillies strung on string.
- For a New Year bubbly, tie on a noisemaker and a bag of confetti stars!

478. Treasure stasher

Disguise jewellery in an unexpected holder:

- Nestle in tissue or satin inside an egg cup.
- Put in an antique bottle filled with potpourri.
- Bubblewrap and hide in a spice jar or tea canister.
- Put in a coffee mug and top with wrapped sweets.
- Place in the bowl of a soup ladle. Wrap it!
- Slip it inside sporting gloves.
- Hide a girl's first jewellery in a toy! Place inside a set of nesting dolls, a CD case or pencil case.
- Use the folds of an umbrella or a favourite shoe!

479. Novelty nuts!

If you buy unshelled walnuts or chestnuts, save those that break open neatly.

- Place a tiny gift – a charm, a luxurious truffle or a single perfect seashell – in the shell case.
- Seal the halves with removable poster glue or old-fashioned paste glue. (Don't use strong synthetic adhesives – the halves should pull apart fairly easily, yet not fall apart while they are closed.)
- Hide them in a bowl of florists' moss or a bucket of popcorn for recipients to dip in.
- You can spray the shells with metallic paint for extra glamour.

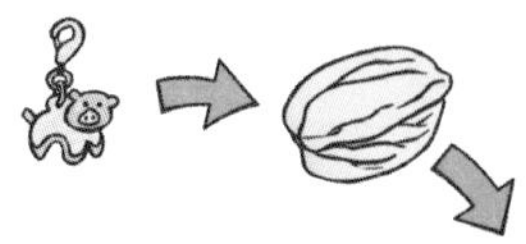

■ Bags of generosity

480. Birthday treasure hunt

Got the birthday boy or girl a big gift? Think beyond handing over the key or instruction manual with a bow on it.

- Arrange a treasure hunt.
- Hand them the first clue in a small wrapped box.
- This should lead them to further clues parked in apt places – for a car, it might be near a poster of a racing car or a favourite childhood toy truck.
- Finally, it should get them to the gift – draped in ribbons, tied with a huge bow or with a cake inside!

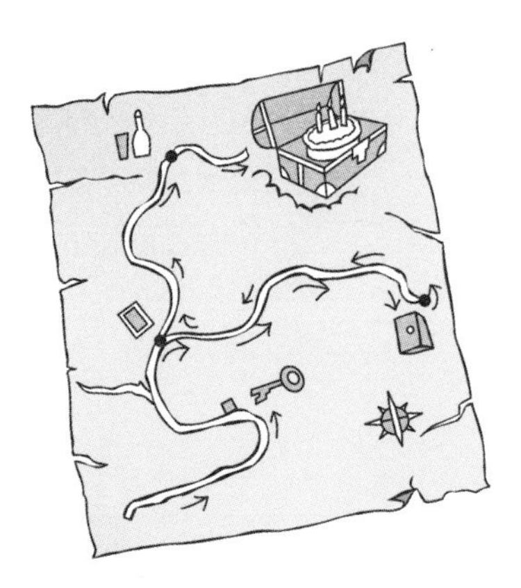

481. Wrap-a-book bag

For a quick gift bag:

- Select sturdy wrapping paper – even greaseproof (for biscuits) or brown paper.
- Wrap a hard-backed book, leaving the parcel a little 'roomy'.
- Secure the paper around the book and at the base, but leave the top flap open.
- Gently shake the book out, slip your gifts in, fold over the top and there's your gift bag!
- Close the flap with a stick-on label or tie a ribbon from base to top, securing the bow just in front of the flap.

482. All sewn up

For dainty presents, sew felt sacks!

- Cut out two identical squares of felt.
- Using a carpet needle and wool or sturdy yarn, stitch the squares together, leaving the top open.
- Turn the pocket inside out and knot the thread; turn right side out to hide the end.
- Add a line of large running stitches about 2.5 cm/1 inch from the top; leave the ends long enough to tie into a bow.
- Slip in the gift, draw the 'cord' in for a drawstring, and tie.
- Embellish with felt appliqués or sequins.

483. Stocking stashers

Knit simple socks to wrap awkward shapes.

- Knit long, narrow rectangles, sewing up one long edge and one short edge to give you a simple sock without heel or toe!
- This will camouflage awkward-shaped objects or hold an assortment of small stuff snugly – bottles and vases, a peculiar paperweight, an assortment of tree ornaments or small toys.
- Add a drawstring near the open end – weave some ribbon through or just tie with some crocheted braid.

484. Well-travelled treat

Giving someone a gift from an exotic point of origin?

- Bag it in a packet made out of a map of the area.
- This is a nifty way to present superlative tea, coffee or chocolate.
- To do this with a wine bottle, you'll need a taller and tougher bag. Laminating the map should do it, if you secure joins with strong double staples rather than adhesive.
- This is also a good way to present a souvenir from your own travels.
- You can seal the gift with a pretty stamp from that country!

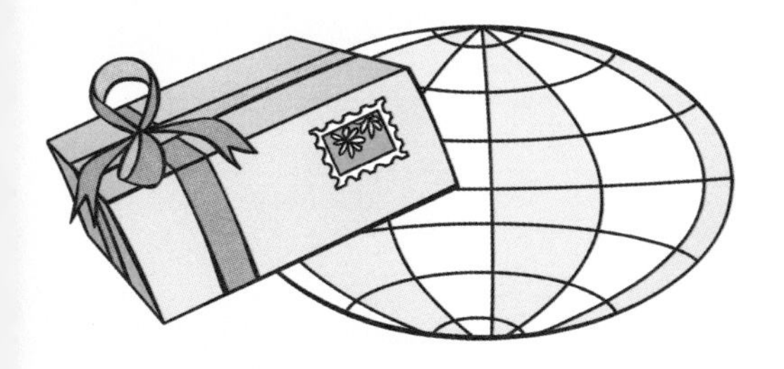

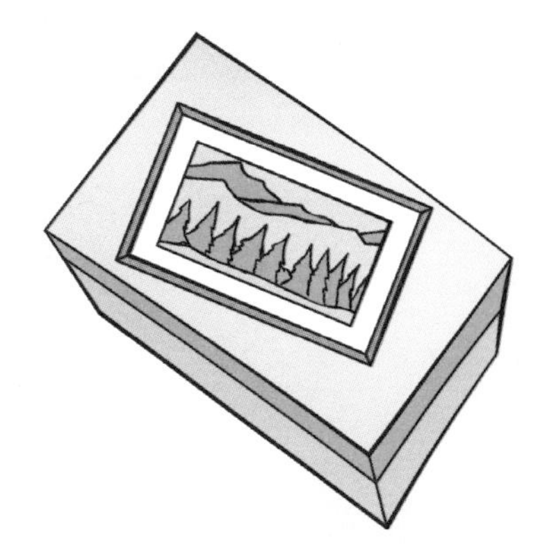

485. The present picture

For a gift meant for a special occasion, use a photographic clue in the wrapping.

- Make a photocopy of the photograph.
- Adjust the size of the image to the area you need to cover.
- Quite a plain container – old coffee tin, tennis ball tube, shoebox – can become wonderfully evocative when this image is pasted on.
- Make it a fabulous reminder – a wedding portrait for an anniversary, a landmark from the part of the world you wish to evoke or a vignette of the occasion or object you are saying 'thank you' for.

486. Gift matching

Consider matching the packaging to the gift – at a slight tangent…

- Put DVDs or videos inside a popcorn bucket.
- Artists' supplies could come in an old paint can.
- Give fireworks in a red fire bucket.
- Put seeds inside a terracotta flowerpot, place an upturned saucer over it, and tie shut with gardeners' twine.
- Got your friend a pedometer? Put inside a pair of sporty socks!
- Present exotic spices wrapped in muslin and bundled inside tea balls.
- Pile liqueur-filled chocolates into a brandy snifter.

487. No boring envelopes!

New covers for coupons, etc.

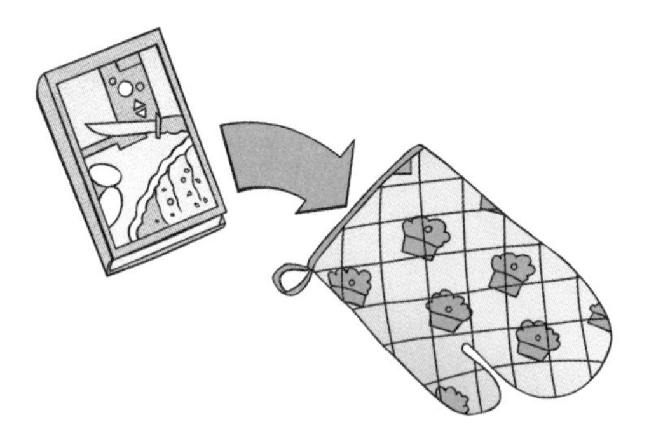

- Giving a cookery course? Slip the brochure inside an oven glove.
- A course in art appreciation? Put in a basic frame.
- Tuck tickets for a holiday in an accessory to match – beach hat or spa slippers.
- Hide an invite to the opera inside a roll of sheet music.
- Secure that gym membership with a terrycloth wristband.
- A pottery weekend? Pop the papers inside a small moulding dough tub.
- Tickets to a movie? Clip to a carton of popcorn!

■ Gifts accessorized!

488. (Heart) warming gift

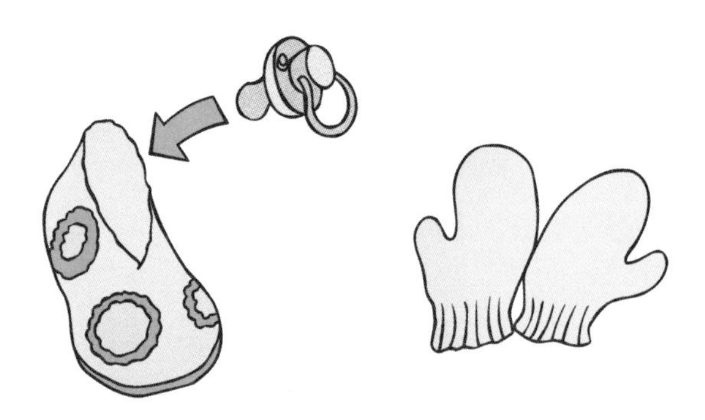

In winter, let the gift bag bring extra warmth!

- For infants, shape the bag into felt booties.
- For children, make mittens!
- For 'little ladies', a party purse.
- For teenagers, cut out a felt scarf, double over and sew up the sides. The recipient picks out the stitches before wearing!
- Adults might like a felt hat tied closed for a bag.
- Line a rectangle of felt with fleece, sew into a cylinder and close the 'bottom' with a separate yarn (unpicking this gives you a muff).

489. Batteries included

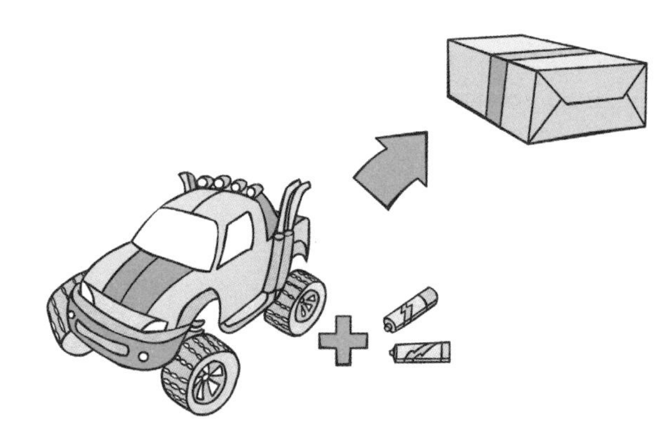

Don't leave the recipient short. Include any must-have item with your gift.

- If you're giving an electronic gadget, especially a child's toy, do include batteries in the right size.

490. Give generously...

... and add some useful extras.

- Buying a book? No one can have too many bookmarks!
- The cheeseboard and knife could do with a wedge of cheese for company.
- Add a colouring book (for children) or a sketch pad to a set of pastels or paints.
- Give a nice notebook with that fancy pen.
- Include a CD with headphones.
- Keys to a new car? Put them on a key ring.
- Gardening tools? Add a tube of hand cream.
- Teapot or mug? Add some good tea.
- Espresso machine or coffee mug? A bag of coffee beans, please!
- A fancy corkscrew? Where's the wine?
- Pop some biscuits in that nice ceramic jar.

491. By the basket

Beautiful wicker or cane craft is a worthy gift in its own right. But it's nice to top up the gift basket! Here are some traditional and some surprising basket fillers:

- Fresh produce – don't stuff the basket or it will seem like it's a gift of groceries; instead, choose a few extraordinary vegetables (perhaps an heirloom variety, or else an unusual exotic, or a surprising shape or colour such as purple cauliflower).
- Some farm-fresh eggs.
- Cut wild flowers *au naturel* – no tying into posies.
- Fresh herb posies tied with ribbon.

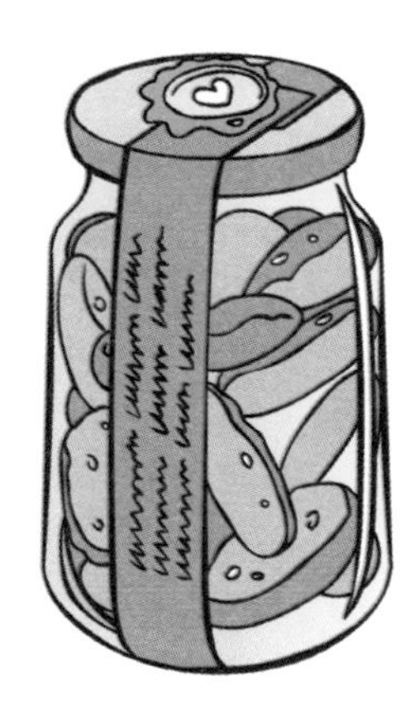

492. Sweetie pile

Smarten up a simple bag of boiled sweets for an easy, yet thoughtful, present.

- Instead of the typical gift boxes, cellophane bags or paper cones, get a small preserving jar to put the sweets in – most supermarkets stock them.
- For smaller sweets, such as jelly beans, you can even use a spice jar or jam jar.
- Add a little scoop or metal measuring spoon – 1 tablespoon or 1 teaspoon, depending on the scale of the sweets – when tying a bow round the neck.

493. Sealed with love

Giving home-made jam or biscuits? Add your own freshness seal and label.

- Wrap a sturdy strip of paper around the jar or box to go across the lid.
- Use an old-fashioned wax seal to secure the edges together on top.
- The paper strip can double up as a label – identify the contents up one side and write a 'use by' date down the other side.
- If your container is more futuristic stainless steel than traditional jars, use label tape for your message and stick on to seal!

494. ID-it!

Take a break from the scrawled names on gift tags.

- Stick on a picture of the recipient, and punch a hole at the top or in a corner to hang off ribbon.

495. Season's greetings from us all

Make your own picture postcard!

- Photocopy favourite snaps of your family. Or use strips from the photo booth.
- Select stiff-ish paper in a bright colour.
- Snip and paste these on your card forms; leave at least half the area empty for writing.
- Cut larger prints into strips an inch wide and reassemble at random.
- For smaller photos, put them together like window panes or line up along the card's bottom.
- Scrawl your messages on the plain background.

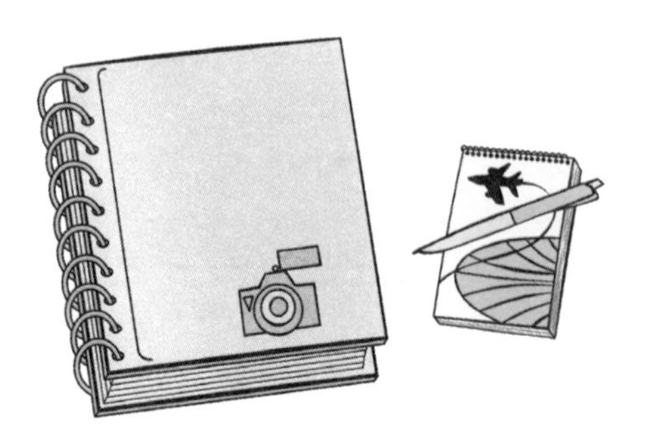

496. Okra greetings!

A quaint vegetable stamp, this!

- Lop the top off a large-ish okra and dip it in paint to stamp.
- Stamp first on a piece of sponge to get excess paint off.
- If it starts to get sticky, slice off another 1 cm/½ inch and continue.
- Stamp pinks and purples on white for summery flowers.
- In winter, stamp with white or silver paint on a midnight blue background for snowflakes.
- Gold on red or red on black always looks festive.

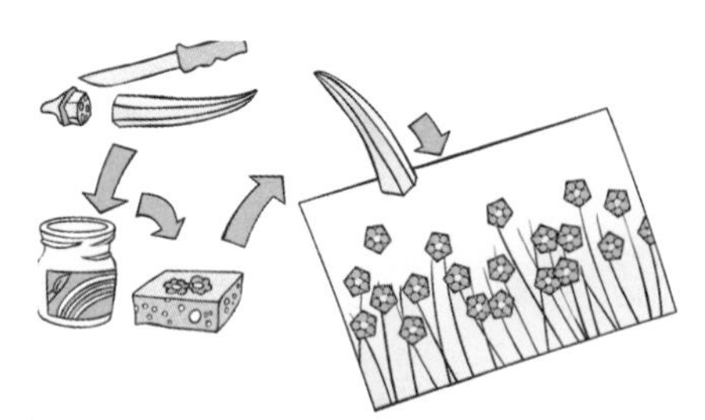

497. Traveller's tales

For a globetrotter who likes recording memories, a notebook is the perfect gift!

- Buy a basic book, spending on good, sturdy cream or wh paper rather than paying for a fancy binding.
- Or get a photo album for the snap-happy tourist.
- Photocopy a picture of a favourite destination, laminate fold over to make a dust jacket.
- Make a sentimental fabric cover that carries memories of home – a parent's signature suit material, a fleece that matches a partner's favourite pullover or a baby blanket.

498. Glasses very full!

ving glasses? Fill them up!

- 'or a hostess gift, present glasses in an open box, ›art filled with water and a single flower floated n each. Instant table décor.
- 'or a birthday or anniversary, fill with popcorn hat hides a liqueur chocolate at the centre of ach glass.
- 'all tumblers for a nifty cook? Add a test tube ›f exotic spice to each.
- 'or the cocktail addict, consider a double-decker ;ift of bar tools slipped into each highball glass!

499. House warmers

Some great ideas for a first bachelor pad or a new couple's first home.

- A tray of potted seedlings.
- A temporary tabletop garden – in a plastic-lined trug, place a container of wheatgrass bordered with pebbles and flowers held in florists' foam. Stick in a 'signpost' with their new address.
- A batch of moth-chasing sachets – stuffed with sage, cedar chips, bay leaves or lavender – rolled up in a fleece throw.

500. Crafty cupcakes

A sweet birthday treat for children, confectionery chefs or crafty types.

- Bake half a dozen cupcakes – with plain white vanilla icing.
- Line up an equal number of sturdy foil muffin cases.
- Fill the foil cases with cake decorations – sugar flowers, shredded coconut coloured blue and green as well as some plain white chocolate curls or chocolate vermicelli, some hundreds and thousands or sprinkles.
- Place in a box and toss in some small ready-to-use icing tubes in the gaps.

Index*

*Please note: The numbers shown refer to page numbers rather than tip numbers.

address books 15
aluminium windows 95
ants 161
arts and crafts 226–8
ashtrays 44, 232

babies 194
bathing 216; cordless phones 215; feeding 211–14; floors 203; furniture 205, 206; gardens 209; hot food 214; kitchens 208; overnight stays 217; period homes 207; pets 171; play pens 216; shelves 204; storage safety 205; tabletops 204; toy hygiene 210; tucking in 220; windows 206
baby wipes 100
back protection 48
bags, fabric 129
baking soda 82, 88, 99
banisters 94
basket cleaning 143
bath mitts 93
bathrooms 85–6
bed maintenance 139
bedlinen 7, 28, 136–137
bees 158
biological detergents 100
birds 164, 193
bites 40
blackboard paint 31, 150
blankets 137
bleach 81, 105
blinds cleaning 90, 141–2
bookmarks 238
books 67, 235
borax 82, 161
bottle display 58
box everything 8
burns 43
buttons 117, 119

candles 45, 57, 102, 107, 152, 153
candlesticks 89
carpets 141
cars 79, 129
cashmere 109, 163
chalk 36
chandeliers 151
chewing gum 103
children's chores 5, 17
children's clothes 221
children's medication 207
children's pets 167, 168
children's safety 50, 55, 194
hot water 201; locking doors 194,196–8; play equipment 211, 219; water containers 196
children's storage 30–1, 205
choking hazards 212, 220
cleaning supplies 80–4
clothes, hanging 25, 26, 122
clothes, pilling 120
clothes, steaming 115, 116
clothes, storage 24–7, 122–3, 163–4
cockroaches 161
coffee filters 66
compost 70
compost bins 68
computers 76, 90, 91
condensation 86
cooking utensils 73
coupons 14
cupboards 9, 19–20, 162
cupcakes 255
curtains 135, 228
cushions 140
cutlery 23
cuts 41

direct debits 14
doilies 24
doormats 93
doors 78, 142, 194, 196–198
drawers 19, 20, 21, 133, 154
dressing 10
dripping taps 147
dry cleaning 112, 137
duvets 104, 137, 139
dye fixing 110

egg trays 63
electric blankets 46, 138
electricity 77, 145, 199
emails 5, 11
emergency drills 55
extractor fans 75

fabric softener 109
fairy lights 150
fences 54, 176
fire alarms 46
fire blankets 47
fire safety 44
fleas 166, 179
flies 156
floors 143–4, 203, 233
flowers 222–4
food containers 103
foot spa 238
fragrance 223, 224, 225, 232–3
freezers 76
fridges 76, 78
fumes 73
furniture 21, 130, 227
babies 205, 206; cane furniture 131; garden furniture 230; polishing 83; removing rings 132; wooden furniture 132–3

gardens 53–54, 209, 229–31
gas leaks 49
gift wraps 241–3, 249–50
baskets 252; batteries 251; extras 252; gift bags 247, 251; gift tags 253; jewellery 246; novelty nuts 246; sacks and socks 248; sweet garland 244; ties 244; treasure hunts 247; wine 245
glass cleaning 87
glassware 23, 74, 88, 89, 255
gloves 38, 124, 146
granite worktops 87
greens 214
guests 232–3, 238–40
children 234; entertaining 235; food 237; overnight guests 235–6, 238; travel guides 240

hand cream 9
hand protection 85
hand washing 109, 111
handbags 63
hardware collection 48, 61
hay fever 213
hems 118
herbs 149, 156
hiccups 215
hinges 148
holidays 18, 52, 218
hot water bottle covers 56
house warmers 255
household hazards 50

ink stains 104
insect repellents 157, 159–61
ironing 106, 112–17, 136

jar gifts 60, 253
jet-lag 239
jewellery 10, 33–4, 51, 149, 220, 246

keepsakes 34, 35
keys 51
kitchen bins 92
kitchen cabinets 22
kitchen gardens 231

lace 120
lampshades 151, 225
laptops 76
laundry 108–11
lavender oil 43
lawns 54, 231
leather 123, 124–5, 126, 129
lemons 82, 83, 133
lighting 77–8, 199–200
fragrance diffusers 225
linseed oil 143
living rooms 97
locks 148
loofahs 62

magnetic board 32
mail sorting 12
measurements 6
medicine cabinets 37
mesh bags 221
mesh scrubbers 65
message boards 7
message mugs 4
metal enamel 126
mice 163
mildew control 86
mites 135, 166
mosquitoes 157, 159
moths 163
motion sickness 217
mouthwash 82
moving house 17, 36
mud-busters 93
mulching 229

nooks and crannies, cleaning 91
notebooks 6, 254

oxidation 101

paddling pools, inflatable 59
paint, water-based 72–3
paperwork filing 12, 13, 31, 35
paving 71
peas, frozen 38
pen and notebook 6
personal security 52
pest control 155–66, 173
pets 167
babies 171; beds 169, 177; birds 193; cats 186–90; collars 176–7; dogs 181–6; feeding 178, 186; fish 192–3; gnawing rodents 191; grooming 169; hair 180–1; home alone 171; house training 181, 186–7, 191; medication 180; play 170; rabbits 191, 192; safety 172–6; settling in 168
picture frames 152, 226
picture plans 5
pillows 140
scented pillow pouch 238
plant pot caps 60
plant pot drainage 62
plants 68
feeding 70; houseplants 72;
poisonous plants 174, 209
plastic bottles 79
plastic cleaning 107
play equipment 211
polystyrene packing 23, 62
post 52
postcards 254
potpourri 224

quilts 139

raincoats 234
ramekin lights 64
rats 162
recycling bins 67
remote controls 29
rugs 141

sand 47
saving tips 16
scorch marks 106
seams 118
service providers 16
sheets 136
shelves 19, 20, 22, 30, 204
shirts 113, 115
shoes 26–7, 59, 125, 126
shoelaces 127; smells 128; tar removal 128; white footwear 127
shopping preparation 8
shower doors 86
silica gel 36
silk 110, 163
silverfish 160
sink smells 88
snails and slugs 165
soda water 102
sofas 131
spice jars 66
spiders 165
spills 98, 101, 102
splinters 41
sponges 93
stains 98–105, 120, 144
stair baskets 97
staircases 94
stamping 13, 153, 254
stings, insects 40, 158
stings, plants 39
storage
behind furniture 21; children's storage 30–1, 205; clothes 24–7, 122–3, 163–4; dowels and rods 32; dressing-tables 65; glassware 23; hangers 34; hazardous substances 49, 155; jars 57; mesh 33; storage cupboards 19–20; tubes 27, 61
string 64
sunburn 39
sunlight 69, 105
sweets 244, 253
Swiss balls 10

tea stains 104
telephones 53, 215
telephone calls 5, 11; telephone numbers 15, 202
thank you photographs 239
throat, sore 42
ticks 166, 179
tidying up 96–7, 219
tools 146
toothache 42
toothpaste 61, 82
towel rails 29
towels 134
toys 210
trousers 113
tumble dryers 45
TV screen cleaning 90

umbrellas 28, 58
utility cupboards 9

valuables 51
vases 148, 227
ventilator fans 75
vinegar 84, 88
vinyl tiles 144
Vitamin E 43
VOCs (volatile organic compounds) 72–3

washing lines 92
washing machines 111
wasps 158, 159
water 74, 218
water butts 71
water heating 75
water-retaining granules 4
wax removal 89, 102, 107
weeds 165
white furnishings 134
window boxes 230
window cleaning 95
window dressing 228
window insulation 69
window painting 147
window seats 20
wine 245
wine stains 101, 102
woollens 109, 117
working from home 11, 16
wrapping, acid-free 122
wrapping, gifts 241–55
wreaths 226

zips 121